TOMMY MALONE

TRIAL LAWYER

Tommy Malone, trial lawyer.

Photo by Larry Patrick.

TOMMY MALONE

TRIAL LAWYER

And the Light Shone Through. . .
The Guiding Hand Shaping One
of America's Greatest Trial Lawyers

VINCENT COPPOLA

MERCER UNIVERSITY PRESS
MACON, GEORGIA
2018

MERCER UNIVERSITY PRESS

Endowed by

TOM WATSON BROWN
and
THE WATSON-BROWN FOUNDATION, INC.

MUP/ H952
© 2018 by Mercer University Press
Published by Mercer University Press
1501 Mercer University Drive
Macon, Georgia 31207
All rights reserved

9 8 7 6 5 4 3 2 1

Books published by Mercer University Press are printed on acid-free paper
that meets the requirements of the American National Standard for Information
Sciences—Permanence of Paper for Printed Library Materials.
Printed and bound in the United States.

All photos herein are the possession of Tommy Malone
and are used with permission.

This book is set in Adobe Garamond Pro.

ISBN 978-0-88146-662-1

Cataloging-in-Publication Data is available from the Library of Congress

Contents

Foreword

by John C. Bell Jr.

Thomas Carlyle, that nineteenth-century Englishman oft-quoted even today, asserted, "The history of the world is but a biography of great men." And so it is with the bar. We are shaped by the lives of the great lawyers, judges, and scholars and have much to learn from their life stories.

I count it a great honor to have played a part in the production of this book. I have now read three drafts and am anxious to read the soon-to-be-published final edition, the one that will include these opening words.

It is a very good book. I have no doubt that you will find this to be so.

On a personal note, my career at the bar has been enriched by my early and enduring friendship with Tommy Malone. We met when I was just out of law school and beginning my clerkship with U.S. District Judge Wilber D. Owens Jr. I was his first law clerk, and though we were based in Macon, he was assigned all cases in the Albany division, and Albany was his hometown.

When the court traveled, many traveled. These included prosecutors and staff from the US Attorney's Office, deputy marshals, probation officers, deputy clerks, the judge's law clerk and the judge's secretary. Tommy Malone was then a young lawyer, just getting his sea legs as a trial lawyer, representing both criminal defendants and injured plaintiffs. He was far from being among the "deans" of the Albany trial bar, but he was the Albany lawyer who would invite all of us for a cookout at his home each time the federal court came to town. He was then, as now, such a gracious host.

I spent two years as law clerk to Judge Owens. I watched many trials and learned so much, lessons that we can label as "how to do it" as well as lessons best described as "how not to do it." I read numerous briefs from big-firm lawyers addicted to string cites of cases that often only tangentially supported the advocated point, and I read briefs from a sole practitioner in Cuthbert, Jessie Bowles, later to become a Justice on the Georgia Supreme Court. His briefs were short and concise, often citing only one or two cases, but those cases were always, always directly on point. I learned from watching trials that the witnesses not to be accorded credibility were those who avoided direct answers and rambled at length. These lessons continue to serve me well. But the most fascinating case of my clerkship was the *Bitterman* pharmaceutical products liability case brought by Tommy and Melvin Belli, addressed at length herein, a case from which I drew lessons that continue to guide my practice. I spent many hours researching the myriad legal issues raised by the numerous motions, most filed by very able defense counsel. That case is described in this book as a seminal event in Tommy's life. It was also for me, but without the financial rewards that flowed Tommy's way.

I finished my clerkship in 1974, returned to Augusta, and hung out my shingle hoping to become a successful trial lawyer with an emphasis on representing the victims of the wrongs inflicted by others. In October 1974, I attended my first Georgia Trial Lawyers Association seminar. Tommy was there and welcomed me into the fold. He has never stopped welcoming me. I have heard him speak at numerous seminars, presented both near and far, and every time that I have heard him speak, I have learned something that made me a better lawyer. I bought his books on *voir dire* and continue to refer to them as I prepare for trial, most recently two months ago. I have been to dinner so many times with Tommy, but I have failed at every attempt to pay the tab.

There are some of us in life who are blessed with many friends, but we never know who will be there when we really, really need them. I have never doubted that Tommy Malone is such a friend. The interviews by Vince Coppola reveal how many others there are who feel the same way. Tommy has centered his life on what he can do for others, be they clients, friends, passing acquaintances, or worthwhile causes such as the Shepherd Center and Mercer University.

No description of Tommy Malone is complete without giving due credit to his lovely wife, Debbie. Dee Dee and I had the pleasure of getting to know Debbie early in their courtship, and we continue to be inspired by her devotion to Tommy and Tommy's devotion to Debbie, particularly in this time of physical challenges—Tommy is without a doubt a very lucky boy.

And now, back to the book. The late Judge Griffin B. Bell played at least two seminal roles in producing this book. He undertook to have a biography written of the now late Anthony A. Alaimo, United States district judge extraordinaire, and he secured noted author Vincent Coppola to write the book. When you have finished reading it, I have no doubt that you will appreciate just how lucky we were to have secured Vince for this task.

Secondly, Judge Bell, along with Chief Justice George Carley and and eminent lawyer Bob Hicks, wisely or not, selected me to serve as President of the Georgia Legal History Foundation, an arm of the Georgia Supreme Court and one that Judge Bell had nurtured, carrying the title of Chairman of the Executive Committee for a number of years.

The Georgia Legal History Foundation was formed in 1985. It publishes the *Journal of Southern Legal History* through the law review staff of the Walter F. George School of Law at Mercer University. The foundation's mission is "to preserve, analyze, and depict the legal history of the State of Georgia, especially that of the Supreme Court of Georgia and other courts of the state and the bar, and to disseminate that history for the purposes of educating the public and the legal community."

We now conduct annual regional seminars that seek to present and to record for posterity the legal lore of a distinct part of Georgia. Great tales are told, and all are recorded for the ages.

This is our first effort to produce a biography. The cost has been fully underwritten by friends of Tommy. Mercer University Press graciously agreed to be the publisher. We thus have many to thank for making this dream become today's reality.

Our goal has been to produce not just a good book about a fascinating lawyer, but an inspirational book both for lawyers and for those who are not within the bar, an inspirational tale of a great lawyer who has done such great good for others, those *others* who are labeled in Scripture as "the least of these."

We would love to hear from you once you have read our book. If you like it, please promote it. Amazon welcomes reviews. Please consider submitting one.

Acknowledgments

We are grateful to all who have by their generous support made this book a reality. Our thanks to Pope, McGlamry, Kilpatrick, Morrison & Norwood; W. Ray Persons; Buddy and Denise Dallas; Searcy Denney Scarola Barnhard & Shipley; Howard E. Spiva; Frank L. Branson; Michael Maggiano; Jack G. Slover; Randall Scarlett; The Honorable Anne E. Barnes; Chad W. Sawyer; Dee Dee and John Bell; The Melvin M. Belli Society; The Honorable M. Yvette Miller; Jeffrey Kaufman; William B. Shearer; R. Adam Malone; Wm. Andrew Haggard; Joel O. Wooten; James E. Butler, Jr.; Edward T. M. Garland; O'Malley & Langan, PC; Peter Perlman; Eugene C. Brooks, IV; Timothy K. Hall, LLC; Roy E. Barnes; O. Fayrell Furr, Jr.; Cook, Noell, Tolley & Bates, LLP; Billy Walker; Bobby Lee Cook; William Q. Bird; Warner S. Fox; Wayne D. Parsons; William Pope Langdale, III; Lance A. Cooper; Charles Guy Monnett, III; Peter A. Law, PC; Earl W. Gunn; Thomas R. Taggart; Fried Rogers Goldberg; S. Bradley Houck; M. Paul Reynolds; Michael G. Regas, II; Vansant & Corriere, LLC; Slappey and Sadd LLC; William S. Perry; Thomas S. Carlock; Richard M. Shapiro; W. Spencer Lee, IV; David B. Bell; Elizabeth Clark; Robert L. Parks; Ira Sherman; Mickey, Logan and Luke Moses; Linley Jones; Berke, Berke & Berke; John Banja; William F. Underwood, II; Virginia R. Sawyer; O. Torbitt Ivey, Jr.; David E. Hudson; Kenneth L. Shigley, and Donald Peck Leslie, MD.

Part I

A Guiding Hand

"I've come to believe I was put on earth to make a meaningful difference in the lives of others, those who've had their lives turned upside down...the catastrophically injured and the families whose loved ones needlessly lost their lives and futures due the failures of others. Without a good trial lawyer, they would not have that difference."

—Tommy Malone 2017

Chapter 1

"And then everything collapsed.... Tucker arrested."
—Lori Sutton on the birth of her brain-damaged son

August 2008. On a sunlit Georgia afternoon, the young professionals streaming into the Ravinia Drive office complex after lunch or a quick foray into Atlanta's bustling Perimeter Mall would not have failed to notice Lori and Landon Sutton. In the hustle and bustle of the workday, the Suttons— blonde, sweet-faced Lori, cradling an infant, and 6' 6" Landon, towering protectively above her—stood separate and apart, clothed in stillness. In that moment, they seemed from another world, a place whereby some marvelous alchemy a fortunate few escape the gravity of human existence, its inescapable cares and unavoidable tragedies, and seem to embody, if only for a moment, our dreams, longings, and hopes for fulfillment.

This was an illusion. The Suttons were reeling, devastated, barely holding their ragged lives together. Catastrophe had struck three months before with the first sharp pangs and contractions of impending childbirth. It was late in the evening of April 21 when Landon hurried Lori to Kennestone Regional Medical Center, half an hour's drive from their suburban home. It was a joyful journey, the culmination of a propitious new marriage and a pregnancy that had progressed smoothly and without complication. Lori's obstetrician, Dr. Gregg Bauer, was well regarded, a physician in whom they invested absolute trust. In fact, Bauer had delivered Zack, Landon's son from a prior marriage. "The only thing we heard when we talked to him," Lori recalled in 2016, "was that Tucker was going to be a large baby." She was 35 years old, and it was not uncommon for mothers in their thirties to deliver large babies.

Seven and a half hours later, Lori was still in labor, straining mightily and hearing no mention of a Caesarean section, a procedure utilized in one of three births in the United States. Anxiety, exhaustion, and the willing surrender to one's caregiver so familiar to every hospital patient were blurring her awareness of what was unfolding—the murmur of the nurses, the rapid acceleration of the fetal heart monitor—even as a deeper instinct signaled something was wrong. Landon spent the long night dutifully moving back and forth from the birthing center to the visitors' room, where his mother, stepfather, and Lori's 5-year-old son, Jay, awaited news.

As endless night gave way to day, Lori sensed a flurry of frenzied activity and a palpable tension among the staff as the monitors continuously signaled fetal distress. Tucker's shoulder was lodged in the birth canal. He'd passed meconium (a bowel movement) in utero, necessitating immediate intervention to prevent ingestion and suffocation. Dr. Bauer arrived and with a deft maneuver, delivered Tucker at 6:47 A.M. Stillborn, his face grey as the dawn. "He was so large and so exhausted that his body couldn't handle it," Lori recalled. "And then everything collapsed." She hesitates in her telling a long moment. "Tucker *arrested*."

In Landon's memory, those fateful hours are a blur of beeping monitors—Tucker's pulse soared to 200 beats per minute—shouts of "CODE," NICU staffers racing in and desperately trying to resuscitate his son. As Dr. Bauer attended to the hemorrhaging Lori, confusion and icy fear gripped Landon's heart. "Because of the duress he endured during labor," he said, "Tucker went without blood or oxygen circulating to his brain for twenty-plus minutes," time enough to cause irreversible brain damage. The team trying to resuscitate the stillborn infant couldn't officially call the time of death: Tucker was delivered at the hospital's shift change, and a neonatologist, who has to be present to make such a determination, had not yet arrived. At that critical moment, a faint heartbeat was detected. Tucker was rushed to Kennestone's neonatal intensive care unit (NICU), where his life hung in the balance. In such an emergency, "cooling blankets," which reduce swelling and can dramatically limit the risk of seizures and damage to a newborn's brain and vital organs by lowering body temperature to 92.3 degrees, are crucial.

Lori was given an IV painkiller and a blissful fog descended for the next hours. The last thing she clearly remembers is Dr. Bauer murmuring, "I don't know what happened." After she awoke, a woman in a physician's coat walked into her room. By some fateful coincidence, this was Dr. Ann Critz, chief of pediatrics at Crawford Long Hospital (today, Emory University Hospital Midtown). Critz had been at Kennestone to visit a family member who was in the maternity ward. She was accompanied by two other women.

"Your son has suffered severe brain damage...," Critz began.

"What?" Lori gasped.

"...and I want to tell you what I'd like to offer."

"We were floored, devastated, paralyzed," Lori recalled. "No one had uttered a word about brain damage or traumatic injury. I remember my father-in-law's quick burst of emotion and then Landon sending everyone out of the room while we cried and then tried to process and decide what to do. We had absolutely no idea."

"We had to hear it," Landon added bitterly, "from a person who's not even an employee of Kennestone Hospital. Dr. Critz kind of froze for a minute. She didn't know that we didn't know."

Critz was proposing moving Tucker to Crawford Long's state-of-the-art Level III neonatal intensive care unit. One of the women with her handed Lori a pamphlet, which she quickly scanned. An Angel 2 Transport Team was already on standby.

"We decided Tucker had to go," Lori said.

Landon accompanied their son to the Atlanta facility, where the eleven-pound Tucker remained, like Gulliver among the Lilliputians, in an incubator with tiny preemies for the next three weeks. Tucker Sutton would be formally diagnosed with Hypoxic Ischemic Encephalopathy (HIE) or birth asphyxia—irreversible damage occurring when a fetus is deprived of oxygen during or near the time of birth, resulting in massive brain cell death. The majority of such infants die at birth. Survivors like Tucker incur long-term neurodevelopmental impairments; i.e., intellectual and developmental disabilities, cerebral palsy, seizures.

So immersed were the Suttons in their grief, they never asked a critical question.

What had caused such a catastrophic event?

***

In Atlanta, there was a man, an attorney named Tommy Malone, who'd spent his life trying to understand why such catastrophic injuries occur, often in state-of-the-art medical facilities overseen by dedicated doctors and medical practitioners. And where there was evidence that a doctor, health-care system, insurance company, or manufacturer of drugs or consumer products had failed utterly in its responsibilities—indeed, had sown pain and suffering rather than promised benefits—Malone sought redress for lives that had been irrevocably damaged or destroyed. He was passionate and unrelenting in this quest, "a true believer," in the words of his peers. Not age, experience, success, or treasure—the bane of idealists—had ever blunted Malone's fierce crusade.

Among plaintiff's attorneys, Malone's was a path much less traveled. When he began his practice, suing a doctor was anathema, amoral, unheard of in civil society, a thing that got a lawyer shunned in his own community. Half a century later, a handful of attorneys—Tommy Malone foremost in Georgia—had blazed a path though this legal and ethical thicket, set important precedents, and won great victories for their clients. They'd achieved celebrity status among their peers, but "malpractice," "negligence," and "punitive damages" were words so manipulated and misunderstood, so charged, that segments of the general public—those, of course, whose lives had not been upended by premature death of a loved one or catastrophic injury—still stubbornly regarded malpractice lawyers with the unease or discomfort reserved for aluminum-siding salesmen and funeral directors. In any event, Malone, a lawyer whose jury awards read like Mega-Millions lottery jackpots and whose lifestyle a handbook for the rich and famous, seemingly occupied a world so unknown and impenetrable to ordinary folks like Lori and Landon Sutton that he didn't exist.

Chapter 2

"This should not have happened.... You need to see an attorney."
—Lori Sutton's pediatrician

In the face of tragedy we instinctively turn inward, to our faith or perhaps some deep well of inner strength and resolve rather than bitterness and frustration. When Tucker was discharged from Crawford Long Hospital, Lori and Landon welcomed him home not with trepidation, but with open hearts and great determination. "I held him so much," Lori remembered. "I promised I was going to love him through his brain injury...love his injury out of him." As weeks and months passed, the magnitude of Tucker's disability and the mounting costs—financial and emotional—of the constant care he needed, began to take a toll. "You didn't get eye contact," she said. "You didn't get smiles. You didn't get coos. You didn't get any of that, so for a long time it was the struggle of giving, giving, and giving."

There were two other boys to care for and limited resources. Lori worked as a special needs teacher, Landon in a family-owned daycare center. There was no thought of blame or finger-pointing. A lawsuit was an alien concept. Dr. Bauer's words—"I don't know what happened"—stayed with Lori, but bad things often happened to good people. The world could be a vale of tears, but you make the best of it. Bauer was a doctor, and like all doctors, a demigod to his many patients. He'd taken the Hippocratic Oath: "First, do no harm." Surely, if he couldn't explain what had gone wrong, there was nothing to understand beyond acceptance. The notion that there were notes and records of decisions made or not made, and precise instruments monitoring the slow starvation of blood flowing to Tucker's brain via his umbilical cord, and precise electronic recordings of his surging and flagging vital signs through that interminable night didn't occur to them.

Tucker arrived home on a feeding tube. He required suctioning to clear his airway. His tiny body was often wracked by seizures. He seemed to never sleep. Rather than musical chimes and lullabies, the amplified rasp of his labored breathing became the background of Lori Sutton's life. "Landon would be with him night and day so that I could sleep and go to work," she recalled. "There was exhaustion and enormous stress and worry. Early on, we had people telling us, 'You should sue. You should sue. This is wrong!' We didn't want to hear it. We didn't want to hear anything bad. We wanted to focus on Tucker and hope and pray he'd recover much better than anyone expected."

In Canton, Georgia, during one of the neverending medical appointments that now defined Lori's and Landon's lives, a pediatrician familiar with the circumstances of Tucker's birth and the mountain of debt the family was accruing shut the door to his exam room, turned, and uttered the astonishing words, "This should not have happened. It's going to be very costly to care for Tucker and it's not going to be easy. You need to see an attorney."

This was a rare thing for a practitioner in a profession that still clings to a code of silence as fiercely as the mafia once enforced *omerta*. The doctor put them—heads reeling—in touch with a local attorney named Patricia Ball. After a preliminary interview, Ball realized the resources and expertise needed to move forward on a potential medical malpractice action of this magnitude were beyond the scope of her family practice. She suggested an Atlanta attorney she'd heard about but had never met.

That man was Tommy Malone.

Malone specialized in medical malpractice, traumatic brain, spinal, and other catastrophic injuries, and pharmaceutical and product liability. He'd successfully handled hundreds of complex actions, often winning verdicts that made "meaningful differences" in the lives of victims and their loved ones. To his clients and a generation of lawyers who studied, idolized, and emulated him, Malone rivaled in ability his mentor, Melvin Belli, the renowned "King of Torts." Unlike the hedonistic Belli, there was a strain of righteous anger, indignity, and perhaps a measure of compulsion driving Malone. "He feels he's been called to serve," said Malone's son and law partner, Adam, a vocation his most gifted courtroom opponents readily acknowledge. To others, adversaries and detractors, the insurance companies and prideful defense attorneys soundly beaten before the bar, Tommy Malone was regarded as a devil, a being to be feared and respected. "He's got the biggest verdicts and he's dangerous," an insurance company executive once warned Laura Deane, director of claims management for

Emory Healthcare in Atlanta. "He won't deal with anybody. It has to be his way or no way."

Of course, Malone is more complex than the trappings of success, notoriety, and a seemingly unending stream of newspaper clippings, awards, and honors could ever explain. He is an astute and incisive legal thinker as well as masterful courtroom tactician. His 1999 book, *Voir Dire and Summation: The Law and the Practice*, detailing the intricate art of vetting perspective jurors to elicit bias and other factors, is a trial lawyer's bible. Malone is an intensely public and yet, ultimately, private person, sprung from a culture where displays of feelings or emotion were anathema among men. His father, Rosser Malone, was a good man, but a man unable to show emotion or affection to his wife and sons, a deficit Tommy has struggled with. If anything, fame and fortune provided a screen that obscured the inner man. He was shaped by the world that was South Georgia in the 1950s and 1960s, but the young Tommy Malone was remarkably like the iconoclast he'd become. "Dad grew up a troublemaker tilting at windmills," said Adam Malone. "He became a defender of people who've been unfairly treated."

There aren't enough walls to catalogue Malone's career highlights. He's been honored as one of the best lawyers in America and trial lawyer of the year, recognized as one of most powerful and influential Georgians, presented the Mel Award by the Melvin M. Belli Society, named a fellow of the International Society of Barristers and the International Academy of Trial Lawyers, and, oddly enough, "Commodore" of the Bimini Big Game Club, a rowdy band of fishermen who made the island's notorious hotel/marina complex their base. Of course, Lori and Landon Sutton had no inkling of any of this as they stepped off the elevator on the third floor of the Ravinia II office tower.

***

The image trial lawyers strive to project—trustworthiness, integrity, and proven expertise—is very close to that of doctors. When the Suttons passed through the doors of Malone Law's imposing suite into the quiet hum of muted conversations and bustling paralegals, every available surface lined with professional awards, certificates, magazine covers, letters of gratitude or recognition drawn from the powerful and celebrated to everyday folks, shelves heavy with legal tomes, and photographs of tall, white-haired Tommy Malone and handsome, dark-haired Adam, the effect was daunting. "We walk in and, 'Oh, there he is with Oprah Winfrey!'" Landon recalled. "I really began to get impressed when I saw the copy of *Georgia Super Lawyers* on his desk. Tommy was on the cover."

This was their first inkling that the man they were about to meet was one of America's premier medical malpractice attorneys. At that moment, Malone was immersed in *Drew Dakota Bianchi v. Gordon Trucking et al.*, representing (with San Francisco attorney Randall Scarlett) a college student who'd suffered massive brain injuries in a wreck triggered by two reckless truck drivers who collided on a twisting mountain pass in California. After a five-week trial, the jury awarded Bianchi *$49 million* in damages. Bianchi was one of a long string of negligence verdicts, including a *$45 million* 1995 compensatory damages award (*Adams v. Kaiser*) against a Georgia HMO for "unnecessary and preventable medical negligence" that cost a six-month-old infant both his legs and arms.

The Suttons were escorted into Tommy's office. The tall, grandfatherly man they encountered abandoned his imposing desk and escorted them to "a big round table" at the opposite end of the room. He had twinkling blue eyes, a head of white hair, and a voice as calm and soothing as a wave rippling across a north Georgia lake.

"Please sit down and let's talk," Malone said.

The details of the catastrophe that had forever altered what had been a happy and hopeful life poured out. What stayed with Lori years later were not the trappings of Malone's celebrity. "Tommy was genuine and warm and caring," she recalled. "No ego, just humility. I felt we could have had the same conversation had he come over to our house." Sutton had touched on one of the qualities that drove Malone's success. "Dad is among the most authentic people you'll ever be around," said Adam Malone. "No pretentiousness. He's a 'what you see is what you get' person, which makes him so powerful in the courtroom. The rest of us walk around with a lot of fear about being accepted, being liked, or being successful. Dad wants those things too, but they don't drive him."

Landon Sutton is one of those rare, gentle, sensitive big men to whom fatherhood is an absolute focus. That day in Malone's office he was struggling with the fact that Tucker "would never be able to catch a baseball or shoot a basketball...never get to go fishing with me for the first time." At the time, a brain scan indicated that rather than growing, the plates in Tucker's skull were collapsing in on each other, another sign of the irreversible loss of brain matter. That encounter did much to lift his spirits. "What I saw in Tommy was that he was such an advocate for Tucker and two people he'd just met," Landon recalled. "He saw *value* in Tucker when everybody else was being so dismissive. You know, 'Oh just pat him on the head.... Love him while you've got him.... He'll live as long as he'll live. And that will be that.'

"Tommy was 'Hell no! Let's make this the best we can.'"

This was no illusion, sales pitch, or studied come-on. Lori Cohen, chair, pharmaceutical, medical device and health-care litigation practice for the firm Greenberg Traurig, has observed Malone as an opponent, mentor, and friend for twenty-five years. "The one thing about Tommy I respect and admire is that he stands head and shoulders above other plaintiffs' attorneys—many of whom I respect and admire—in his passion and commitment to his cases, his clients, and more broadly, justice. He's for the 'little people,' never wavers, never puts himself or his wallet first."

Malone promised the Suttons he'd look into what had unfolded that tragic night at Kennestone Hospital, but added, prudently, that he couldn't take a case without merit. Given the time, energy, and enormous resources he'd have to expend in pursuit of an unpredictable outcome—the Suttons lived in conservative Cherokee County, a hotbed of anti-trial lawyer and pro-tort reform sentiment—his battles might best be fought elsewhere.

Mel Belli had warned Malone that working on contingencies was the biggest gamble in the world, but Tommy was also an inveterate gambler who'd bet on everything from poker to Bahamian fishing tournaments. With more than forty years in the law, he knew how to narrow the odds. He chose his battles carefully and assumed the opposition appreciated whom they were facing off against. He'd need all his skill suing Kennestone Hospital, part of a powerful health-care conglomerate that viewed a close examination of its practices and inner workings as unwelcome, invasive, and disconcerting as a fungal infection among its patients.

Malone was willing to wager his own money—enormous sums—to cover the research, hiring of expert witnesses, staff costs, travel, and any number of ancillary expenses necessary to prepare a high-risk case like the Suttons'. "He'll take a case in which somebody's life has been catastrophically changed through circumstances Tommy believes are wrongful," said Chris Searcy, a friend and past president of the International Academy of Trial Lawyers. "This client, if he had any money before, sure doesn't have any now. Tommy may have to shell out $100,000, $200,000, or $500,000 to cover litigation costs and several years of work. If he doesn't win, he gets nothing. It's a very high risk, entrepreneurial type of thing. If you're good enough, you can have a high enough success ratio and consistently do well in this arena. If you're not very good, you go bankrupt very quickly."

There was more to Malone, Searcy explained, than a riverboat gambler in a tailored suit: "Boldness, self-confidence, resourcefulness, and a willingness to risk terrible loss and humiliation to fulfill your duty to your clients. It's a very special thing to be the one behind all the expense and everything else to try these cases. But the one that's risky, the big loss that can ruin you, is also the one that can bring justice to these horribly injured individuals."

In his seventh decade, Tommy had come to believe he "was put on earth to make a meaningful difference in the lives of others who've had their lives turned upside down...the catastrophically injured and the families of those whose loved ones needlessly lost their lives and futures due to the failures of others, who without a good trial lawyer, would not have that difference." He meant this with all his heart—his career was a testimony to his values—but if pressed, Malone might also admit that there was something exhilarating about rolling the dice and risking everything to battle against a blind and unjust system—however one defined that system—that rolled right over the Lori, Landon, and Tucker Suttons of the world. He was still tilting at windmills.

***

There was still another calculus at work, one not easily quantified. Growing up in rural Georgia in the late 1950s and early 1960s, where conformity to community norms was as regular as spring planting and late summer harvest, Malone had rebelled. At first, his rebellion was inchoate and unconscious, drinking, gambling, carousing, and causing trouble in and out of school—the familiar and permissible alpha-male misbehaviors of the era. Later, as a young lawyer, he rebelled again, this time against his own privileged status and the hypocrisy of a white establishment that had abused its prerogatives and fostered injustice and racism as a status quo. Like Sampson among the Philistines, Tommy was willing to accept the wrath his rebellion brought upon his own head and the long-term emotional costs of social ostracism. "My father is a heroic character," said Adam Malone. "A unique human being with qualities you don't see in other people. He's not without flaws, but there's a strength and charisma that draws you to him."

In South Georgia, Tommy Malone became a rebel *with* a cause and the innate gifts, determination, and budding experience to mature into a masterful lawyer determined to fight injustice. It wasn't criminal law that ultimately became his passion, though as a young man he'd defended criminal cases by the hundreds, many successfully. Nor was it simply ego, the challenge of lawyerly combat against formidable opponents, nor a consideration of pecuniary reward that made Tommy accept the challenges inherent in the Sutton case. It was a simple and telling reason that captures another side of Tommy Malone. His unexpected and outsized sensitivity— what his wife Debbie Malone calls Tommy's "marshmallow heart"—so rare and unexpected in the harsh, black-and-white world he inhabits. Years later, when asked why he took on the Sutton case and all its inherent difficulties, he put it succinctly:

"My heart went out to them."

Chapter 3

Sutton v. Bauer
"Tommy Malone was this combination of my granddad and Matlock.
So nonchalant and yet working with an X-Acto knife, surgically precise
and country simple at the same time."
—Landon Sutton

Three years would pass before the Sutton family had its day in court. Exceedingly tough years. Alone and unsupported save for a tight circle of friends and family, Lori and Landon struggled to keep the financial and psychic costs of caring for Tucker from overwhelming them. They lost part of their income when Landon left his daycare job to care for Tucker and the boys. Whatever was left seemed to go for the endless medications and equipment necessary to keep their boy alive. Within months, they were forced out of their home and into a smaller house someone offered in return for a modest mortgage payment—a house ill-equipped and inaccessible, given the demands of a special needs child. "The family was reduced to abject poverty," Tommy Malone remembered. "The house was as bad as could be imagined. You'd have tears in your eyes if your children lived there."

Credit card bills piled up. A relentless collection agency operating out of an attorney's office wiped out their bank account and their last $2,000 in savings. (A few years later, the agency became the target of a federal Consumer Financial Protection Bureau investigation and ultimately agreed to pay—without an admission of wrongdoing –more than $3 million in penalties.) They survived that crisis only to have Lori called in by her school system administrators, who advised her that her paycheck was being garnished. "It got so bad," Landon recalled, "I was selling my guitar gear to keep the power on and the water flowing...grabbing up change to go to the supermarket's CoinStar machine to pay for gas."

Sutton v. Bauer got underway on August 2, 2011, in Cobb County State Court. The Honorable Kathryn J. Tanksley presided over a courtroom thick with curious lawyers and other notables who'd come to witness what promised to be prodigious battle; among them, the judge's husband, former state senator Charlie Tanksley. Tommy and Adam Malone represented the plaintiffs; defense attorney Daniel J. Huff for defendant Gregg Bauer, MD, and his group, Marietta OB/GYN Affiliates; David A. Sapp represented WellStar Health System Inc., Kennestone Hospital's corporate parent.

In simple terms, the case revolved around whether Tommy Malone could convince a jury that Dr. Bauer and the nurses on duty in the delivery room in the early morning hours of April 22 were negligent in not responding immediately to clear signs of fetal distress—among them Tucker's consistently elevated heartbeat—and not proceeding with an emergency Caesarian section. A C-section, the plaintiff's argument went, would have prevented Tucker's becoming lodged in the birth canal, avoided traumatic oxygen deprivation and a long sequellae of devastating events that would continue for the rest of the Sutton family's lives.

The defense would counter that Dr. Bauer had no precise way of determining Tucker's outsized (eleven pounds) weight and the complications it would entail and that fetal heartbeat was not sufficiently elevated to signal an emergency. Therefore, a C-section was not indicated and no standards of care were violated. "There is no question that Tucker had permanent brain damage," Daniel Huff stipulated. "This case is about whether Dr. Bauer caused it."

Tommy Malone's opening statement reflected the skill and demeanor that had carried him to the pinnacle of his profession. Towering over the jury, he came across as gentle and welcoming. He was meticulously prepared, knowledgeable, and seemingly as conversant with medical terminology and procedures as a doctor, reducing arcane terms and complex events to a simple and understandable timeline of actions taken or not taken, decisions made or unmade that inevitably led to disaster. He spoke in a soft, resonant voice that reporter Katheryn Hayes Tucker, covering the trial for the *Daily Report*, called "almost intimate."

"Honesty plus vulnerability equals authenticity," explained Adam Malone. "Dad is incredibly honest and self-deprecating, which appears as vulnerability. He's got an authenticity that's real and unpretentious. Most people respect him for that even if they don't like him. It makes him very powerful in a courtroom."

A clear, finely honed strategy underlay his arguments. Malone's style is not to fire a scattergun blast at the defendants, but rather to point out that these were good people who'd made bad, but avoidable, mistakes. "This case is about promises made and promises broken with disastrous results," were his opening words. "This family counted on Dr. Bauer and counted on WellStar." He left those words hanging in the air, and then promised proof of these broken promises "beyond the standard." To assist the jury in such a complex undertaking, Malone transformed the burden of proof to commonplace metaphors and images. "We don't have to score a touchdown," he said. "We just have to be in the opposition's territory at the end of the game." (He used other examples, such as fine-tuning the dials of a stereo system. "You don't have to have all the lights lit up.")

He relied on storytelling rather than rancorous argument and frontal assault to move the jury. "I've been waiting to tell you this for a long time," he said in that soft hypnotic voice as he invited the jury to listen in. His tale began more than a year before Tucker Sutton's birth with Lori meeting Landon at his family's daycare center and the two falling in love like innocent, star-crossed lovers in a Shakespearean tragedy. Each had a son from a prior marriage and wanted another baby. "They were all about children," Tommy said, noting Lori's eighteen prenatal visits with Dr. Bauer, with Landon often in attendance. And then, he added, undercutting the poetry with practical knowledge the jury would need to know: "Whether you want to or not, you're going to get to be an expert on fetal monitoring strips."

Over the next several days, Malone would introduce evidence showing that Kennestone physicians and staff repeatedly violated standard-of-care guidelines. Unbeknownst to the Suttons, labor and delivery nurses in the birthing center had adjusted Tucker's fetal monitoring upward so as to silence the alarm (triggered by a heart rate that sometimes approached 200 beats per minute [bpm]) to avoid upsetting other women in various stages of labor. "This is critical," Malone told the jury. "The alarm was set to go off at 180, but the nurses silenced it twice by moving the triggering standard to higher rates." (Normal fetal heart rate at term is between 120 and 160 bpm.)

He targeted hospital policies, not hospital staff. "I know you're a good nurse and you care," he told one witness, and then elicited testimony that if she'd been in charge that night, she would not have allowed the nurses to turn off the alarms without supervisory approval. "WellStar could train their nurses better," he said to drive his point home. "And these things wouldn't happen if they trained their nurses better, and if they called them in and said, 'Nurses, we don't keep secrets from patients.'" In the 1990s, Emory Healthcare, the largest health-care system in the state of Georgia, had adopted a policy of full disclosure in interactions with its patients. Such transparency should be the standard in health-care systems everywhere in the country.

Malone also shredded a likely defense argument that obstetrician Bauer was closely monitoring the developing situation, communicating with delivery nurses from the hospital's "On Call" room. Evidence suggested Bauer had spent only twenty minutes with Lori after she arrived, and he appeared in the birthing center only after it was apparent that Tucker was *in extremis*, his shoulder wedged in the birth canal (dystocia). Only then did Bauer deliver the stillborn Tucker. In advance of the trial, Malone had sent a photographer to the hospital. The photograph he displayed to the jury depicted a door with a sign that read "Physicians Sleep Room," not "On Call."

Tommy closed by describing Lori and Landon's commitment to the child. "Burdened as he may be, there is no more loved child, but it is love that comes with quite a burden," he said. "The expenses are going to be in the millions and millions of dollars. I wish they weren't, but they are because Tucker is profoundly damaged—and didn't have to be."

***

In his opening statement, defense attorney Daniel Huff took a sympathetic and compassionate tack while laying out a very different scenario: Lori Sutton had always planned on a vaginal delivery, and during the night Tucker's heartbeat, while elevated, was not, in itself, "a reason to change that plan." Dr. Bauer, an experienced and highly regarded OB/GYN, handled the dystocia efficiently, delivering the stillborn infant in less than two minutes. (As mentioned, the NICU team resuscitated Tucker but after nineteen minutes without a heartbeat.) Defense experts would testify, Huff said, "that a C-section would *not* have prevented Tucker's problems." The elevated heart rate and neurological damage most likely was linked to a maternal strep infection which spread to the placenta and could have been going on for days. "This is what caused the brain damage," Huff said. (Malone deemed this a "fantasy defense.") "This is a very sympathetic case," Huff acknowledged, but "keep an open mind."

David Sapp, the hospital's lawyer, hoped to build an unbreachable wall around WellStar. He devoted part of his opening statement to praising the nurses in the birthing center and the NICU team's "valiant and heroic efforts" in resuscitating Tucker. "There is no question the team brought his child back from the dead." There was no negligence and therefore no liability. Sapp concluded by asking for "a verdict in favor of the nurses at WellStar," an appeal to a hometown jury. "They met the standard of care. We don't have the burden of proof. They do."

The hip feint didn't get past Malone. With the jury out on a lunch break, he complained to Judge Tanksley that Sapp's characterization of the lawsuit as targeting the nurses was wildly inappropriate. "No nurses are being sued." When Tanksley asked what remedy he sought, Malone replied sourly, "Tell him please don't do that anymore."

"Yes, your Honor." Sapp agreed, but the exchange unveiled a no-holds-barred defense strategy. For the next two weeks, Lori and Landon Sutton looked on in amazement as Huff and Sapp introduced medical experts who offered alternative-universe explanations for what they believed was unassailable evidence. Worse, they were forced to watch the tragedy they lived and breathed every day of their lives sliced, diced, and devalued until it became nothing more than empty words echoing off a courtroom wall.

In these existential moments, away from the media glare, peer approbation, and the alcohol-fueled retelling of grandiose "war stories," an attorney must prove his or her worth, a measure of honesty, fidelity, and commitment to the trust he holds. Here, Tommy Malone proved a rock, reassuring the Suttons with his homespun, conversational approach to witnesses that belied the razor-sharp workings of mind. "He'd take the most complex medical explanation and stand there," Lori remembered. "And then it'd be, 'All right, what you're saying is....' He'd lay it out so everyone could go, 'Ah, now I get it!'"

"Tommy Malone was this combination of my granddad and Matlock," Landon added. "So nonchalant and yet working with an X-Acto knife, surgically precise and country simple at the same time." He'd use humor if a light touch was called for. "There were times when the jury would actually laugh at things Tommy would say," Lori remembered. "One time, I don't know what the questions were, but a defense witness kept giving these long, long responses that didn't answer the question. Tommy just stood there nodding his head, letting him talk until he finally stopped."

"Doctor," Malone asked, "You got a plane to catch today?"

"Yes, sir. I do."

"Doctor, if you don't answer my questions more directly, you're probably not going to make that flight."

Lori Sutton: "Everybody's like, '*What* did he just say?'"

Beneath the jauntiness, Malone worried about the viability of his case. Nothing would grant Tucker a normal existence—he'd never go fishing or throw a baseball—but the lawyer fervently *believed*—the essence of his calling—that the 3-year-old was entitled to a judgment that would make a "meaningful difference" in his fragile life. This would require a multi-million-dollar award by a Cobb County jury, a signal victory given that Cobb is a place where politicians regularly campaign on reining in "greedy" trial lawyers. Malone was facing another hurdle, one that went all the way back to his days as a young lawyer in Albany, Georgia, when he dared sue a well-regarded physician whose negligence had utterly destroyed the lives of a teenage girl and her family. Physicians and hospitals occupy a privileged position in their communities—rightly so—and juries are loathe to hold them accountable or award heavy damages often when the evidence is clearly against them.

Malone used a tool that had served him well in the past, a life-care plan that put all the zeros in the multi-million-dollar awards that juries often found off-putting into context. Malone projected $20 million in healthcare expenditures over the course of Tucker Sutton's life. He then broke these expenditures down into detailed purchases, for example, of specially adapted wheelchairs, medical equipment, medications, foodstuffs, and so forth. By way of comparison, he cited Tucker's $20 million against a $299 million severance package given to a Lehman Brothers executive—"one of the jerks who got our economy in the shape it's in." He threw in the mega-million-dollar salaries of the CEOs of the Coca Cola Company and the American Family Life Assurance Company (Aflac) for good measure.

The case was in the jury's hands.

***

Friday August 12. After two days of deliberation, the jury foreman sent a cryptic note to Judge Tanksley. They'd reached agreement on one defendant but not the other. The note provided no specifics. Tanksley sent them back for further deliberation. A verdict on one defendant, she feared, would run counter to state apportionment requirements and could lead to a reversal. "We're in uncharted territory," she acknowledged. "We could have a mess." After three hours and no progress from the jury, she declared a mistrial.

Malone tried to convince Judge Tanksley to take the verdict on the one defendant. Interestingly, no one knew for sure against which of the defendants they'd reached the verdict. Malone assumed the jury had found *against* the hospital. He proposed an "arrest of judgment" motion to place the damages' award on hold until the state supreme court could unwind the apportionment question. The defense claimed it was outraged by such a novel use of an arrest motion. Quoting Melvin Belli, Tommy said his motion was "hoary with age, but modern as tomorrow."

The judge declined. She again urged a settlement. When nothing materialized, Malone then offered to release Dr. Bauer from the case and take a verdict on the hospital. Throughout, the Suttons had insisted on sparing Bauer any undue personal or career harm. "There was no hate or revenge in our hearts," Landon said. "We were doing this for Tucker."

Judge Tanksley vetoed Tommy's proposal.

***

When the courtroom cleared, Tommy and Adam waited outside, hoping to talk to jury members. Lori, Landon, and Tucker, in a specialized stroller, were there with them. Tommy held the little boy's hand. As the jurors passed by, Tommy approached and said, "You don't have to talk to us, but we'd appreciate it if you did." A handful gathered uncertainly around him. Malone asked the question that was plaguing him:

"You reached an agreement on the hospital. Will you tell us what it was?"

"We found for the defense," a juror answered.

"*For the defense?*" Malone tried to hide his astonishment.

He pressed further, asking whether the jurors believed the Suttons should have been alerted to Tucker's distress during labor and offered the possibility of a C-section. The male jurors shrugged. They found no fault with the hospital staffers' actions. Malone asked if anyone felt the doctor had been negligent, a lone female juror stepped up.

"I did."

"An expensive focus group, but we learned from it," Malone said. "We've got a good case, just the wrong jury. We'll try it again." He reminded himself to take a long, hard look at the men in the next jury pool.

WellStar was less sanguine with the mistrial. After discovering the jury had been prepared to rule in its favor, the hospital appealed. Armed with supporting affidavits from three jurors, WellStar asked the court to set aside the mistrial and declare in its favor. Judge Tanksley again declined.

On appeal, WellStar found itself arguing against its own attorney's insistence on a unanimous verdict. The Court of Appeals decided WellStar was in no position to complain. "Even if there were any error, it was invited by WellStar," wrote Appellate Judge Christopher McFadden. "WellStar twice joined with co-defendant Bauer in arguing to the trial court that if the jury reached a verdict as to one defendant and remained deadlocked as to the other, then a mistrial was warranted."

Chapter 4

*"The days of our years are threescore years and ten. And if by
reason of strength they be fourscore years, yet is their strength,
labor and sorrow."*
—Psalm 90:10

January 2014. Another two-and-a-half years would pass before *Sutton v.
Bauer* was retried, Judge Tanksley presiding. Tommy Malone spent those
years doing lawyerly things, working on other cases; networking and socializing with peers; continuing Malone Law's philanthropic outreach to the
Shepherd Center, a private, not-for-profit hospital specializing in treatment,
research, and rehabilitation for people with spinal cord injury, brain injury,
and other neuromuscular conditions; supporting Mercer University, his
alma mater; attending or lecturing at gatherings of the more than twenty
professional organizations he holds membership in, the International Academy of Trial Lawyers, American Bar Association, Belli Society, Southern
Trial Lawyers Association, and Georgia Trial Lawyers among them; working dutifully to get suitable judges and politicians of both parties elected;
and expanding published articles and papers. And as often as he could, es-
caping with Debbie and friends to his estate on Abaco Island in the Bahamas, where he pursued fishing with the rapturous joy of a Hindu mystic.
Mostly being Tommy Malone, hosting extravagant parties, promising himself he'd get into shape, playing poker, traveling, imbibing Crown Royal, his
whiskey of choice.

When *Sutton* restarted, he was approaching his seventy-second birthday, already beyond the "threescore and 10" years a man is allotted in the
Bible. Malone is not formally religious, though descended from sturdy Baptist stock and grew up in a church-going family. His great-grandfather on
his mother's side was a well-known Baptist minister and educator. A soul-
searing medical malpractice case, *Bitterman v. Johnson* (chapter 17), Malone
tried in 1966 had soured him on organized religion after ministers from
Albany, Georgia's, First Baptist, First Methodist, and First Presbyterian
churches showed up in court to embrace a physician—he sang in the Methodist choir—whose negligence had cost a Jewish teenager any hope for a

normal or productive life. (The lead defense attorney taught Sunday school at the Presbyterian Church.)

"I became fed up with modern-day Christianity and churches," Malone said. "I'm not proud of that. I just went a different way." In his maturity, Malone had become deeply spiritual, conscious of a "guiding hand" that had shown him the path forward at every crisis and critical juncture in his life. "I've always been a devout believer in God," he added. "I've known for a long time, so long I can't remember when I came to realize it, that a higher spirit...a divine-intervention type of thing, has drawn me to do all the things I've done and the people who've been brought to me."

In 2014, Tommy could not know that another crisis of faith was looming, a personal medical catastrophe that threatened to end all that he was and everything he still hoped to accomplish. The Bible's admonition that a man's later years would demand "strength, labor and sorrow" was proving prophetic. In 2016, Tommy Malone was diagnosed with inoperable cancer. Since that time, he'd been undergoing extensive rounds of chemotherapy.

"I'm not questioning," he said. "I'm just accepting. There must be a reason."

***

When the second trial began, Tucker Sutton was 5 years old and had the appearance of a 3-year-old. His medical bills had surpassed a million dollars, offset by health-care insurance and, later, Medicaid. Lori Sutton, a sparkling, upbeat woman who can fill a room with pure delight, had not recovered from the ordeal of the first trial. "It affected me way more than I thought it would," she admitted. "I hadn't been angry until the night the judge said, 'All right, we're declaring a mistrial.'

"*Mistrial?*"

"We'd been sitting there trying to deal with the trauma of having to relive all these details and hearing—because it wasn't until the trial that we learned that Tucker would have been okay had he been delivered by C-section at 3:58 A.M.—the experts say, 'This is where Tucker is being deprived of oxygen.... Here's where Tucker is starting to decline.' I'm watching my child die, and I'm so angry at the hospital and they're so dismissive.

We *wanted* to settle. We would've been happy to settle. They wouldn't even talk about it. By the end, it was pretty emotional. I just couldn't understand why they wouldn't *want* to do the right thing."

Tommy Malone's charge was to make sure they did. In the first trial he'd focused on the series of breakdowns in the birthing room—the nurses' failure to alert Dr. Bauer when Lori developed complications, the turning down of the fetal monitoring alarms, etc. Now he developed a fresh line of attack. Expert testimony and a devastating deposition of the hospital's administrator made it clear that WellStar's neonatal intensive care unit (NICU) wasn't prepared to handle the cascading challenges surrounding Tucker's birth. In fact, the infant's survival had everything to do with Dr. Critz's near-miraculous appearance and Tucker's subsequent evacuation to Crawford Long Hospital.

WellStar advertises "world-class childbirth services for a safe and healthy journey to motherhood." Indeed, Lori had chosen WellStar because of the claims made on their website. As mentioned, no neonatologist was on duty when Dr. Bauer delivered Tucker. He was revived after nineteen minutes without a heartbeat. "Those facts scared the hell out of WellStar," said another attorney familiar with the case.

The possibility of a jury awarding tens of millions of dollars in damages because of these lapses was enough to spur a settlement. "WellStar's attorney sent us a letter with an offer, but there were two parts to it," Malone remembered. "The second part made me realize *we* needed to settle. There's this thing in the law that if you're offered a settlement and refuse, and go to court and lose, you can be responsible for defense costs up to a point. It was a double-whammy." Malone did not push the offer on his clients. "Now, I can probably go back and get you a little bit more, but here's what I want you to do," he told the Suttons. "Look at this amount of money [he broke out court costs, his fee, and what would be left]. If it's enough to make a meaningful difference in your life, think about accepting it."

In simple terms, Malone was foregoing the possibility of a mega-recovery in favor of his clients' best interests. "To me, it's significant that in this day and age where lawyers have expanded, grown, gone for volume and bigger, better, brighter, shinier objects," said defense attorney Lori Cohen, "Tommy stayed committed to his view of justice and remains an advocate for his clients."

"The hospital's offer was a game changer because it gave us peace," Lori said later. "Part of me didn't want to accept because I didn't want to let Tommy down. That's how much love and trust and faith we had in him. But if you get a bad jury, there is nothing you can do. We sat down and looked at a budget, what we could put away for Tucker and what we'd have left for a house and other necessities. Then we considered the stress of having to go through it all over again.

"We accepted."

Malone negotiated the offer upward, and WellStar happily dropped out of the lawsuit.

***

The second trial began on January 6. A high/low agreement Malone had worked out before the mistrial was still in place. (A useful hedge in high-stakes cases, high/low agreements give both plaintiff and defendant a measure of protection. The defendant agrees to pay the plaintiff a minimum recovery—low—regardless of verdict, and the plaintiff agrees to accept a maximum figure—high—no matter how high a jury's award.) As a result, the Suttons were assured of a monetary cushion, and Bauer and his partners insulated against a devastating verdict. As it turned out, $2 million was the upper limit of the group's insurance coverage, and neither Malone nor the Suttons wanted to press for more.

This time around, Malone vetted the jury exceedingly carefully after a couple of inadvertent misfires in the first trial. When jury selection was over, the foreman was a father whose children had been delivered via C-section. Another male juror had a three-week-old daughter. These would be significant players.

In opening, Malone again insisted that Tucker's brain damage could have been avoided had Bauer responded quickly to a number of warning flags: Tucker's elevated heart rate, his size, Lori's age (36), and the presence of meconium in the amniotic fluid, which can cause asphyxiation. "The failure to do a C-section is what it's all about," he told the jury. When the crisis developed, Lori's OBGYN was at the end of a twenty-four-hour shift. "We're going to prove that Dr. Bauer should have paid more attention,"

Malone continued. "We are going to prove Dr. Bauer should have been more involved.... He spent far too much time in the Sleep Room."

The trial ran ten days, a battle of dueling expert witnesses. Bauer's side emphasized his reputation—the obstetrician had delivered more than 4,000 babies in the course of his career—arguing there was no medical reason to intervene surgically in Lori Sutton's delivery. Defense attorney Daniel Huff implied Tucker's brain damage was caused by the fever and infection she'd developed in the last days of her pregnancy: "C-sections are not risk free. They carry with them their own complications, especially when infection is present, like with this mom."

Once again, the jury deadlocked 10–2.

Facing a second mistrial and an interminable run-up to a third, Malone came up with a creative solution: in effect, a coin toss. Poll the jury, and if the plaintiff's side has ten votes, award the Suttons the high end; if the defense has ten jurors, the Suttons would settle for the low figure. After some back and forth, both Huff and Judge Tanksley signed off on the deal. (This was not without precedent. Malone, in fact, had tried a case in California where a verdict was taken based on a majority of eight jurors.)

After the puzzled jurors returned from lunch at a nearby pizza restaurant, Judge Tanksley queried them.

"Which side does the ten favor?" Tanksley asked.

A hush settled over the courtroom.

Landon Sutton remembers being "the most scared I'd ever been in my life."

"The plaintiffs'," the foreman announced.

Knife-edged tension gave away to acceptance, even relief. Malone and Daniel Huff shook hands. Judge Tanksley thanked and dismissed the jury. As it turned out, Malone's *voir dire* had been spot-on. Both men with young children he decided not to strike during jury selection had sided with the plaintiffs. As the courtroom emptied, a trembling Lori Sutton hugged Tommy Malone and whispered something to him. Then sobbing, she gently carried her silent, blond-haired boy to his stroller and walked away.

It was over.

Part II

Beginnings

Family and place are essential to understanding Thomas W. Malone. In his maturity, place came to mean the Malones' expansive north Atlanta home, where his birthday parties and annual Christmas blowout became the invitations of the season in Georgia's legal and political whirl. Place is also the magnificent waterfront homes in North Palm Beach and Marsh Harbour on Abaco Island in the Bahamas. Ultimately, place for Tommy Malone is rooted in the sandy loam of southwest Georgia, its cotton fields and scrub pine forests, in the sharecropper shacks sprung like weeds in the shadows of great antebellum plantations—now hunting preserves for the elite—in its courtrooms and jailhouses, bars and backrooms, where powerbrokers' deals are done, all glimpsed fleetingly and often uncomprehendingly as a much younger man, and later with a jeweler's eye.

Tommy was born in the provinces, Albany, Georgia—Gaul to Atlanta's Rome—but was never provincial, never the country boy gawking at the city slickers in Atlanta. His mother was descended from a line of scholars and preachers running all the way back to the American Revolution. Petrona (Toni) Malone schooled Tommy and his older brother, Ross, in the gentlemanly arts. Tommy's father, Rosser Malone, was of rougher stock, a self-made man, lawyer, state judge, and lifelong political aficionado.

Tommy was of a generation of middle-class, white Southerners grown up on the wrong side of the racial divide, insulated as caterpillars in a cocoon, a thing inexplicable to outsiders, but undeniable to those who lived through it. "We weren't racists," insisted attorney Spencer Lee, a lifelong friend of Malone's. "We were so segregated back in high school I didn't even know where [all-black] Monroe High School was." In Dougherty (Albany) and neighboring Lee, Mitchell, Baker, Calhoun, and "Terrible Terrell" counties, racism was endemic. African Americans were isolated—purposefully—by a white establishment that denied them even the meager political and economic progress being made in Atlanta and elsewhere. For a black man living in South Georgia in the early 1960s, Martin Luther King Jr.'s dream was as insubstantial and unreachable as a cirrus cloud over a field of cotton. Easier to touch the sky. This is the crucible in which Tommy Malone was formed. The suffocating context he refused to let define him. Strip away the surface glimmer of success, popularity, and lawyerly renown, this is who he is.

Chapter 5

*"The best is not good enough for my friends. And hell is
not hot enough for my enemies."*
—Rosser Malone, Tommy's father

More than most of their countrymen, Southerners define themselves by family, history, and tradition while the rest of us are increasingly rootless, willing, even eager to leave the past behind and reinvent ourselves. Faulkner's oft-used depiction of the South is no cliché: "The past is never dead. It's not even past." This has as much to do with the fiercely independent, clannish, and self-reliant Scots-Irish culture that took root in the region as it does with the Civil War and its bitter aftermath. The past is also prologue. What's gone before is significant in the present and often bleeds far into the future. Like the seasons that nourish and ravage the soil, life in the South is cyclical.

Malone family roots run deep in southwest Georgia. Rosser Malone, Tommy's father, was shaped by searing familial events that began unfolding before his birth, things whose impact he could not fully comprehend and spent his whole life determined to ignore. Young Tommy would be shaped by forces complex and disruptive: he was born, innocent, like all of us, into a world defined by unspoken verities and the overpowering, even suffocating rhythms of a privileged life in a small Georgia city at the dawn of an era of great social upheaval and racial awakening.

In the 1950s and '60s, Albany (population approximately 77,000), was a curious place, more medieval fiefdom than Southern city, with more than its share of banks, churches, bars, gambling dens, and lawyers. As for its economy, cotton was king. Albany lay 180 miles southwest of Atlanta, below the "gnat line," athwart the Flint River along one of the north-south roads connecting Florida to the Northeast in an era before the interstate highways were constructed. It had a robust military presence— US Marine Corps Logistics Base, Naval Air Station—and a historically black college, Albany State. As for race relations, majority black Dougherty County and its environs had a very bad history.

***

Late in the evening of November 2, 1942, Petrona (Toni) Underwood Malone gave birth to her second son, a strapping, nine-pound boy named Thomas William, at Phoebe Putney Hospital in Albany. Earlier that Monday, when Toni experienced the first pangs of childbirth, her husband, Rosser Adams Malone, a 36-year-old attorney, dutifully dropped her off at the hospital and then went off to play golf or cards—the details are lost to time—with his buddies. This was a simpler time, and in any event, Rosser Malone was not a man given to displays of husbandly affection. Tommy's was an easy birth, but like much that would unfold in his life, it was not without complication. As Toni was leaving the hospital, the assisting nurse somehow managed to drop the newborn on his head. The rest of the drive home was uneventful.

It was a grim season. The Japanese were still ascendant in the Pacific nearly a year after the devastating attack on Pearl Harbor. In North Africa, the British were locked in a desperate battle at El Alamein trying to dislodge Rommel and his Afrika Korps from Egypt and deny Hitler access to the Suez and the vital oil fields of Persia and the Middle East. At home, it was a time of fear and uncertainty, of food shortages, ration books, blood drives, and families dutifully dipping into scant savings to purchase war bonds. In Albany and surrounding Dougherty County—the heart of southwest Georgia's historic "black belt"—Gold Stars blossomed like poisoned flowers in the windows of both affluent and impoverished, in farmhouses and the tree-shaded streets on either side of Oglethorpe Blvd. Like millions of able-bodied Americans in every city and small town, Rosser Malone enlisted after Pearl Harbor, joining the navy. Stationed in Oakland, California, he was not assigned overseas duty.

Malone was a solidly built man, about 5' 11" with Scots-Irish features—big ears, long nose, fair skin, and thinning hair. Hardworking and family oriented, he was determined to provide his wife and children a better life than he'd known as a child. He was an avid hunter and fisherman, a man's man to be sure, and quick to anger. "He'd hold a 'resentment' forever if crossed," said his grandson Adam Malone. "The best is not good enough for my friends," Rosser liked to say. "And hell is not hot enough for my enemies." Recalled Adam: "My grandfather lived by that. If you crossed him, there was no crossing back to the other side again." (A trait Rosser seemingly passed on to Tommy, who's been known to recall courtroom injustices and less-than-fair play by defense attorneys decades after the fact.)

Rosser was raised an orphan, though both his parents were living. In 1914, according to family legend, his father (also named Rosser Malone), a man of tempestuous moods and impulsive behavior, left for Central America to work on the Panama Canal. "I was told my grandfather was an engineer," Tommy Malone recalled. "That he departed Key West on a boat bound for Panama and abandoned his wife and four children on the dock." As the story goes, Tommy's grandmother made her way back to Georgia and exacted her revenge. She sent her husband a "Dear Rosser" letter announcing she'd fallen in love with his best friend. Another variation has Rosser (Tommy's father), then aged 7, and one of his brothers running away in Key West and living for a time in a cardboard box. Discovered by the local authorities, they were shipped by train back to Albany, where they were taken in by their paternal grandmother. Their mother apparently moved to Alabama, leaving all four of her sons behind. "On the surface, my grandfather was this jovial guy who did what he wanted to do," said Adam, who as a child spent a lot of time with his grandparents. "But he'd had a lot of pain. You could see what he'd suffered in his face."

Tommy picked up the tale. "My grandfather came back from Panama. According to the story, he saw his best friend on the post office steps and shot him dead. He was arrested, convicted, and sent to federal prison." Malone paused, then added, "I always wondered why federal prison. I figured the post office was government property." A classic Gothic tale of betrayal, double-cross, and revenge, except the story, overheard by Tommy in bits and pieces growing up, wasn't true. The truth was elusive and slippery as a snake. Tommy had no luck drawing the facts out of his father or his uncles.

"One holiday, I came home from college and said, 'Daddy, tell me about Grandfather Malone, I never knew him.'" Tommy continued.

"Ain't nothing to tell, Son."

"Daddy, I know there's *something* to tell. Please tell me."

"Goddamn it, Son! I said there ain't nothing to tell!"

Rosser went back to reading his newspaper. Many years later, Dr. Hudson Rogers, Tommy's cousin, the family genealogist, solved the mystery. "Turns out my granddaddy didn't kill anybody in Albany," Tommy said. "He killed somebody in France. Toward the end of World War I, he was in the Quartermaster Corps. He'd gone over there as a captain with a boatload of 250 horses and more African Americans than that. He was sent over to work the horses and the African Americans. Being from South Georgia, he knew how to do both.

"Back home, a *stranger* had married his wife after her divorce. As fate would have it, my grandfather's driver, or somebody who worked for him, discovered that a lieutenant with that man's name had arrived and was stationed in a nearby town. My grandfather got his gun and had his driver take him over there. He found the man."

"Come outside."

"I know who you are," the man said. "Rosser Malone."

"Come on out. I need to talk to you."

"The man came out," Tommy continued. "Two minutes later, there were four shots. My grandfather got back in the car and his driver drove him away. He was arrested, court-martialed, sent back to the US. He got a life sentence for killing the guy. I actually have a transcript of the court martial.... So why would my uncles tell this bullshit story about the post office and not the truth? Why do families tell these kinds of stories?"

Why indeed?

Elsewhere, the murder and his grandfather's eventual pardon and death in 1936 would have been likely forgotten, carried away by the swift flow of events, the dislocations of the Depression, and the onrushing Second World War. But the South is enduring, and such stories are the currency of family life. That reckless act and its repercussions would cascade through the Malone family for the better part of the next century, ebbing and flowing, but ever present.

With their father imprisoned, and "effectively abandoned" by their mother, young Rosser and his three brothers were split up. Two, Lyman and Freddie, were adopted by a family somewhere up north, named Mueller. Rosser and Harry were raised by their grandmother. Their paternal uncle, Hudson Malone, helped out where he could.

Rosser never forgave his mother. Adam Malone, then a child, remembered a scene that unfolded at his grandparents' house. "Somebody came and knocked at the front door. It was a man wearing a suit. My grandmother got up to answer. She came back and told Granddaddy who it was."

"I won't see him," Rosser declared.

"I later found out," Adam continued, "it was someone who'd come to give Granddaddy his part of the inheritance from his mother's estate. He had not spoken to her. He had no relationship with her and would not accept the gift or any part of her life. I remember thinking as a little kid, 'Everybody makes mistakes. Too bad she didn't come to him before her death to say she was sorry, but she remembered him in her will.' He wouldn't have anything to do with it."

Chapter 6

"It's a damn poor road that don't run in both directions."
—Judge Rosser Malone on justice

Tommy's father, Rosser Malone, began his law career in high school working part-time for an attorney named Kruger Westbrook, who shared an office with a wealthy cotton broker named John Billingsley. (Cotton casts a long shadow in Georgia; today, the state ranks second in US production behind Texas.) Teenaged Rosser was rough around the edges, fatherless, abandoned by his mother, raised by an impoverished grandmother, but Billingsley and Westbrook were so impressed with his diligence and determination they loaned him the money, barely enough, for law school. At the time, an undergraduate degree was not a prerequisite for a Juris Doctor or admission to the Georgia Bar. Rosser jumped from high school to law school, from living with his grandmother to sleeping on the floor of the Athens YMCA. He graduated from the University of Georgia's School of Law, arrived back in Albany, rolled up his sleeves, and went to work. Sixty-five years later, sturdy as a mule, he was still hard at it.

Rosser served for more than twenty years as Dougherty County Solicitor, a part-time job which positioned him for a judgeship should city court judge Clayton Jones, whose tenure ran fifty years, ever retire. "My father would never run against Jones," Tommy recalled, "because he was the lawyer who got my grandfather out of prison." The city court was later reconfigured as the state court of Dougherty County. In these years, Rosser Malone focused on building a private practice, handling real estate transactions, and brokering insurance company-backed loans on real estate, divorce, and probate, mostly flying by the seat of his pants. "I remember when I first started practicing with my daddy," said Tommy. "I went to pull one of the law books off the shelf in the library." (He spread his thumb and forefinger.) "The dust was that thick."

Like every small-town lawyer of the period, Rosser Malone was a generalist—you had to be to keep your shingle hanging on the door—a dealmaker, a negotiator, a common-sense counselor, certainly not a "book lawyer" who'd read the law and would complicate matters with precedents and legal minutiae. "Grandfather had a deep sense of right and wrong," added Adam Malone, the third generation of Malone lawyers. "And he kept things pretty simple." Southerners are storytellers *par excellence* and Rosser had his share of yarns and country aphorisms. "It's a damn poor road," he told young Adam to illustrate his notion of justice, "that don't run in both directions."

Rosser had a lifelong affinity for public life, was very active in local and state politics, and maintained a tight circle of lawyer friends and politicians—Taxi Smith and Asa Kelly among them—who held and handed off the mayor's job in Albany as smoothly as runners on a relay team. In that circle, James "Taxi" Smith (Smith, Garner, Kelley, & Wiggins) fancied himself "Everyman's Lawyer," a showman who'd "ride the elephants in the parade when the circus came to town." Smith was wily and shrewd, never one, as Tommy would learn to his dismay, to stick his neck too far out. "Taxi was the go-to lawyer down there," Tommy remembered. "If he sued somebody for divorce, the defendant would say, 'My wife's got Taxi Smith! Do you think I have a chance?'" According to legend, Smith, at the time a Georgia Tech freshman, earned the "Taxi" sobriquet by hailing one after tiring while running a road race.

Judge Asa Kelley, another former mayor, once browbeat Tommy—fresh out of law school—in front of a jury for asking too many questions during cross-examination ("Not moving things along efficiently"). "He hurt me very badly," Malone recalled. "Afterward, I went to see him. I had tears in my eyes. I said, 'Judge, I may be asking more questions than a seasoned lawyer would, but if you don't ask some questions, you've got no way of winning.'"

***

In the best of circumstances, South Georgia is a harsh, unforgiving place. Its economy—tied to cotton, corn, peanut, and tobacco harvests—is at the mercy of gyrating markets and implacable bankers, plagued by drought, flood, erosion, and infestation. Yet one generation's tribulations can drive success in another. "My father grew up really, really poor," said Tommy. "He didn't have a father providing for him, so his mission as a father was providing food, shelter, clothing, and the other trappings of happiness and success he'd wanted as a boy."

Such a childhood would have crippled most men, but Rosser drove himself regardless. Sometimes, the bitter memories seemed tales from another man's life, things of no consequence in the present, to be ignored or denied ("Ain't nothing to tell, Son."). Such a man, never having had affection, would, understandably, be uncomfortable with affection, introspection, or sensitivity. Tommy Malone, in his seventies, can count the times his father hugged him. "I can remember seeing my father kiss my mother on the cheek one time," Tommy said. In Rosser Malone's world, *provider* was the role of a husband and father. Career, wealth, respect, influence, power, and acclaim are what drive ambitious men.

***

Rosser married up. Pretty, vivacious Petrona (Toni) Underwood was an elementary school teacher from Early County, fifty miles southwest of Albany. Her grandfather, John Levi Underwood, was a Baptist minister, aspiring poet, and essayist (trained in Presbyterian seminaries) who'd studied in Heidelberg and Paris and later served as a chaplain in the Confederate Army. Underwood, who went on to teach and practice law, wrote a paean to the Lost Cause: *The Women of the Confederacy*. Toni's father, John Lancelot Underwood, was a merchant who owned a dry-goods store in Blakely, Georgia. When times grew harsh, as they often did in southwest Georgia, and Underwood could no longer survive selling clothing, fabric, ribbons, and thread, he turned to truck farming. Toni's family, despite financial reversals, revolved around music, the arts, literature, and the social graces, gifts that she insisted on inculcating in her sons.

John Lancelot Underwood had married into the Howard family, another noteworthy line that counted doctors, dentists, teachers and other members of the professional class in its ranks. In the South, social status can be a state of mind, of family history, education, and past glories, quite distinct and distinctly superior to recently acquired wealth. To the up-from-the-bootstraps Rosser Malone, an "Underwood from Blakely" meant something. In Petrona, it meant an illustrious pedigree—she was an active member of the Daughters of the American Revolution and other civic and service organizations. She'd earned a college degree, graduating with honors from Shorter College in Rome, Georgia, at the time a rare thing for a woman anywhere in the country. She was president of that school's Polymnian (literary) Society and later, the Shorter College Alumnae Association. A debutante, Petrona capped all the social cachet and well-rehearsed rituals of her class with a sparkling intelligence, generous nature, and a deep love of books, theater, and poetry. In Albany, she was a major force behind the Charity League, Debutante Club, and Junior League. She was a woman of her era, wife and mother with duties and responsibilities very distinct but complementary to her husband's more quotidian concerns. In Albany, it was easy to recognize the two: Toni was perfectly coifed, charming, a sparkling conversationalist and storyteller; Rosser was the gruff lawyer who arrived at work in hunting season dressed as if his office was a deer blind.

Toni gave birth to her first son, Rosser (Ross) Jr., in 1939 and Tommy in 1942. "She was warm, loving, all those wonderful things that you can say about a mother," Tommy recalled. "She did the social things for the family, the charitable things. She played bridge three or four times a week with a group of ladies. She sang, played the piano, and enjoyed having a couple of drinks. She called them 'bumps.' Only one ounce, but if you poured two, she didn't complain. She kept a beautiful home with the assistance of the maid. She was very happy under her circumstances and the times she lived in." During the boys' childhood and adolescence, Tommy Lee Williford and Evelyn, Toni's long time African American maids, were considered part of the family. "Bominitius" was the yard man. One time, Toni, who paid his wages in cash, found herself short and offered to write a check.

"How do you spell Bominitius?" she asked.

"That ain't my name."

Toni stood there perplexed. "But when you first came to work I asked what I should call you."

He stared at her blankly. "By my initials!"

As his practice grew, Rosser moved the family to larger, more comfortable, though still modest, homes—first to 730 Seventh Avenue, and then a new, four-bedroom, 3,000-square-foot brick house at 1219 Hilltop Drive near Crown Hill Cemetery. He and Toni drove late model cars. She shopped regularly at the Rosenberg Brothers' department store on

Washington Street and treated herself to an occasional shopping spree at
Rich's in Atlanta. Rosser never missed a hunting season or a chance to go
fishing in Georgia's plentiful lakes and streams.

"As far back as I can remember," Tommy said, "my father worked in
every governor's race." One of Tommy's earliest memories is clambering on
his father's broad shoulders to tack campaign posters on telephone poles
touting whatever conservative Democrat—the range of the political
spectrum in 1960s Georgia—Rosser had gotten behind. Politics was
intensely local and personal. "Governor Sanders stayed at our house when
he was campaigning in South Georgia in 1961," Tommy recalled. Urbane
and forward-looking, war hero, scholar-athlete Carl Sanders was the avatar
of the "New South" leadership *Atlanta Constitution* editor Henry Grady had
famously promoted. Sanders campaigned flying his own airplane around
Georgia and once took star-struck Tommy for a ride, perhaps inspiring—
once his rodeo fantasies had faded—his becoming an instrument-qualified
pilot with a string of airplanes.

Rosser Malone went on to handle the legal affairs of the moneyed
outsiders who owned the enormous plantations and hunting preserves
spread across South Georgia. R. Charles (Charlie) Loudermilk, for example,
grew up in Atlanta without an indoor toilet and went on to found Aaron
Rents, a billion-dollar furniture rental business. Loudermilk owned
Woodhaven Plantation in Coolidge, a 5,000-acre spread capped by a
20,000-square-foot mansion complete with Doric columns and wrap-
around porches, fifty miles south of Albany. "My grandfather's business
evolved around doing real estate closings for these rich landowners," said
Adam Malone. "He ended up spending time with those people and they
became his friends. I don't know that he really fit in, because they grew up
so differently, of a different social class, but he'd become part of that class."

In a long career, Rosser Malone would win elective office. He'd serve
as a gubernatorial appointee to a coveted state commission, but he'd never
be rich. "We always lived so that the people in the community would think
we had plenty of money, but we were just barely within our means and
bumping the limit," Tommy said. "The truth is we were not wealthy." If
the specter of Rosser's childhood haunted him, it was offset by his rising
status in the community and enhanced by Toni's charitable work and social
prominence.

This was an America of expanding horizons. Your children were *supposed* to live better than you did. "Daddy said to me and my brother," Tommy recalled, "'I'm going to educate you to be anything you want and accustom you to the finer things in life.'.... We'd go to a restaurant and I could order lobster, prime rib, or whatever. It was never the kids' menu." The family dined out once or twice a week, often at Merry Acres or the Radium Springs Country Club, southeast of town. Developed in the 1920s as a spa and casino to lure tourists traveling along Highway 19, a main route to Florida, Radium Springs, one of Georgia's "Seven Natural Wonders," was the place for Albany's white families to relax, swim, dance, and dine out. It was rumored to glow in the dark; there were trace radioactive elements dissolved in its icy, clear waters. As a teen, Tommy Malone worked there as a towel boy, making 13 cents an hour and all the girls he could pick up.

Chapter 7

"I wanted to be treated like 25 when I was 14. That probably really explains a lot of my frustration." —Tommy Malone, teenage rebel

Tommy was a tall, striking child with brown hair and angelic features. A quick study, he could read and write by age 4. "My mother was instrumental in my taking 'Expression,' a kind of speech class," he recalled. The memory instantly triggered a flashback: 74-year-old Tommy reciting in a lilting, little boy's soprano:

"See that angel peeking through that lace? Oh my, ain't that a pretty face! God knows it's mighty like a rose."

At 5, he was reciting poetry in public. "I had no fear standing up before a crowd and talking," he said. "In fact, I liked it. Later, when the opportunity presented itself, I *wanted* to be in a courtroom speaking and communicating on my feet." That ability, the gift of speaking to a jury of ordinary citizens simply but intimately, and reducing complex arguments and facts to bite-sized morsels, became one of Tommy Malone's great strengths.

In high school, Tommy, though a woeful student and perennial discipline problem, never doubted he'd become a lawyer. He hung around his father's office running errands and assisting Robert (Bob) Drake, Rosser's associate, search titles at the County Clerk's office. Mostly, he listened to the people, the businessmen, local politicians, and litigants, who paraded in and out, and not just the joshing and silver-tongued bombast of the lawyers, but the fearful, tremulous tones of ordinary people who'd been wronged and were hoping for redress. Tommy did dream of riding in a rodeo. He painstakingly fed, groomed, mucked, and gave riding lessons on the horses Rosser purchased for his sons, though elder son, Ross, had scant interest. As one story has it, Toni dissuaded Tommy from his equine aspirations by suggesting lawyers attracted a better class of woman than broncobusters.

Toni lavished love, affection, and a schoolmarm's dedication on both boys. Favored by the complex and unknowable interactions that define family dynamics, Tommy clearly was the favored son, a status he'd claim for the rest of his life. His mother carefully inculcated the virtues, manners, and social graces a proper gentleman required. At the time, Tommy might not have cared, but he likely knew the difference between a dessert fork and a salad fork. An idealist who saw the world as perfectible and full of light, Toni parented the way she lived, with kindness, delight, and gentility. Rosser lived in the real world, a darker place. Blunt, plainspoken, and dictatorial, his honesty and homespun wisdom resonated with his younger son. "Daddy believed that a man is no better his word...that credibility is everything," Tommy recalled. "He taught me to cut through the bullshit and confusion and get to the essence of things."

Tommy is the child of both parents. Over time, in a place where a man's worth was judged by the color of his skin, where the remnants of an antebellum ruling class had evolved into a paternalistic, self-perpetuating establishment controlling all political and economic power, where a renegade Yankee media lord named James Harrison Gray filled the airwaves and the editorial pages of the *Albany Herald* with toxic racial spew, Toni's sweet idealism and Rosser's hard-nosed pragmatism, the real and the ideal, justice and injustice, what he was taught and the evidence of his eyes, clashed and jarred in Tommy Malone's head.

That tension surfaced in high school. "I'd been a teacher's pet and made top grades all the way through seventh grade," he remembered. "In the eighth grade, I kinda went to riding bucking horses, drinking beer, and not being a good boy. I guess I was becoming a rebel." A therapist might have recognized "cognitive dissonance," stress generated by having to reconcile contradictory impulses, thoughts, beliefs, and attitudes. He was hardly alone. The whole white population of the South was in extreme denial. Psychotherapists were *rara avis,* not only in Georgia but anywhere in the country. Treatment for psychotic disorders was essentially medieval. As an adult, Malone would bring a lawsuit against Georgia's most famous psychiatrist, the man who gave the world *The Three Faces of Eve.*

***

A century after the Civil War, descendants of the plantation owners and the collaborators slavery had relied upon—lawmen, legislators, functionaries, clergy, and the mercantile class—still controlled the great-grandchildren of slaves. Tactics had changed. Lynchings—at least 122 public lynchings have been documented in South Georgia—had ceased; Jim Crow laws were eroding. But the white ruling class, a tiny fraction of the southwest Georgia population, was determined to cling to mastery. Consciously or unconsciously, in polite whispers or fierce exhortations, that belief was communicated from one generation to the next.

"My father and all the white people I knew in Albany were segregationists, you might even say racists, but they didn't think they were," Tommy said. "My father would have slapped my face if I used the n-word, but he wasn't about to call a black female a lady or 'Missus.' I believed our community was run the way it should be because my father and his patriarchal friends felt that our way of life was the appropriate way of life and that everybody treated everybody honorably."

Tommy's angst was unnoticed in the zeitgeist, but it was there, nameless and unsettling, just below the surface of his very busy, seemingly careless, teenage existence. His was the era of Elvis, James Dean, and Marlon Brando, of bored teens chugging beer and circling aimlessly around small-town squares and big-city parks in flathead Mercs and chopped Ford coupes, lake pipes rumbling, searching for something elusive and inexpressible to give meaning to their lives. Dislocation and rebellion blared nonstop from Albany's WALB "Johnny Reb" radio. In the 1953 film *The Wild One*, a girl named Mildred addresses Johnny, the surly leader of a motorcycle gang newly arrived in town.

Mildred: "What are you rebelling against Johnny?"
Johnny (Marlon Brando): "Whadda ya got?"

Most rebels are doomed to settle—if they survive—into the humdrum routines of ordinary existence. Tommy Malone and at least two of his Albany peers were among the exceptions. They'd travel very different paths. Best friend Spencer Lee, the idealistic son of an FBI agent sent South by J. Edgar Hoover himself to keep an eye on racial unrest, would become a legal aid attorney for twenty-six South Georgia counties. Hamilton Jordan, a brilliant political strategist, would map out Jimmy Carter's successful 1976 run at the White House and serve as Carter's chief of staff. On the other side of town, a long-suffering African American attorney named C. B. King would earn his way into the annals of the civil rights struggle and gift the South with generations of his brilliant offspring.

***

At Albany High, Malone was an underachiever, the bright, restless kid eager to get on with the expansive life he envisioned for himself; a smartass ("discipline problem"), but not mean-spirited or violent. "I wanted to be treated like 25 when I was 14," he said. "That probably really explains a lot of my frustration." He recalls his ninth grade English teacher ordering him to the principal's office for cutting up in class. Tommy stood up and politely asked, "May I ride on your broom?" The teacher relented, no doubt concerned the quip might resonate among the faculty. Outside of class, he avoided the apple-polishers and overachievers in the Beta Club and gravitated toward the rebels and brawlers—Ish Verner, Edward Lewis, John "Gruber" Griffin, Harry "Rug Head" Ort—who hung around the Pig 'N Whistle on Oglethorpe Blvd. and would happily, after half-a-dozen beers, put "a Ked upside your head" should you cross them.

Among the cars Tommy drove was a white Plymouth Fury with a 45-rpm record player mounted on gimbals under the dash—the technological equivalent of today's rolling boom-boxes—Little Richard and Brenda Lee blasting. "We'd ride through 'The Pig' and girls would come right up to us," laughed Spencer Lee, Malone's sidekick in many misadventures. "Tommy must have worn out two motors playing that music." To hear Spencer tell it, Malone was a young Apollo in his chariot, a nimbus of nubile women trialing in his wake. Big brother, Ross, shared none of these traits. Tommy's good looks, outsized charm, and popularity triggered a rift that would divide them for the rest of their lives. Tommy was also a pool hustler and crapshooter, drawn to the less-than-savory characters who indulged in these vices, a passion that undoubtedly made his father gnash his teeth. Like Rosser, he'd go dove hunting—a big pastime in South Georgia—but never developed his father's zeal for hunting. In later years, hunting on his Albany farm, Tommy found himself staring at two deer grazing peacefully by a waterhole. He turned away. He couldn't bring himself to pull his rifle's trigger.

A black man taught Tommy to shoot pool. Oscar Cutts was one of those indelible characters who so often round out white middle-class lives in the South. At the time, Rosser Malone was the solicitor (prosecuting attorney in the "lower" court) in Dougherty County. Oscar ran "Cutts' Place" and some other joints where music blared, men played pool, and women played the men. Beer and whiskey flowed, the occasional fight erupted. This was literally Albany's "Harlem" district, a strip of bars and honkytonks south of Oglethorpe. Paradise to a big-eyed kid from the white side of town. "Oscar was close to my daddy for some reason," Tommy remembered. "Way back when I was 9 or 10, he'd pick me up after school in his big yellow Buick convertible and drive me home. Sometimes he'd sit in the back and let me drive. Nobody could see me peering out between the top of the steering wheel and the dashboard."

Oscar would roast hot dogs and for Tommy, Spencer Lee, and the boys as they lounged, Huck Finns, on the banks of Kinchafoonee Creek. The two became inseparable. "I spent more time with Oscar than I did with my father," Tommy said. A generation later, Tommy's son Adam had a parallel experience with Jeanette, Tommy's African American maid. "I spent more time with Jeanette than either my mom or dad."

Driving around Albany with Cutts, Tommy would have wondered about the shotgun shacks, broken streets, and ramshackle shops clustered on the black side of town. Separate surely, but hardly equal. He might have noticed C. B. King's law office tucked behind the funeral parlor on South Jackson Street. There, momentous things were underway. On warm days when he walked past the Dougherty County Courthouse on the way home from school to his daddy's office, he could literally hear the lawyers arguing through the open windows. It might have registered that the defendants were overwhelmingly African American, the juries never.

Tommy's descriptions of his times with Oscar are not gauzy recollections, but signs of a growing awareness that the world was not the *equitable, honest and just* place Rosser Malone proclaimed it to be. "Oscar raised me," Tommy said, but his words suggest consciousness as much as parenting. It's also possible that behind the teenager's growing rebelliousness lay a bruised innocence that, looking back, is almost painful. Make no mistake, Tommy loved Rosser Malone, which made the dissonance more acute. "I'd ask my daddy why we didn't we have some

black boys going to school with us so we could have a better football team,"
Tommy remembered. "He said, 'Son, we believe in separate but equal.
They have just as good teachers, just as good books at Monroe High
School.'"

Tommy also believed, against the evidence of his own senses, that men
like "Gator" Johnson, Baker County's notorious sheriff, and Dougherty's
"Cull" Campbell enforced the laws fairly. In high school, he often
accompanied his father to the courthouse. They'd park out back and walk
up the stairs to Sheriff Campbell's first-floor office. Prominently displayed
on the inner office wall was a photograph of six black men hanging from a
tree. Tommy asked his father about the lynching. Rosser explained "that
one of the black men had raped a white farmer's wife while her husband was
out in the fields." The sheriff roused his dogs and deputies and chased the
alleged assailant to a cabin. There, they rounded up six black males. "The
dogs couldn't identify who was the guilty man," Rosser continued. "So they
hung all six. White farmers out in the fields need to know that their wives
are safe. They had to do it."

"I accepted the things my daddy told me to be true," Tommy said. "I
learned later that a lot of what he said wasn't the way it was." Young
Tommy also believed that preachers were men of God and married couples
never cheated on their spouses, notions that would pop like soap bubbles
when, as an attorney, Tommy Malone came home to try his first cases.

Chapter 8

"I suddenly realized the brakes didn't work. I was about to run onto
Slappey Boulevard, a big four-lane road. I cut right and then left,
right into the back wall of the Palmyra Pharmacy."
—Tommy Malone at 16

In high school, one of Tommy's chores was to drive out to a subdivision his father had developed and collect the monthly water rent. "I'd go door to door like a newspaper boy collecting from the homeowners," he said. "It was like a dollar or two a month." Oftentimes, even that modest payment was beyond a family's means. One afternoon, he recalled hopping into his WWII-vintage jeep, picking up a buddy, and heading out to the east Albany subdivision. Somewhere along the way he got diverted.

"Like to go out on the sand dunes?" he grinned.

Albany is more than150 miles from the Gulf of Mexico. "We've got these dunes because at one time, the sea was there," Tommy explained. "It's like the beach only without water. You can find fossils and sea shells." Malone wasn't looking for fossils; he was reliving the exploits of Sgt. Sam Troy, star of his favorite TV show, ABC's *The Rat Patrol,* imagining he was crashing through the dunes of El Alamein in hot pursuit of Nazis. "They showed soldiers driving jeeps in the desert flying over dunes and stuff like that," he added. "I was going to show my buddy what it felt like when I'd driven over this rise in the dunes with a guy named Rusty Kaliher." At one point, the worried Kaliher had literally jumped out of the jeep before it landed harmlessly on the other side of the dune.

This time, in his excitement, Tommy didn't register that a work crew with earthmovers had come in and removed truckloads of sand from Tommy's desert. "So we're bumping along.... Going faster. Having a lot of fun.... I can't tell that the back slope of this big dune is literally gone." Suddenly, as he was yammering away, "Right here is where Rusty jumped *ouuuuuut!!!!"*

What happened next was more *Road Runner* than *Rat Patrol.* The jeep went straight out until it lost its momentum and then straight down practically at a right angle. "My buddy, whose name is lost in the sands of time, tried to jump and ended up half-in and half-out," Tommy said. "He broke a bunch of ribs. I stayed behind the wheel and ended up with a lick on my shin and my head where I'd hit the dash." The boy was hurt badly, undoubtedly going into shock. Blood dripping in his eyes, Tommy staggered a mile to the closest house and called an ambulance. Both boys were rushed to the hospital. Tommy was patched up and discharged. "I probably called my daddy right after that." Tommy paused, then added, "He thought I was trying to kill myself." Weeks later when the jeep was repaired, Tommy grabbed another buddy to pick it up. "On the way back from the shop, I suddenly realized the brakes didn't work. I was about to run onto Slappey Boulevard, a big four-lane road. I cut right and then left, right into the back wall of the Palmyra Pharmacy."

Around this time, Tommy's sophomore year, the phone rang at the Malone residence. The call was from the Albany High School principal's office. (You can almost hear Rosser groan and slam down his newspaper.) "The principal asked my parents to come meet with him," Tommy recalled. "Daddy wouldn't even go. Mother goes off to the meeting, and the next thing I know I'm being shipped off to military school! I'm a discipline problem, and Georgia Military College has this prep-school program."

Milledgeville is Georgia's antebellum capital. The city, 135 miles northeast of Albany, was home to the infamous Georgia State Lunatic Asylum (established 1842) and the prison from which Leo Frank was kidnapped in August 1915, driven to Marietta, Georgia, and lynched. Frank's trial and conviction in the murder of a 13-year-old mill worker named Mary Phagan was national news. His lynching touched off outraged cries of anti-Semitism, a mob assault on the Governor's Mansion, and controversy that continues to this day, long after Leo Frank was exonerated of the murder.

For Tommy, military school might as well have been prison. In the dreary confines of the barracks, he continued to outsmart everyone. "I learned you could stay out later, 11 P.M. or something, if you made the Merit List," he remembered. "So I made the list every time the grades came in. They'd also give you disciplinary hours for not shining your shoes or talking back to an officer. The only way to clean those up was to walk an hour on the 'bullring' with your rifle on shoulder. I set the record for more 'To Walk' hours than anybody." It was literally the gulag for a kid whose

first impulse was to challenge authority. He buckled down, continued to
made good academic grades, but at year's end, he was a lowly private adrift
in a sea of newly minted sergeants and lieutenants.

"So I headed on home."

At Albany High, Tommy's chance at making the varsity football
squad—one of Rosser's fervent hopes—had evaporated. Other players had
moved up while Tommy was walking circles in Milledgeville. He was a
6' 3" junior forced to play on the junior varsity. "Playing behind people I
knew were scared of me," he grumbled. "This added to my resentment." To
his credit, Rosser Malone understood it was only a matter of time before his
son triggered the next upheaval. What he didn't realize was that it would
come *after* Tommy Malone had finished law school, passed the bar exam—
Rosser's fondest dream—and was practicing law and "supposedly settling
down" back home.

Chapter 9

*"You can't turn the important decisions a grand jury must make over
to a bunch of uneducated people."*
—Rosser Malone to Tommy Malone

Tommy graduated from Albany High in the spring of 1960. In a class of 400, in a majority black city, in an overwhelmingly black county, not a single African American was among the graduates. Desegregation was years away and would not arrive without a struggle. That summer, Tommy and Spencer Lee wiled away the days boating and skiing on Lake Worth, readying themselves for the pilgrimage University of Georgia freshmen had been making for 175 years. At 17, Tommy was a young man with a plan: pledge a fraternity, party, study what caught his fancy, never intending to earn an undergraduate degree, simply accumulate the hours he needed for law school admission, and move on. The future glimmered bright and full of possibilities.

In the larger world, Massachusetts Senator John Fitzgerald Kennedy was en route to the Democratic National Convention in Los Angeles, where he'd win the party's nomination and face Republican Richard Nixon in November. One of the speakers in Los Angeles was James H. (Jim) Gray, chairman of the Georgia Democratic Party. Gray, a highly unlikely Georgian, was born in Massachusetts and graduated from Dartmouth College in New Hampshire. He'd married a Southern heiress and settled in Albany after World War II. At the convention, speaking in a broad New England accent startlingly similar to John Kennedy's own, Gray astounded fellow Democrats when he delivered the party's so-called "Minority Report," a segregationist screed denouncing even the tepid civil rights plank the party had adopted.

In Albany, Gray *was* the establishment. Ultraconservative, elitist, and an unashamed segregationist, he owned WALB, the second largest television station in the state, was editor and publisher of the leading newspaper, the *Albany Herald,* served more than a decade as Albany mayor, and ran unsuccessfully for governor in 1966. On one hand, he was a civic cheerleader and relentless booster of his adopted hometown; on the other, a harsh and virulent opponent of the nascent civil rights movement. Gray was also a man who liked a drink in an era when liquor was *the* social lubricant. He tended to bellow his opinions. One night at the Continental Room, Gray roared, out of the blue, at the hapless Spencer Lee, who happened to be standing nearby: "I'm gonna kick that son of a bitch Jimmy Carter's ass! I know you like him. I don't!" Not surprisingly, Gray traveled with a driver/bodyguard, a man known to Tommy, Spencer Lee, and their circle of friends as "Bo Monkey."

Gray and his sons, the Haleys, Weatherbees, Billingsleys, and Barretts, the physicians and administrators at Phoebe Putney Hospital, and the landed gentry and corporate executives, rounded by the raft of rotating lawyer-mayors—Motie Wiggins, Taxi Smith, Asa Kelley among them—controlled Albany. Rosser Malone was part of this cohort but not in the first ranks. In a few years, Tommy Malone would reject this hermetically sealed world. In turn, he'd be ostracized and banished. He and James Gray would clash repeatedly over the pervasive injustice privilege creates, a thing young Malone did not fully comprehend but would not abide.

Racism ran deeper than the chill waters of Radium Springs and wider than the segregated schools and whites-only water fountains and bus station and doctors' waiting rooms, reflective of all the daily indignities the black man was made to endure. Racism was the economic and political engine that kept the white men of the "establishment" in power. Of course, Albany was a microcosm of a toxic system supporting white power and privilege throughout the South and, while not formally codified, everywhere in the country. Under Georgia's county-unit system, rural voters perpetuated segregation by diluting the votes of moderate whites and African Americans living in population centers such as Atlanta, maintaining a corrupt, self-sustaining cycle. In congressional, state, and multiple-county races, for example, the county-unit system granted rural Calhoun, Baker, and Terrell counties, where registered voters were overwhelmingly white, disproportionate weight over more populous Dougherty, negating what little African American turnout there was and any hope for political change. Dougherty County was also part of a four-county state judicial circuit; it had four votes in elections while the other three counties each had two. "There was no way we could elect a superior court judge or district attorney, two of the most powerful people in the county," Tommy Malone recalled, "because the three smaller counties always ganged-up against the big county."

There was a wink-and-nod shamelessness to the depths to which the power structure would sink. Jury selection is a case in point. Jury commissioners were charged with selecting upright and intelligent members of a community to serve on grand juries as well as petit (trial) juries. As Rosser Malone explained to Tommy, "You can't turn the important decisions a grand jury must make over to a bunch of uneducated people." Of course, 90 percent of the African American population was poor and "uneducated." In some parts of South Georgia, the story went, when jurors were summoned, their names would be put on a slip of paper. The papers would be put into a box and brought into open court, where the presiding judge would reach in, take out a slip with a juror's name on it, and hand it to the clerk.

"Well, the whites were on rough paper and the blacks on slick paper," Tommy discovered. "So a judge could tell which was which. They didn't think they were doing things as bad as this obviously was, and appears today, but they sure weren't about to turn over important decisions like appointing the registrar to African Americans. They wanted to maintain that control."

Chapter 10

Change, dizzying and gut-wrenching, was in the air.—Albany, Georgia,
1961

Segregationists such as James Gray refused to see it, but change, dizzying and gut-wrenching, was in the air. Many years later, Andrew Young, former Atlanta mayor and congressman, would describe the feeling of the tumultuous civil rights years as a "freedom high." In southwest Georgia, freedom was a long time coming. In 1918, a returning World War I veteran named Chevene (C. W.) King organized an Albany, Georgia, branch of the NAACP in the hope of boosting black voter registration, the first step to securing civil rights and political power. At the time, barely a handful of African Americans were registered voters in Albany, and many of these were merchants and professionals unwilling to challenge the system. C. W. King's fragile hopes withered in the face of Jim Crow but were revived again in the late 1940s as a new wave of veterans returned home seeking the rights citizenship guaranteed and their service demanded.

In 1960, when Tommy Malone headed off to college, most African American residents of Albany had never voted or served on a jury. Their children attended dilapidated schools and studied from ragged texts castoff by the all-white public school system. Malone had never questioned his father's assurances that the black schools might be separate but equal. "Outside agitators were coming in and stirring up things," Rosser assured him. "Our community is run the way it should be." And so, to most whites, the sorrows, hopes, and joys of black people were invisible.

Four years would pass before the landmark civil rights and voting rights acts were signed into law as part of Lyndon Johnson's "Great Society" initiative. More years before Rev. Martin Luther King Jr. and his Southern Christian Leadership Conference propelled civil rights onto the national agenda in the aftermath of the savagery of Birmingham and Selma. In Albany, the first cracks in the facade appeared in the winter of 1961 when Student Nonviolent Coordinating Committee (SNCC) organizers Charles Sherrod and Cordell Reagon arrived and began an outreach to students at

Albany State College. The plan was to organize open-ended, nonviolent marches, sit-ins, and protests, draw support from local black churches and community organizations, and register enough African American voters to force concessions from Mayor Asa Kelley and the city council.

If the organizers envisioned sympathetic media coverage—civil rights was fast-becoming a national story—James Gray made sure those hopes were dashed. Chronicled in civil rights' histories as the "Albany Movement," the protests that erupted over the next eighteen months resulted in 2,000 arrests and drew in Dr. Martin Luther King Jr. but failed to desegregate or even ease the systemic racism in Albany. There was no national media outcry against police brutality because Laurie Pritchett, the city's chief of police, responded to civil disobedience not with police dogs, beatings, and fire hoses, but with swift and nonviolent arrests. He jailed the protesters and warehoused them in neighboring counties, rendering them, like pawns swept from a chessboard, *hors de combat.*

When Martin Luther King Jr. arrived to join the marchers, he was arrested, but according to the histories, King allowed himself to be bailed out, erroneously believing Albany's city fathers had agreed to the protesters' demands. They hadn't. The following summer, King and Ralph David Abernathy returned to Albany for sentencing, *determined* to serve jail time, only to find their fines had been paid "anonymously." The Albany Movement stalled and King moved on.

Chevene Bowers (C. B.) King would be the avatar of Albany's civil rights struggle. No inspirational preacher or rabble-rousing organizer, C. B. was a lawyer, honest, rational, and unyielding as granite. He'd graduated from Fisk University in Nashville. After being denied admission to Georgia's all-white law schools, he earned his JD degree at Case Western Reserve University in Ohio. In the mid-1950s, he returned home to practice. In Albany and its environs, he worked cases like any other lawyer, but King was, by definition, an outsider in his own town, and the establishment, to its shame, would do whatever it took to thwart him.

A contemporary of Rosser Malone, King was one of a handful of African American lawyers in Georgia, the only one practicing south of Atlanta. By existing accounts, C. B. King was eloquent and adept, with a near-Shakespearean mastery of the English language and a photographic knowledge of the law. His lawyering left opposing lawyers and most judges flummoxed by his vocabulary and outraged by a black man's audacity. Civil rights icon and Georgia Congressman John Lewis—whom King defended after his arrest in a protest in Americus—once joked that "C. B. used words only C. B. understood."

C. B. King joined the battles swirling around him. He worked to block literacy-test voting requirements, to integrate Albany's schools, polling places, and public accommodations, to open up the pool of city employees to include African American jobseekers, and to integrate the jury selection system. Against the odds, King was able to grow his practice, secure a measure of justice for his clients—Martin Luther King Jr., Ralph Abernathy, and Andrew Young, among the more notable—and serve as a model and mentor for a host of young students from the nation's finest law schools, who flocked to Albany as interns when the civil rights struggle captured the zeitgeist. In 1971, C. B. King hired Herbert E. Phipps, a young African American lawyer born in nearby Baker County. Phipps, who'd attended segregated schools and studied from tattered, out-of-date textbooks cast off by the white schools, never owned a new school book until he enrolled at Atlanta University's Morehouse College. After earning his law degree from Case Western Reserve University in Ohio, he'd come home determined to wield the majesty of the law in the civil rights battle. He'd go on—after an unlikely boost from Rosser Malone in 1980—to be appointed magistrate judge, juvenile court judge, superior court judge (the highest level of trial court in Georgia), and ultimately, chief judge of the Georgia Court of Appeals.

***

Shameful barely describes C. B. King's treatment at the hands of law enforcement, the courts, and fellow attorneys. Court officers thwarted him from sitting inside the bar until his case was called or tried to exclude him from the courtroom altogether. When King dared visit one of his clients, a jailed white protester named Bill Anderson, who'd been assaulted by his cellmates, C. B. was attacked by Dougherty County Sheriff "Cull" Campbell. (South Georgia sheriffs seemed to favor names like "Gator," "Screws," and "Cull.") Shrieking "Nigger!" again and again, Campbell beat King senseless with a wooden cane. A news photograph of King, head bandaged and bleeding, flashed around the country. He'd won a victory, but at terrible cost.

More often, it was the little indignities the man endured. The bar association literally split its meetings into business and social components. They handled business in the courtroom and excluded King from the socializing. "They weren't about to share food or drinks with C. B.," Tommy remembered. When King came into the courtroom, he was not permitted to sit in front of the rail like all the other lawyers. Once, when testimony ran overlong in the sweltering Dougherty County Courthouse, King requested a glass of water and was brought a bucket and ladle. When Laurie Pritchett addressed King as "C. B." rather than "Mr. King," the manner of address accorded white men in court, King countered by referring to the police chief as "Laurie." Lambasted for carrying "a chip on your shoulder," King replied, "I beg your pardon. I have the law on my shoulder."

***

Tommy Malone came to maturity in this through-the-looking-glass world, the evidence of his senses denied or distorted. In time, reality came crashing through, exposing many of the things he was taught to think, feel, and believe as illusion. Reality shock can be transformative, opening one's eyes to truths that for many reasons we dare not see. It's possible to imagine young Tommy, thirsting for approval, accepting Rosser's explanation that the lynching on display in Sheriff Campbell's office contained a moral, an exemplum, not so different from the sermons Albany's preachers might deliver on a sunny and peaceful Sunday morning.

"Son, the farmers working in the fields need to know their wives are safe."

"Yes, Daddy," Tommy answered, meaning every word, even as the *dissonance*, the contradictions that would drive rebellion against his teachers, role models, and preachers, Cull Campbell, Jim Gray, everything the poisoned Albany establishment represented, roared in his head. "I accepted my daddy's explanation for the hangings," Tommy recalled more than half a century later. "That there was no alternative."

***

Years later, when Tommy was practicing in his own Albany law office, he took a call from his father, now a state judge. Rosser was none too happy.

"Son, somebody told me they saw you going into C. B. King's office south of Oglethorpe."

"Yes Sir. That was me."

"You don't go into his office. He comes up to yours."

"Well, Daddy, now we've got black jurors and we've got white jurors. And I know that C. B. and I could try cases and do better than either one of us could do alone."

"'Least make him come up to your office."

"No, Daddy, I'm not going to do that."

Tommy persisted. In fact, despite his father's disinclination, he somehow convinced Rosser to appoint Herbert Phipps—still working with C. B. King—to the Dougherty County Magistrate Court. As a state court judge, Rosser Malone had the authority to appoint magistrates and also make them associate judges of the state court to help with his caseload. Phipps, who wanted to continue his civil rights work, later said he accepted the appointment because he realized it would be significant to have "a black judge in South Georgia." (He was the first.) Tommy assured Herb that he had the talent and ability to go much further, "to be a judge in the state's highest courts," a conversation both men remembered many years later. "There was a lot of quiet resistance," Phipps recalled. "A lot of influential people in the community didn't want Judge Malone to do it. Tommy was the one who persuaded him. Tommy planted the seed, and along the way, I always had his encouragement and support. He'd become well known and well connected with the governors and others who were making these appointments."

Chapter 11

*"None of us realized the significance of what we were witnessing.
History was being made and we were oblivious."*
—Tommy's college roommate, Buddy Dallas

Tommy and Spencer Lee arrived in Athens, Georgia, in September 1960. Tommy, cool behind the wheel of his Plymouth Fury. The Ventures' twangy guitar anthem, "Walk—Don't Run," was near the top of the charts, chasing Elvis's "It's Now or Never" and Chubby Checker's "Twist." Two 17-year-olds, straight out of rural Georgia, could not have been more unprepared for the tumultuous world they were about to enter. Or cared less. "We didn't even unpack our bags in the dorm," Lee recalled many years later. "We headed straight to Chili's to shoot pool and drink beer. That's how we entered college, and that's what we thought college was all about."

Fraternities dominated life at the University of Georgia. Then as now, the frat houses were raucous islands of elitism and reactionary politics afloat in a sea of conservatism, essentially a microcosm of Georgia itself. In 1958, Governor Ernest Vandiver Jr., a UGA graduate, had been elected under the slogan "No, not one!," promising no black child would ever sit next to a white child in a public school. In Georgia, fraternity membership was a particular rite of passage for any young man planning to move into the spheres of law, politics, or business. At UGA, frat membership often numbered generations of the same family (no different than Princeton or Yale). Taken together, this created an intricate skein of familial, commercial, and political connection that survives to this day. Within the all-white Greek system, secret societies and closed groups abounded. In Atlanta, everything from the Governor's Mansion to the State House, to the Coca-Cola executive suite, to elite law firms such as King & Spalding and Alston & Bird seemed to have an umbilical to Athens that flowed much deeper and blood-rich than an affinity for Bulldog football.

Tommy Malone pledged Alpha Tau Omega (ATO), a fraternity founded in post-Civil War Virginia, and whose white-columned house suggested *Gone With The Wind*, but its vibe *Animal House*. Never a shrinking violet, Malone threw himself headlong into Athens' raucous party scene. His years at UGA would be no replay of Rosser's Malone's joyless sojourn at the Athens YMCA. "I was a party *animal*," Tommy admitted with some understatement. Indeed, one of his pledge brothers remembered the towering freshman sporting pegged pants, tennis shoes, and a tee-shirt, pouring sweat and gulping beer as he "absolutely rocked out" to Ray Charles's jittering "What'd I Say!" Rosser Malone, a complicated man, expected no less of his son. Ross, the eldest, had disappointed him by choosing to attend archrival Georgia Tech, intent on becoming an engineer. Rosser absolutely *wanted* his offspring to enjoy all the pleasures of campus life and kept Tommy's finances liquid with money drawn from the "water rent" collected on his properties.

"My father was reliving his college life through me," Tommy said.

That would change.

Malone's roommate, prelaw student Albert (Buddy) Dallas, remembered the autumn day an ATO contingent descended on the Clark County Fair. As one might imagine, the boys had scant interest in champion hogs or prized heifers. "In the South, there's always a particular tent that the men go to," Dallas explained. "I'd never been to one. In Lincoln County where I grew up, you weren't about to be seen going into a place like that. Of course, the tent was our first stop." Dallas eagerly paid the few dollars admission. Inside, through a pall of cigarette smoke and whiskey breath, he found himself staring at a belly dancer "in all her glory." Half-heartedly gyrating on a tiny stage, the woman was naked except for a smear of bright blue mascara around her eyes. "You could hear a pin drop," Dallas remembered. "For me, seeing a nude young lady was an accomplishment in its own right.... But then, the lady started doing something with a cigarette in a certain portion of her body. She could blow smoke rings! I was experiencing a bit of heaven or hell at the same time." From somewhere among the dumbstruck, overheated frat boys a voice rang out:

"Hey girl, does your mama know you've got all that blue shit around your eyes!"

It was Tommy Malone. "He brought the place down," Dallas recalled. "Only Tommy could have gotten away with it."

Elsewhere on the frat circuit, Tommy met and began dating Joan Beall, a very pretty but equally immature sorority girl from the Atlanta suburbs. Like every male of the period, Tommy's ideal woman was a caricature torn from the pages of *Playboy*. To her delight and her sorority sisters' envy, Joan found herself dating a tall, fun-loving, good-looking Big Man On Campus. The relationship progressed over the next years, but like so many eyes-wide-shut college romances, the marriage that followed would be star-crossed.

Spencer Lee's no-nonsense father, William (Billy) Spencer Lee III, had finished law school at UGA and joined the FBI. Like Tommy, Spencer would take a more circuitous route. Trailing a string of incompletes and short on money, he never made it past second semester. Lee dropped out— he said—to buy a car, got married, came back, dropped out again, until finally making it through law school. For his part, Tommy was in a hurry to pass the bar exam but had little interest in an undergraduate degree. "Just trying to accumulate hours," he recalled. "Back then, you needed three things to get into law school—135 hours, an adequate grade on the Law School Admissions Test (LSAT), and a C-average. I went from the business school to the journalism school taking whatever courses I found interesting."

***

On January 6, 1961, as Tommy Malone was beginning his second quarter, US District Judge William Augustus Bootle stunned Southern segregationists by ordering the admission of two African American students, Hamilton Holmes and Charlayne Hunter, to the University of Georgia, effectively ending 170 years of state-enforced segregation. Judge Bootle's ruling, enforcing the Civil Rights Act of 1957 (the first since Reconstruction), is considered a defining moment in history. Like a tumbling row of dominos, the order, backed by the renowned US Appellate Court Judge Elbert Tuttle, would throw open the doors of institutions of higher learning throughout the South, but not without a struggle.

In Georgia, Judge Tuttle triggered a constitutional crisis. In 1955, the state legislature had passed a constitutional amendment mandating an immediate cutoff of funding for any white educational institution that desegregated. Governor Vandiver was now faced with a daunting challenge: either he ignore state law or shutter his state's premier educational institution

(Vandiver's own alma mater) along with the rest of Georgia's public school system. In 1960, Griffin Bell, Vandiver's chief of staff and confidante, suggested the governor create a commission of political and civic leaders charged with exploring public sentiment regarding desegregation, in effect putting the "decision" in the hands of the people. Atlanta businessman John Sibley was named commission chairman.

The Sibley Commission's hearings and carefully orchestrated report (some would say "doctored," as 60 percent of Georgians actually favored massive resistance to integration) is remembered as laying a political foundation for desegregation and averting the kind of showdown with the federal government then unfolding in Mississippi and Alabama. At this point, Judge Bootle effectively threw Georgia a fig leaf, issuing a restraining order "prohibiting" the legislature from denying funding to any integrated school. Vandiver quickly adopted the Sibley Commission findings and later that winter initiated successful legislation repealing the defunding amendment.

On Monday, January 9, Holmes and Hunter arrived on campus under heavy security and accompanied by a contingent of national media bristling with microphones and TV cameras. One of the student reporters covering the crisis for the campus newspaper, *The Red & Black*, was Tom Johnson, later president of CNN. In his memoirs, Johnson clearly remembered "state legislators calling fraternity members urging them to resist integration."

"Two-Four-Six-Eight! We don't want to integrate!" the chant echoed across the campus.

"Two-Four-Six-Eight...."

On Wednesday, January 11, as Tommy arrived at the ATO frat house after a basketball game, a mob waving makeshift signs and banners was surging toward Myers Hall, Charlayne Hunter's dorm, a stone's throw from fraternity row. "People were going around shouting, 'The Governor says the more people get arrested the better!'" Malone recalled. "The higher-ups in the fraternity were passing out cherry bombs and firecrackers to throw." Buddy Dallas was with him. "We were not looking to go over there," Dallas insisted, "but there were phone calls being made to assemble. Today, it would be called a flash mob."

A senior ("one of the men I had to follow," Malone recalled) shouted, "We need to get up to Myer's Hill!"

"So we went up there," Dallas added.

They were met by a cordon of local police and Georgia state troopers. "There was hooting and hollering," according to Tommy, "but at that point, nothing riotous." At that moment, one of the seniors thrust the corner of a hand-painted sheet into Malone's hand. "I'll tell you why it hurts," Tommy said in 2016. "It's one word."

"*Nigger Go Home!*"

"None of us realized the significance of what we were witnessing," Dallas said. "History was being made and we were oblivious. There just were thousands of kids chanting and yelling in the streets. Honestly, if someone had told me to hold the corner of the sheet instead of Tommy, I would've done it without a thought." Dallas paused and added, "All of it really bothered us later."

Dean William Tate, a courageous man careless of his own safety, waded into the surging crowd demanding student IDs. In the midst of the growing turmoil, Tommy Malone was arrested. "As far as I know," he recalled, "I was the first one in jail." After he was hauled off, police and state troopers waded into the crowd. A full-blown riot ensued. Bricks and bottles were thrown, cars overturned, hateful epithets shouted, and tear gas floated across the campus.

At the police station, Tommy made a fraught phone call to Rosser Malone in Albany, who hired an Athens lawyer named Rupert Brown to defend him. "Rupert was probably 90-years-old at the time," Tommy said. "When the time came, we went to court as required. The judge on the bench said, 'Everybody who's here for obstruction,' or whatever it was, 'step forward.' I had to punch Rupert on the arm to wake him up."

"You know what's happening, don't you?" Tommy hissed.

"What?"

"They're about to try all of us at once!"

"You don't want to do that?"

"No, sir! I want to be tried by myself."

Rupert nodded, got to his feet, and approached the bench.

"Lo and behold," Malone remembered, "they couldn't find any witnesses so the charges were dismissed."

But the worst part, the thing that undercut Tommy's trust in so many things he'd been taught to believe, occurred when he returned home to Albany later that quarter. "I was crossing the street with my daddy—he always parked behind the courthouse—and it took me twenty or thirty minutes to shake hands with everybody congratulating me like I was a local hero."

At 74, Tommy Malone is still troubled by events that unfolded on a winter's day when he was 18. Over the years, he has done much personally and professionally to undo the pain he may have caused, but the unease still nags at him. "I was just a naïve freshman who'd pledged a fraternity," he said. "I didn't know how bad it was. I didn't even know who I was."

Chapter 12

*"I began to realize that whatever Tommy dug into was not going to
be ordinary because there was nothing ordinary about
Tommy Malone."*
—Buddy Dallas

In some ways, Buddy Dallas was Tommy's polar opposite. He was the son of a struggling logger in rural Lincoln County and the first in his family to attend college. "My parents could barely scrape together the $25 a week I needed to survive," he recalled. Dallas was bright, ambitious, and focused, as only a man born with few options could be. "I went to UGA to become governor of Georgia," Dallas said bluntly. "And to win every academic award and honor I possibly could. Tommy was there because Rosser Malone told him, 'I went to college and I'm not having you laying [*sic*] around the house!'" True to form, Tommy's grades went straight into the toilet, a trajectory that convinced Rosser that perhaps his wayward son still had some growing up to do.

Dallas was a joiner, a networker, and natural politician of considerable talent and enthusiasm. In short order, he was elected secretary and then president of the UGA student body. He was a member of the Gridiron Secret Society (a "Who's Who" of Georgia leaders in government, law, business, and medicine), the Bulldog Club, the Dean's List, and a half dozen other organizations. After law school at Mercer University, Buddy would return home to Lincoln County, start a practice, and devote himself to keeping the family farm above water. He never did become governor, but he did spend two decades as James ("Godfather of Soul") Brown's personal attorney. He and Tommy would stay friends for the rest of their lives.

In Tommy, Buddy sensed a powerful magnetism, a potent mix of sensitivity, likeability, and recklessness that—much magnified—had propelled James Dean to fame. "The fact that I was president of the student body was no big deal," Dallas said. "Girls wanted a guy who was ready to party. That was Tommy." Dallas and Malone shared quick minds, raucous humor, and a taste for high-speed living. "Tommy and I never thought we'd make it," Dallas said in 2017, at the time struggling to recover from a horrific highway accident. "By age 40, we'd worn out three bodies." By age 24, James Dean was dead.

By Malone's sophomore year, Rosser's fantasy of somehow reliving his college life through his son's exploits had evaporated. He penned what Tommy's friends and family later came to call the "Dear Son" letter. As Adam Malone paraphrased:

Dear Son:
Your grades have arrived. You are obviously having more fun than anybody else who ever attended the University of Georgia. Do not change a thing. But between now and the next time your grades come out, I would advise you to give strong consideration to which branch of the service you want to join because I will not support this party for another quarter.

"Back then, no one would have picked Tommy Malone as the guy 'Most Likely to Succeed,'" Dallas recalled with a chuckle. "Then his daddy's letter arrived.... I guess rooming with me, seeing me trying to accomplish something other than drinking all the beer in Athens, registered." Buddy also saw a glimmer, a longing, a need to put aside childish things in his freewheeling roommate. At one point, he used his influence to name Tommy secretary of the Pre-Law Club (Buddy was president). Malone's grades immediately ticked up. "No one had ever asked Tommy to do anything responsible," Dallas remembered. "I swear it was an aligning up of planets. He saw an opportunity to solve his grades' problem with his daddy and actually put on a responsible face. He worked hard to be the best secretary there'd ever been. And he was. After a while, I began to realize that whatever Tommy dug into was not going to be ordinary because there was nothing ordinary about Tommy Malone."

When Tommy was elected secretary of the pre-law club, Rosser and Toni celebrated like he'd garnered a nomination to the Supreme Court. "It totally revolutionized the attitude my parents displayed toward me," he remembered. Next, he was named president of the Demosthenian Literary Club, a debating society founded by the university's original graduating class in 1803. Debate brought together the elocution, the public-speaking skills, and the love of the spotlight Toni had nurtured in her son in his preschool years. The club provided Tommy a forum to hone the tactics and tools that would make him so formidable a courtroom general. More importantly, it gave him a taste of success as intoxicating as all the beer in Athens.

Almost.

The man could ace a test. Tommy had taken the SATs as a high school junior and scored in the top percentiles. Now he took the Law School Admissions Test (LSAT) a year early. He did so well that he sent an application to the law school's admissions office, where it eventually made its way to the desk of the formidable J. Alton Hosch. Hosch, a fixture at UGA, had been law school dean so long Rosser Malone knew him from his own years in Athens. "Daddy asked Dean Hosch to please let me in," Tommy recalled. "He said he'd make sure I'd have the required hours. He said didn't want me wasting a year sitting around doing nothing—and having to support me, I guess." A year later, Tommy was still short ten hours. Piling on summer school credits wouldn't put him over the top. Resigned to another undergrad semester, he took a summer job working for Lawyers Title Insurance in Atlanta. Out of the blue, a letter arrived *welcoming* him to law school. "I called my father," Malone remembered. "'Daddy, they've made a mistake. I've got this letter here inviting me to come to class. If you want me to, I'll go, but if they catch me they might kick me out.'"

"Give it a try," Rosser said.

Tommy charmed the ladies in the registration office into changing his campus ID from "3" (junior) to "6" (graduate student), and after passing the sophomore equivalency exam, he registered and strode into class with the confident air of a young Clarence Darrow. Unfortunately, the robust work ethic he'd displayed in the Pre-Law Club dissipated like mountain dew. "I was in the fraternity house," he explained. "I was secretary of the fraternity. I partied. I did everything I did in undergraduate school. Obviously, I was *born* to be a lawyer, so I didn't need to buy all the books." At this point Malone paused in his tale.

"Let's just say by the end of the first quarter, I was very disappointed in my grades."

He made a B in Legal Method, D+ in Criminal Law, F in Agency. Such grades do not go unnoticed. Chastened, Malone bailed out of the fraternity and moved into a house peopled by nose-to-the-grindstone law students. He next attached himself to Scott Charlton, the school's top student. "When you saw Scott on campus, you saw Tommy. I didn't let him out of my sight. We studied together for every course." The turning point was an eight-hour contracts course taught by Dean Hosch. "He gave a test at the end of the second quarter," Tommy said. "He was reputed to not even *look* at tests. He gave you your average. So Scott got an A+ and I got a D+. When we debriefed each other, we'd quoted almost the same cases, made the same answers. I could believe a B, even a C+, but a D+? No way!"

Stunned at the injustice, Malone went to see the dean. "Hosch won't even talk about my test," he remembered. "Instead, he tells me I don't have enough hours to even be in law school." (He didn't.) "'You shouldn't be here.'" Then there was Catch 22: if Tommy ended the year with a D average, no accredited law school in Georgia would admit him. "I was trapped," he said. "My father graduated from this school. I wanted to graduate from this school. I *wanted* to be a lawyer." Hosch advised he go back to undergraduate school, get a degree, and reapply. "'Then we'll consider whether to take you.'"

"It would have taken me *two more years* to earn my degree," Malone said. "All he can promise is to consider me?"

Fate intervened. As president of the Demosthenian Literary Society, Tommy developed a friendship with Dr. Albert B. Saye, the club's faculty advisor. Saye is the historian and political scientist whose scholarship had upended the old canard that Georgia was founded as a penal colony. At the time, he was on a committee tasked with revising Georgia's criminal code. One of his colleagues on the committee was James Quarles, dean of Mercer University's Walter F. George School of Law, a school that numbered Judge Augustus "Gus" Bootle and future Attorney General of the United States Griffin B. Bell among its alumni. Quarles seemed the polar opposite of the irascible Hosch. "Courteous, soft-spoken, moderate in word and deed, generous, serious when required, piquantly humorous when appropriate, unerringly true to his word," according to his obituary. A man who might give a troublesome but gifted young man a break. "Professor Saye asked Dean Quarles if he'd give me a chance," Tommy said. "Thankfully, he did." It was the beginning of a beautiful relationship. In October 2015, Tommy Malone took office as chairman of Mercer University's Board of Trustees.

Over the years, according to those familiar with his philanthropy, Malone has donated more than a million dollars to the university and funded the Tommy Malone Distinguished Chair in Trial Advocacy.

Chapter 13

"Son, when the Governor calls, you have to serve."
—Rosser Malone

1963. Tommy Malone snared a summer job in the Washington, DC, office of Georgia's all-powerful US Senator Richard Russell thanks to the influence of Earl Leonard, Russell's press secretary. Hamilton Jordan, Tommy's boyhood friend who'd become President Jimmy Carter's chief of staff in 1976, was also in Washington that summer, young men began to weave the intricate skein of connection so vital in a state like Georgia. Hamilton was exceedingly well connected. His maternal grandfather, Hamilton McWhorter Sr., was president of the Georgia state senate; his uncle, Hamilton McWhorter Jr., served as senate secretary; a cousin, Robert H. Jordan, was chief justice of the Supreme Court of Georgia. In Albany, Toni Malone and Adelaide McWhorter Jordan, Hamilton's mother, worked together on numerous social and charitable functions. Not all patronage jobs are equal. Hamilton worked as a Senate page. Tommy ran an elevator and folded mail in the senator's office. "I'd go over to the office and there'd be a stack of signed letters and a stack of envelopes with addresses on them," he remembered. "My job was to fold the letters, stuff them into the envelope, lick 'em, and have them ready to be mailed. The last words in all those letters that went to all the constituents were, 'I fear we will lose this battle, but I assure you it will be in the last ditch.' Senator Russell was talking about the Civil Rights Act."

Tommy began Mercer law school in September 1963. John F. Kennedy's assassination and the fall of Camelot were just months away. This was a new Tommy, studious, serious, and determined. The party animal consigned, at least temporarily, to the wings. On the personal side, obedient to custom and the laws of attraction, Tommy proposed to Joan Beall and she accepted, another attractive young couple taking a preordained step on the path to adulthood. Like so many others, neither was capable of understanding the sacrifices and demands necessary to build and sustain a loving, long-term relationship, how precious such a commitment was, or how a dysfunctional relationship would reverberate, ripple, and repeat itself over the years. This was a world in which love was no more deeply defined or examined than a country song or an image projected on a drive-in movie screen. Divorce would soar over the next decades until marriage itself offered no better odds than a roulette table in Las Vegas. Tommy was particularly naïve. "What was a wife for?" he asked rhetorically. "My father was a chauvinist. I didn't grow up learning the value of women. Anybody who could play bridge, handle charitable events, keep the house clean with the help of a maid, raise the children with nannies, could be a wife. All I paid attention to were nice figures and pretty faces."

At Mercer, Tommy rose to the top third of his class. His first summer at Mercer Law ('64), he landed a job with Georgia Attorney General Eugene Cook. "Back then," Tommy said, "you could take the bar exam under one of three conditions: you'd worked in a lawyer's office for two years; you'd gone to any law school, accredited or otherwise, for two years; you'd been under a lawyer's tutelage for two years." He took it in his second year. Joan and Tommy married in June 1965. While they were honeymooning in Puerto Rico, *the letter* arrived in Albany. Rosser gave Tommy the news when he called to check in. He'd passed the bar. "I didn't have an undergraduate or a law degree," Tommy said. "It didn't matter. I could be a lawyer, get sworn-in, and start practicing. Only now, I *wanted* a degree to make my parents proud." Back from his honeymoon, the newly minted lawyer started his summer job in 1965 with Arthur Bolton, who'd replaced Cook as state attorney general.

Tommy graduated in 1966. That year, on November 28, a son, Thomas William Malone Jr., was born. For a young lawyer with an eye on bigger things, the first step is a clerkship, the more prestigious the better. Tommy was hoping to clerk for Appellate Court Judge Homer Eberhardt, a conservative and very influential jurist and a man whose law clerks were routinely recruited by the big firms beginning to dominate the scene in Atlanta. Tommy had a recommendation from Attorney General Gene Cook in his pocket. "Had my application in," Tommy recalled. "And a pretty good shot at that clerkship."

One morning, a classmate approached.

"I didn't know your father was in state politics," the guy said.

"He's not. He's in local politics. Always has been."

Rosser Malone had worked on political campaigns as long as Tommy could remember. In fact, one of his ambitions was to persuade the Georgia legislature to authorize a separate judicial circuit for Dougherty County. If it happened, Albany would no longer be in thrall to its smaller neighbors. Who better than Rosser, a former solicitor, to serve on the bench of a newly formed superior court?

"Well, I just heard on the news that your daddy is the new director of the Georgia Game and Fish Commission."

"I can't imagine."

Curiosity piqued, Tommy got on the phone.

"Son, when the Governor calls, you have to serve," Rosser allowed.

Certainly, Rosser Malone was an avid outdoorsman, but he also had bigger fish to fry. The commission was no minor patronage plum. Rosser was a man with a plan. "Anyone in government who has employees all over the state is a power," he told Tommy. It didn't hurt that the newly elected governor was his old buddy Carl Sanders. Rosser was packing to move to Atlanta. Toni opted to stay behind.

"Son, you've got to get back to Albany to keep the law firm going."

"Daddy, I've got an application to clerk on the court of appeals...."

"Can't do it, Son. Got to keep the firm together."

Was this destiny, fate, or just another chapter in the never-ending adventure of being Rosser Malone's son?

"I withdrew my application with Judge Eberhardt," Tommy said. "Looking back, my career might have been very different had I taken that clerkship. Daddy said he planned to stay in Atlanta six months. He stayed three years."

Back in Albany, Tommy discovered how much he liked the day-to-day feel of lawyering, forging human connections, researching precedents, marshalling arguments, and matching wits with intelligent and motivated adversaries in the pursuit of an admirable and elusive goal. Law was as familiar and comforting to Malone as his father's musty office or the big round table at the Gordon Hotel where Rosser and the older lawyers gathered to drink coffee, shoot the breeze, and flirt with the waitresses who gave as good as they got. "One of the older lawyers told our waitress he wanted his pie *a la mode*," Tommy remembered. "She pointed to his belly and said, 'If I had that on me, I'd skip the *a la mode.*' To which he replied, 'The last woman that was on had no complaint and I am confident you would have none either."

For the majority of young, idealistic law students, the law is not a backdrop against which to practice and make a good living, but a mechanism, vital and alive, for arriving at justice and righting wrongs in a world rife with injustice. Certainly, Tommy felt that way. What set him apart, knowingly or unknowingly, is that he would never change.

Chapter 14

"When I came back, I was not a kid who had to accept what I was told. I was a man. Not just a man, but a lawyer-man who could make up his own mind about what cases to accept and reject."
—Tommy Malone

Sometime in 1962, Tommy had a memorable conversation with Carl Sanders. The gubnatorial candidate was passing through southwest Georgia on a campaign trip and stopped in to visit with Rosser. Tommy was 19 at the time and duly impressed by the personable and magnetic Sanders, a candidate different from the backslapping, grits-and-barbecue-eating old-boy politicians he'd seen. "I asked him why a successful lawyer from Augusta would even want to get into politics with all the criticism and sniping and stuff that goes on," Tommy remembered. Sanders' answer resonated with a young man seemingly determined to live in the arena, meaningfully and on his own terms: "Tommy, let me tell you something," Sanders said with a wink. "Ain't no dogs barking at parked cars."

"Those words saw me through my life," Tommy said. "If you don't do anything, you won't be noticed, but if you do, you run the risk of getting bit, or at least barked at."

***

The sign in the law office above the U-Save-It Pharmacy now read "Malone, Drake & Malone." Tommy and Joan had arrived in Albany. Rosser was busy traveling around the state for the Game and Fish Commission. With Rosser away, Tommy was experiencing a freedom high of his own, determined to strike out in new directions. "I'd take everybody," he recalled. Bob Drake was handling real estate work; Tommy focused on new business—that is, showing up mornings for arraignments at the city armory (a facility utilized during the construction of a new courthouse) and volunteering to represent indigent defendants. "I'd get them all to sign a $50 note not expecting anybody to ever pay me, but I'd get whatever I could—$10 or an old car," he said. "I represented folks charged with everything from rape to child abuse to murder. It really was *pro bono*, but the *bono* was the trial experience I got handling these cases and dealing with people."

The newlyweds bought a three-bedroom house on Barnesdale Way for $750 down and a $19,000 assumed mortgage. At work, Tommy wasted no time sprucing-up Rosser's rundown office. The institutional green linoleum was so worn the wooden flooring showed through in places. Rather than law books and hunting prints, a "huge rattling air-conditioning machine" greeted clients coming through the door. "Nothing succeeds quite as well as the appearance of success," his mother had advised, so Tommy—never adverse to spending money—pulled up the linoleum and had new carpeting installed.

"What in hell have you done?" Rosser demanded when he took in the renovation.

"Daddy, it was embarrassing. We had holes in the linoleum..."

"Goddamn it, Son! Now nobody will think we need the business!"

Rosser may have had a point. In a few years, Tommy would decide he needed a private airplane, anticipating the demands of an expanding personal-injury practice scattered all over the state, but equally likely indulging a passion for bigger-faster-better toys that began with speedboats and a jeep and led to Aerostar aircraft, Striker sport fishing boats, and Jaguars and Jensen-Healey sports cars. "It'd take me two days to do a deposition in Augusta if I flew commercially," he explained. "Or I'd have to make the gruesome drive from Albany to Augusta and back. A plane became indispensable." As it happened, Tommy was playing poker (gambling is not just a metaphor in his life) with a flight instructor who owned a Cessna 150. They got to talking. "He told me he'd teach me to fly," Tommy said, "if I'd check a title and close a loan." Tommy soon owned a quarter interest in a Cessna 172 and over time, a string of larger, more sophisticated aircraft. He'd log more than 4,500 hours before handing the stick to a professional pilot.

***

Not much had changed in Albany. James Gray still spewed racist diatribes sprinkled with chamber of commerce bromides on the *Albany Herald*'s editorial pages. Black voter registration still lagged woefully. The white power structure, a tiny minority of the population, was firmly in place. C. B. King kept plugging away, trying to make his cases in the courts and in the court of public opinion. Young people, the leading edge of a trend that would accelerate throughout the state, were pulling up stakes and moving to Atlanta seeking better jobs and opportunity. Activity at the Marine Corps' logistics base and the Air Force's Turner Field was picking up as the country began a disastrous adventure in Southeast Asia. Teenagers continued drinking, flirting, crashing, and scuffling outside the Pig 'N Whistle, a handful getting kicks racing through the Albany State University campus tossing beer cans and racial epithets. "Albany was always a troublesome place," remembered Adam Malone, who'd engage in his share of mischief a generation later.

Tommy and a cohort of politically active young lawyers and Jaycee-types now did their drinking at the Victory Club, Sand Trap, Library, and the Monkey Palace. Then as now, lawyers loved to talk shop and hobnob with the big dogs. "Peter Zack Geer was the most well known," said Jack Slover, an Atlanta-born attorney who'd moved to nearby Camilla, Georgia, to work for the Twitty Law Firm (now Twitty & Bangston). "Peter Zack was the youngest lieutenant governor ever in Georgia, a swashbuckling, very articulate lawyer." The word on Geer was that "he was the best lawyer in Georgia when he wasn't drunk and the second-best when he was." Taxi Smith ("Everyman's Lawyer") and the old-guard lawyers were beginning to move, albeit unwillingly, off the stage. Tommy was considered a young man on the move. "He was well spoken, well liked, and quite a social animal," added Slover, today an Atlanta defense attorney who'd face off against Malone many times in the decades ahead. "A guy you'd want to get to know."

Education, experience, and exposure to people and ideas in the larger world were triggering a transformation in Tommy. "When I came back, I was not a kid who had to accept what I was told," he said in 2016. "I was a man. Not just a man, but a lawyer-man who could make up his own mind about what cases to accept and reject."

Chapter 15

"If Tommy comes in here with a case he's coming with a brass band and 50 cheerleaders."
—Judge Robert E. Lee Culpepper Jr.

The criminal cases piled up—Albany was indeed a troublesome place—and the defendants Malone represented ran into the scores, then hundreds. They were white, black, and impoverished, and few had hope, opportunity, or any path forward. In the 1960s, Georgia's jails and prisons were literally hellholes. (A decade later, the state would come under federal court order to improve conditions in its prison system.) Faces and names faded, but Malone's awareness that *he* was their advocate grew, and with it a sense of responsibility that was almost personal. Under such caseloads, young criminal defense attorneys often become cynical, no doubt a psychological defense against crushing caseloads and the human carnage around them. Tommy stayed constant. "All these people with their lives in my hands," he recalled. "Just me standing between them and disaster." That awful sense of responsibility would define him throughout his career.

He won a great many criminal cases in state court, but rarely in federal. In the beginning, he accepted the adverse verdicts by telling himself, as all trial lawyers do, "Juries just were not buying what I was selling." On the civil side, he was determined to work harder than his adversaries, delve deeper in research, hone his arguments and briefs to surgical precision, and push the boundaries where he could. He'd do pioneering work. "Tommy was way ahead of his time in his presentations using demonstrative evidence," remembered Jack Slover. "This is before plaintiff's attorneys brought in a lot of visual aids and things." In fact, it was a time when comportment was so rigid, lawyers were forbidden from even listing their names in bold print the phone book. Oration was paramount, the more spellbinding and stem-winding the better. Some lawyers were folksy (country lawyers); others affected what might be called a "classical" approach, that today sounds like the Duke and the Dauphin perorating in *The Adventures of Huckleberry Finn*. Still others were dry and flat as Georgia clay. "Tommy's courtroom style wasn't out of line," Slover remembered. "It wasn't bullying or hateful. It *was* flamboyant. As a defense attorney, you had your hands full with him. Some people didn't like his style. I thought he was great." The late Judge Robert E. Lee Culpepper Jr, whose circuit included Mitchell, Baker, Grady, Calhoun, and Decatur counties—adjacent to Dougherty County—is remembered for his classic take on the young Malone: "Well, if Tommy comes in here with a case," the judge said drily, "he's coming with a brass band and 50 cheerleaders."

"Articulate," remembered Slover, "and very intimidating. I remember the first time I faced him. I'm 5' 8 ½." He's 6' 4" and already well known. Beautifully dressed, he looked like something out of *Vogue*." For all that, Malone was, in many ways, innocent. Across the state in Glynn County, a young lawyer named Anthony Alaimo was witnessing revolving-door justice firsthand. Alaimo (later the US district court judge who ordered a massive restructuring and improvement of barbarous conditions in Georgia's prisons) recalled appearing in county court for a routine hearing and noticing three capital cases, each involving an African American defendant, ahead of his on the docket. He was about to file a motion for a continuance when the county clerk leaned over and whispered, "Don't worry they'll all be done by noon."

And they were.

That something wasn't right with the justice system in South Georgia was equally apparent on the civil side. In Tommy's first major wrongful death case, he represented the parents—Billy and Helen Jennings Black—of a 5-year-old boy who'd been struck and killed by a speeding motorist in the middle of the Albany State campus. The child's father, Billy Black, was a professor and later president of Albany State University. The defendants were a car salesman named Stanley Brown and the owners of Aultman Cadillac, the Albany dealership whose vehicle Brown was driving. As Malone recalled, the evidence clearly indicated Brown was speeding, never swerved to avoid striking the child, never blew his horn, and left 300 feet of skid marks when he finally braked. He shouldn't have even been on the campus road running through the campus, a common shortcut for white motorists headed to Radium Springs, a close-in suburb of Albany.

Malone's first inkling of trouble came when he walked into the courtroom. "There were two African Americans out of the whole sea of prospective jurors," he said. "How shocked I was." This was 1967, two *years* after the federal Voting Rights Act passed into law and six years after the voter registration drives triggered by the Albany Movement. "And yet African Americans had not registered and could not appear on juries."

Rosser Malone and Peter Zack Geer, a courtroom magician, had cautioned Tommy not to question potential jurors in any detail during *voir dire*, lest they feel "you're putting them on trial." With that in mind, jury selection for the Black case ended with Malone not finding out very much. "*Voir dire* was unheard of back then," he said. "The judge would ask the fundamental questions and that was it."

Had he probed, Tommy would have struck John M., an insurance agent who made his living writing policies for Albany businesses. Instead, John M. became jury foreman. During deliberations, he pointedly asked the judge for clarifications on a number of questions that served to undermine Malone's case in the minds of his fellow jurors. "If Mister Brown did anything wrong," John M. asked at one point, "why are we trying a civil and not a criminal case?" The deeper implication, widely accepted at the time, was that monetary damages were not a proper remedy in a civil death case. An argument, despite the obvious negligence and the terrible loss the Blacks had suffered, that took root. "It became clear to me," Malone said years later, "that if you don't do thorough *voir dire,* you can't win." A message so vital to all trial lawyers, Malone would write two books on the subject, the second a 500-page legal tome.

The defendants were exonerated, but the thing that stayed with Tommy was not the pain of losing a well-argued, fact-based action—he'd lose many over the years—but the fact that Billy and Helen Jennings Black, whose lives had been shattered by the death of their little boy, "never had any expectation of winning." For Tommy, it was a watershed. "I never did think racially until I lost that first case," he said. "This was the way they treated the African American community. I started thinking very seriously about jury selection. As long as the power structure determined the composition of a jury, you'd never get twelve individuals to find for a lower socio-economic person against a member of the power structure. There were few black jurors. Lower-class white jury members knew better than to challenge the powerful."

After the loss, Tommy remained friends with Billy and Helen Jennings Black and worked to build bridges to Albany's black community, an outreach that won him no love in white-controlled Albany. He'd work with the African American lawyer and activist C. B. King on cases, and later on some very lucrative actions with C. B.'s lawyer son, Chevene King Jr. He'd serve on Albany State's Board of Directors, and after moving his practice to Atlanta, Tommy donated his office building to the university.

Chapter 16

"There were few black jurors. Lower-class white jury members knew better than to challenge the powerful. They could lose their jobs. They'd have their loans called at the bank, all kinds of bad stuff."
—Tommy Malone, on practicing law in Albany, Georgia

Malone soldiered on, "taking good cases all around southwest Georgia, trying them and losing them." *Albany Herald* publisher James Gray, who registered everything, would have followed the Black case closely. Tommy also raised eyebrows with the courthouse courtiers and chamber of commerce types, surely among the well-heeled diners at the Radium Springs Country Club, always eager for a whiff of scandal, particularly now that Rosser was out of pocket living in Atlanta. They appreciated Tommy's history of rebelliousness. The kid was hard to get a handle on. His daddy knew that better than anybody. Besides, who could blame a young man with fire in his belly for stretching his father's stodgy real estate practice and tapping some new, albeit unwanted, clients. In the end, Tommy was one of them. He'd come back into the fold.

Instead, he started more trouble. The Dougherty County Commission had proposed—and voters approved—a referendum funding the construction of a new city-county government center on Pine Avenue. "The old courthouse had burned down after the vote," Tommy recalled. (There'd be no outlay for land on the new project.) One morning, picking up the *Herald*, he noticed a quote from Dougherty County Commission Chairman Paul Keenan to the effect that he was looking for a low bid of x-dollars for construction. Keenan's hoped-for low bid for the construction alone "was the exact amount of the bond issue intended to cover construction, equipment, furnishings and so on."

Tommy was a very active member of the Jaycees, the leadership training and civic organization that drew young, idealistic volunteers from all over the state. "We did a lot of good charitable work," he remembered. "And we were very active in politics." Tommy and a group of Albany

Jaycees decided to confront Keenan on the apparent overrun. They cornered him in the lobby of the First State Bank.

"Commissioner, how can you possibly accept a construction bid that alone will cost what the people voted for the whole project?" someone asked.

"Don't bother me, boys," Keenan said, pushing past them. "We're going to build y'all a wonderful courthouse. When it's done, you'll be happy."

"We weren't happy," Tommy said. "In fact, we filed a lawsuit."

Malone is the attorney of record in the action brought by one of the Jaycees against the City of Albany, Dougherty County, the individual city commissioners, the mayor, and Keenan, the commission chairman. As Malone remembered it, "We had a preliminary hearing and the judge says, 'I'm going to have to rule in favor of the *plaintiffs*.' Then Jay (Jay-Bird) Walters, the county attorney and establishment enforcer, talked some more, and the judge nodded and said, 'Well, I'm *still* going to have to rule in favor of the plaintiffs.' At that point, the nonplussed Walters interjected, 'Your Honor, may we have until morning before you issue your final order?'"

"You may."

Next morning, Walters appeared in court with a construction bid—apparently magically arrived at overnight—less than the figure Keenan cited in the newspaper. The lawsuit was rendered moot and dismissed. Tommy and the Jaycees celebrated a victory against cronyism and corruption, but years later, a more hard-bitten Malone came to a different realization. "I'm sure what they did was cut something out, then did an add-on later. I wasn't that savvy in those days. That's the way they did things. 'We are the power structure. Don't mess with us, boys.'"

In the larger world, such a lawsuit would have been a ripple in the ebb and flow of local politics, but through the distorted lens the Albany establishment used to view the world, it was a very troubling development. Rosser's son had crossed another line from which there was no going back. "Suing the city and the county was a huge statement," Malone said. "It identified me in the minds of others. To some, I was the vehicle through which the young Jaycees and other people interested in the community were given a voice." To Keenan, Jay-Bird Walters, and Jim Gray, 25-year-old Tommy—"a pipsqueak who wouldn't acknowledge he was a pipsqueak"—was now an enemy, a traitor to be crushed.

"I didn't realize any of this," Malone recalled, "until the newspaper took after me." By now, Gray, the *Herald's* publisher, was excoriating Malone around town as a "smartass," apparently an unforgiveable sin to a social-climbing Yankee carpetbagger. Though of different generations, Malone and Gray ran in roughly concentric circles with mutual friends and associates and were likely—Albany is a small place—to bump into each other over drinks at the Hotel Gordon, the courthouse, a public hearing, wedding, or political event. At one point Gray was chairman of the Georgia Democratic Party. According to Spencer Lee, who was on good terms with Gray and his son, James Jr., the elder Gray at first recognized Tommy as a young man with dreams and goals and the wits and guts to pursue them, much like his own younger self. When Tommy began making outreaches to the black community, when he challenged the power structure Gray viscerally embodied, the man moved against him. "I won't say James Gray was bad," Tommy said many years later. "He was a segregationist of the highest order and he was a tyrant and he had money and power and control. That makes him a pretty powerful person."

He was a man who never hesitated to use the power of the media as a cudgel. Gray struck in the aftermath of a case in which Tommy had negotiated a plea arrangement for a man charged with counterfeiting, a federal crime. Tommy and the defendant, R. Whaley Hughes, were, as Malone recalled, "very good friends." Not unusual in a small town where everyone knows everyone and their family before them. US District Court Judge Wilbur D. Owens Jr., another Albany native, presided over the case. Even with the plea bargain, Hughes was sentenced to a stretch in prison. One of the truisms of the penal system is that convicts with too much time on their hands will inevitably fall in with "jailhouse lawyers," other cons with a smattering of legal knowledge who claim they are qualified to revisit the circumstances of arrests, charges, pleas, trials, and incarceration, the whole criminal justice process, looking for reversible errors or arguments justifying a new trial. If they can afford the fees of these "counselors," convicts file what are often "nuisance lawsuits," baseless allegations of violations of their constitutional rights that, at least on the federal level, can swamp a judge's calendar. If they decide to go after their own attorneys, they file actions alleging malpractice, conflict of interest, or some variety of malfeasance.

Hoping for a new trial, Hughes sued Tommy Malone. This was big enough news to merit an *Albany Herald* reporter calling Malone on a Friday afternoon. After the interview, Tommy locked up the office and drove to Panama City, where he'd planned to spend the weekend with his buddy Bill Davis, editor of the *Albany Journal*, the city's weekly newspaper. Tommy innocently mentioned the encounter to Davis. "The guy was so nice," Malone added. "He said he was going do 'as favorable a story as he can.'"

"He's going to gut you!" warned Davis. "They hate you."

"What?"

Davis thought for a moment. "If the story runs in Saturday's paper, you may not have a problem. No one reads the Saturday paper much." Everyone read the Sunday paper. Sunday morning, Tommy picked up the *Herald*. The front page headline, in bold, six-inch letters above the fold, screamed at him: "Lawyer Conflict Charges Surface."

In due course, Whaley Hughes's lawsuit was dismissed. He appealed and the appellate judge noted Hughes was both "guilty *and* disgruntled." In the honored tradition of innocent individuals who've been keelhauled by the media and seek redress, Tommy paid an indignant visit to the *Herald*'s office, a converted department store on Washington Street. There, he confronted James Gray Jr., editor of the paper. Gray was so nervous— Malone towering over him—he had trouble lighting his cigarette. Tommy demanded that a second story *exonerating* him be given equal play as the first. Gray agreed, but what he printed was a story on the inside front page, less likely to grab attention. "That first headline would have run me out of town if I hadn't been a multi-generational Malone," Tommy recalled. "And if I hadn't been the fighter I was."

He'd get the fight of his life in his next big case, an encounter that crystalized the hypocrisy lurking beneath the unruffled surface of small town life and the lengths to which upstanding citizens—pillars of society— would go to protect their own. It would tear away Malone's tattered illusions about fairness and justice in South Georgia and focus the discordant energies churning inside him. *Bitterman v. Johnson* was not just a civil lawsuit argued before the bar, it was the catalyst that altered the trajectory of Tommy Malone's career and shaped the man he'd become.

Chapter 17

Bitterman v. Johnson
"If a doctor cut your father's head off down there, you wouldn't
consider suing him and you couldn't find a lawyer to do it.... It would
be like saying something against the Church or the Lord."
—Atlanta Attorney Jack Slover

It began, as momentous things often do, simply. Taxi Smith, a fixture in Albany's legal circles, invited Tommy Malone to drop by his office. He had a *proposition* to discuss, something that might be mutually beneficial. Such an offer might have been a red flag, but Tommy was 24 years old and still shedding his innocence. Smith, for his part, was too smart to sue a powerful doctor. Taxi was a negotiator, a dealmaker, happy behind the scenes. Tommy, on the other hand, seemed to relish combat. Smith told Malone he had a plaintiff who wanted to bring a malpractice lawsuit against a local doctor. In 1966, this was a rare thing anywhere in the country. In southwest Georgia, conservative and tradition-bound, it was unheard of heresy. Taxi was suggesting an action against Dr. Thomas Johnson, MD, a highly regarded Albany internist with Hollis, Johnson, Guillebeau. The case was not so much an action as it was a feint to win a quick insurance settlement in what could be a very ugly lawsuit. Tommy jumped at the opportunity to try such a case with Taxi Smith.

The plaintiffs were local merchants, the parents of 15-year-old Carol Bitterman, a high school student and twirler in the Albany High band. Carol had suffered, Smith explained, a catastrophic injury under Dr. Johnson's care. It was irreversible and indisputably linked to negligence. Taxi had written a letter to Dr. Johnson and his insurers expecting a quick resolution. The insurance company had blown him off. "Taxi gave me the file, and all it had in it was the letter," Malone recalled. "He told me to file the suit and they'd pay us $100,000 straightaway. Lawyers didn't study the law all that much in those days, but I'd later realize that Smith came to me to be the 'name on the complaint.' I went ahead and prepared this great complaint."

Taxi looked it over, nodding in approval. "Amazing!" he told Malone. "Great job, but I want you to change one thing."

"What's that, Mr. Smith?"

"Take my name off it."

"What?" Malone said in astonishment. "I can't try this case without you. I'm wet behind the ears."

"Don't worry. No trial. They'll pay."

He filed the suit. The $100,000 was not forthcoming.

At this point, Smith departed the scene, leaving Tommy Malone to spend the next years wrestling with a bear of a lawsuit. At the heart of the case was Dr. Johnson's decision—despite the fact that other medications were proving effective—to treat the teen, whom he'd diagnosed with ulcerative colitis (more likely, a less severe condition known as Irritable Bowel Syndrome) with the standard treatment, a sulfa-based drug. "It was documented in Johnson's records that he knew Carol was allergic to sulfa," Tommy said. "In fact, her mother even reminded him."

Fifty years later, Tommy, who has near-total recall of the facts of his major cases, reconstructed that conversation:

Mrs. Bitterman: "Azulfidine? Doctor, does that have sulfa in it?"

Johnson: "Yes, why do you ask?"

"When she was born, the hospital told us never give her sulfa. She's allergic."

"This is a new kind of sulfa. Anything unusual happens, be sure to let me know."

The drug triggered a nightmarish allergic response. Two weeks later, young Carol Bitterman was hospitalized, her body covered with blotches that grew into "huge, hanging water blisters," her flesh peeling and her nails, eyelashes, and hair falling out. Her agony was such that nurses at Phoebe Putney Hospital, at a loss as to what to do to ease her pain, applied cornstarch to the sheets to keep the girl's skin from sticking to her bed. A month later, Carol Bitterman, continuing to decline, was transferred to Emory University Hospital in Atlanta, and when no relief was forthcoming, to Peter Bent Brigham Hospital (today, Brigham and Women's Hospital) in Boston. The country's top specialists were helpless. "She developed an ascending paralysis that stopped at the umbilicus and left her permanently paralyzed, motor as well as sensory," Malone recalled.

***

Like other *rarae aves*, small-town doctors are a protected species. "They were sacrosanct," recalled Jack Slover, who at the time represented the Mitchell County Hospital Authority and some of the doctors who practiced in Camilla, Georgia. "We wrote their wills, assisted when they purchased land, things like that. Nobody dared sue them, especially in South Georgia. It would be like saying something against the Church or the Lord. Doctors saved people's lives, looked after old people, did all kinds of good things. I understood these things [medical negligence] occurred, but at that time, you just didn't do it. If a doctor cut your father's head off down there, you wouldn't consider suing him and you couldn't find a lawyer to do it."

Sure enough, no Albany doctor was willing to testify against Johnson despite evidence that his actions constituted a textbook definition of medical malpractice. He'd violated applicable standards of care. A patient had suffered a grievous, compensable injury caused by that substandard care. Behind the hard facts was the greater consequence: Carol Bitterman's life, her schoolgirl hopes, dreams, and aspirations—college, marriage, a family—had been destroyed. Her loved ones faced a future laced with pain, grief, and hardship; no amount of money could alter that—and no one in the medical community seemed to care. In the months ahead, that callousness would prove much more widespread.

To Tommy Malone, the case would prove more troubling than local politicians looking to line the pockets of their cronies. It wasn't racially tinged like the Billy Black lawsuit, though the Bittermans happened to be Jewish. (In every small Southern town, shops and stores invariably run by Jewish families who first arrived as itinerant peddlers are commonplace.) Tommy would find himself peering through the looking glass at a community—his own hometown—whose impulses were not only at odds with compassion and common decency, they reflected an alternative reality. Wrongdoer and victim somehow reversed places. This repulsed him and unleashed a deep-seated and righteous anger, more intense because it was grounded in shame and disappointment. "Tommy always had empathy for these kinds of people," Slover continued. "He's brash, bold, and very confident, but he has this side where he'll take up for people whom nobody else will. And give voice to those who are voiceless. That's very admirable, and it may sound like a fairy-tale, but he's got it in him."

A doctor, a personal friend at the time, advised Tommy that nobody "would get mad if he *didn't* go out of town to get hired guns" as expert witnesses to testify against Dr. Johnson. In effect, asking him to scuttle his case. "Of course, they wouldn't get mad," Malone said, "because nobody in town was going to testify *for me*, my client, or our side of the case." Ironically, it was a group of outcasts—the chiropractors—who rallied to Malone. Considered quacks and interlopers by a medical establishment that despised them and lobbied, among other things, to ensure claims filed by chiropractic patients were not covered by medical insurance. At least one Albany chiropractor grasped the David-versus-Goliath aspect of the Bitterman action. One of Albany's more recognizable characters was a silver-haired, Bible-spouting chiropractor named Bill Harris. "He'd come to my office," Malone said, "and get down on his knees and we'd pray together. He'd tell me he'd been to the mountaintop and there were great things in store for me." Tommy wasn't convinced that Harris was sent to him by God, but he happily handled the bread-and-butter whiplash cases (injuries caused by a sudden distortion of the neck triggered hyperextension) the man referred.

One day, Harris appeared out of the blue, insisting that Tommy fly with him to Miami. There, he promised to introduce Malone to the great Melvin Belli, the internationally renowned attorney, whom he claimed to know quite well. At the time, the San Francisco-based Belli was among the two or three best-known lawyers in the country, maybe the world. Harris convinced Malone that Belli would know precisely how to proceed in the Bitterman case. "Well, I ended up going to the Belli Seminar in Miami," Tommy recalled. "Sure enough, there he was, Melvin Belli, introducing all these wonderful speakers and talking about all the topics of the day." Tommy was dazzled by Belli's ease and style, his razor wit and obvious intellect, his global footprint, but also his passion and dedication to his clients. Here was a role model a young lawyer could emulate. At the seminar's close, Tommy, briefcase stuffed with Bitterman material, was standing in the hotel lobby when Belli and a scrum of admirers breezed by like a king and his court. (Indeed Belli prided himself as the "King of Torts.") Bill Harris stepped into his path and made a quick introduction.

"How're you doing?'" Belli said, eyes darting to the next expectant acolyte.

"And then," Tommy recalled, "Melvin Belli brushed me off."

One of the speakers at the Miami seminar was Dr. Roger Palmer, chairman of the pharmacology department at the University of Miami's school of medicine. Palmer was a larger-than-life figure, a man who called to mind the phrase Keith Richards used to describe his bandmate and fellow Rolling Stone, Mick Jagger: "a lovely bunch of guys." Palmer was an academic, world traveler, womanizer, raconteur, big drinker, and hardcore sport fisherman. He and Tommy were instantly drawn to one another. Dr. Palmer's resume included numerous courtroom appearances as an expert witness testifying on adverse drug reactions and their *sequellae*, i.e., consequences and complications. Another intriguing figure at the seminar was Dr. Andrew Cyrus, a neuropathologist who specialized in identifying diseases and ailments of the nervous system, experience that aligned nicely for the case Tommy planned to make in the Bitterman trial. Dr. Cyrus was an African American from Wisconsin; he'd undoubtedly appear as startling as a Martian in a South Georgia courtroom. After Tommy laid out the facts of the Bitterman case, both agreed to travel to Albany to testify as expert witnesses.

The Bitterman trial was the launching pad for a decades-long friendship between Malone and Roger Palmer rooted in loyalty, raucous behavior, drinking, and—once Tommy was hooked—a monumental addiction to sport fishing in the Bahamas. Over the years, Malone would serve as best man at two of Palmer's many marriages. (He declined a third invitation, assuming by then he was bad luck.) They'd share numerous escapades and adventures, including what Tommy graciously called "side stories" at the Miami Playboy Club.

Palmer recommended a few other medical experts who might contribute to the case. Malone flew home feeling much better about his prospects. He didn't have the Great Belli, that flamboyant magician whose very appearance would give a defense pause, but the facts and the law were on his side. "I had my liability doctor and I had my causation doctor," he remembered. Cyrus, the neuropathologist, would testify that the etiology and progression of Carol Bitterman's paralysis were identifiable as Stevens-Johnson Syndrome (SJS), a rare, life-threatening disorder of the skin and mucous membranes typically linked to an adverse drug reaction. "According to them," Malone said, "it was a slam-dunk."

And so it seemed.

Chapter 18

"First Baptist, First Methodist, and First Presbyterian preachers came into the courtroom and patted Dr. Johnson on the back and nodded to the jury.... If anyone made the mistake of sitting behind us, somebody would get up and escort him to sit on the doctor's side."
—Tommy Malone, the Bitterman Case

In his opening statement, Tommy Malone began to weave the forthcoming testimony, evidence, and indisputable facts of the Bitterman case into a seamless and seemingly irrefutable whole. Outside the courtroom, Bitterman was big news in Albany. The *Herald* churned out stories, WALB aired reports, gossip flew, and rumors and speculation spread like chicken pox. Onlookers, the curious, the concerned, and the unsettled, buzzed around, eager to weigh in on the trouble Rosser Malone's boy had stirred up this time. Never shy, Tommy reserved a private room at the six-story, red brick Hotel Gordon for the duration of the trial and dined with his team behind the big plate-glass windows in the lobby restaurant. Rosser Malone showed up to look in on his son. "He ate lunch with us every day," Tommy remembered. "Except the day Dr. Cyrus, my neuropathologist, testified. Daddy wasn't going to eat with an African American."

As expected, a number of local doctors testified for the defense. Flying in the face of scientific evidence, one swore he'd "prescribed enough sulfa to fill up the courtroom and had never seen nor heard of a bad reaction," testimony that likely sent visiting Judge Wendell Horne and members of the jury back on their heels. Then the ministers showed up. "First Baptist, First Methodist, and First Presbyterian preachers came into the courtroom and patted Dr. Johnson on the back and nodded to the jury," Malone remembered. "It was a relatively small courtroom. They had crowds coming in, business people, wives, everybody. If anyone made the mistake of sitting behind us, somebody would get up and escort him to sit on the doctor's side." The unfolding spectacle would have had the feel of a medieval puppet show with "good" characters arrayed against "bad" ones, with the jury and Judge Horne a captive audience. "It seemed that anybody who knew somebody on the jury showed up," Malone added, "all nodding and giving assurances. I didn't realize what was happening while it was happening, but I put it together later—after we lost the case."

Tommy put up a powerful case. The trial took six full days, the jury all of a Saturday to find for the defense. The Bitterman family was distraught and disheartened. Tommy was so devastated he avoided his office and stayed home "crying myself to sleep, wondering if I'd be better off selling shoes or something." He nearly convinced himself that he didn't have the makings of a courtroom lawyer, but what he'd lost was not a lawsuit but his innocence. "This was one of my early, early trials," he said in 2016. "I believed in justice and truth and fairness and all that. I could have understood losing the case in front of the rail, though this was a case nobody should lose. I lost it *behind the rail* with all those people who came to court. I was brought up in the Baptist Church and have always been a devout believer in God, but when those preachers came to influence the jury to hurt that Jewish girl, I was fed up with modern-day Christianity. I have seldom been in a church since unless to honor someone at a funeral service."

Taxi Smith couldn't backpedal fast enough. Before the trial even got underway, Smith handed Malone, Judge Horne, and the defense a letter signed by every member of his law firm disclaiming any financial interest in what he realized was about to become a toxic case. "Taxi didn't want to be seen suing a doctor," Tommy realized. "If you did, all the doctors would hate you. They wouldn't testify in any of your cases. They wouldn't treat you or members of your family. I became one of those hated lawyers, the only one in South Georgia. At the time, there was another lawyer, Charlie McCranie [Ross & Finch] in Atlanta, who sued doctors. It was just the two of us in the whole state."

***

Some days after the Bitterman verdict, a dispirited Malone was walking over to the Malone Law office at 202 ½ Pine Avenue just across from the courthouse.

"Tommy! Tommy!"

He stopped and turned. A guy he recognized as one of the Bitterman jurors was hurrying toward him.

"Man," the ex-juror blurted out. "I just want to tell you how good it makes me feel to know that there's a lawyer of your ability in Albany who'll take on the establishment and kick ass like you did."

"Buddy," Malone managed to say, "there's something wrong with this conversation. You were on the jury. In case you forgot, we lost."

"Anywhere other than Albany you'd have won."

The words struck like a thunderbolt. *"Anywhere other than Albany..."*

"This is a man who sold real estate—small farms and big houses for a living," Malone realized. "The medical community and their friends are his clientele. He couldn't possibly vote in my favor and expect anybody to ever give him any business. He saw *potential clients* come up and pat Doctor Johnson on the back and then nod to him in the jury box." That same scenario was unfolding, Tommy realized, in every trial, every jury selection, every deliberation, and every verdict that had an establishment—however one defined it—connection.

A day would come when jury pools reflected the true makeup of the population of South Georgia, black, white, rich, poor, middle, and working class. Only then would the establishment's stranglehold be broken (perhaps to be replaced by another set of powerbrokers) and verdicts reflect the honest judgment of the people. That day was a long way off, perhaps too long for Tommy to keep tilting at windmills. In the meantime, he told himself, he'd make a good living handling the flood of civil and criminal cases and clients his bravura courtroom performances began to attract.

The Bitterman affair was not over. Tommy researched the applicable statutes and decided he'd file a "loss of services" complaint based on a statute that traced its origins all the way back to English Common Law. In simple terms, parents are entitled to the services of their children whether (originally) working in the fields or otherwise contributing to the family's financial well-being. "If somebody hurts your child," Malone realized, "you can sue for loss of service and also to recover medical expenses." At the time, costs for Carol Bitterman's hospitalizations and transportation to Atlanta, Boston, and back totaled $38,000 (astonishing by 2017 standards, which would be in the millions). Today, a loss of services action would be filed as companion to the original complaint. "Back then we filed it separately," Malone added. "It's a good thing we did."

This time he'd be ready. Peter Zack Geer could say what he wanted about alienating potential jurors, but Malone had come to realize that *voir dire* was not a fancy French phrase for a routine procedure; it was a tool—among the most powerful in his toolkit—that could help level the playing field for a plaintiff. "It seems so obvious and I should have known it," he said. "But I didn't really appreciate it." In later years, he'd become a Zen master of the intricate and subtle dance in which bias, conscious, unconscious, or hidden, is elicited, and potential bad actors are eliminated before they can do harm. "This time, I examined the jury so effectively that the judge excused about forty people for cause," Malone recalled with a laugh. "They had to go out in the streets and bring in more." As the trial got underway, the preachers and other influencers once again began filtering into the courtroom. This time Tommy handed out subpoenas. "I might need to call on you in for rebuttal," he announced, and they howled in protest. "For now, you can go home, wait in your office, or sit in the Witness Room." They disappeared. Throughout the litigation, the defense hammered Malone for talking to the media about the case. "They tried to intimidate me, threatened to sue me, report me to the bar, all sorts of stuff," he recalled. "Of course, they'd use the press when it worked to their advantage. It was me against them."

Bitterman II barely got past jury selection. As Malone recalled, "I was called back to Judge Horne's chambers. The defense was offering $10,000 to settle. I knew I couldn't get but $38,000 on the best day and I really thought we were going to lose again. Going forward, we'd have to spend more money with the experts coming in to testify. So we agreed to settle."

At that point, an odd thing happened. "Say, Tommy," the lead defense attorney asked, "how 'bout we knock a dollar off?"

Malone was puzzled. "You mean pay us $9,999.00?

"Yes."

"Okay," he shrugged. "That's fine, I guess."

Next day, the *Albany Herald* ran a front-page story to the effect, "Local Malpractice Case Settled for Nominal Amount—under $10,000."

Jim Gray had struck again.

Tommy used the $9,999 settlement to pay his expert witnesses. Of them, Roger Palmer refused all payment so Malone, knowing Palmer was a fisherman, purchased a $600 fighting chair for the professor's Bertram 31 fly-bridge fishing boat. He spent another $600 having it delivered to Andros Island in the Bahamas.

Bitterman continued to trouble him. Tommy could not forget Belli, that whirlwind of ego, energy, and mad brilliance he'd glimpsed at the Miami seminar. "I figured if I could get Mel Belli to come to Albany and try a case with me against Pharmacia, the New Jersey drug company that manufactured Azulfidine, it wouldn't make any difference that Carol Bitterman was Jewish. Now, she'd be the local girl who was paralyzed by a New Jersey drug company."

Chapter 19

"Dad was a giant of a man to a little child. He rode horses and taught
us how to ride. He took us to the ocean and the beach and had a
beach house and a farm with animals."
—Adam Malone, growing up with Tommy

In his twenties, Tommy Malone's dreams were Technicolor, larger than life,
rodeos of possibility with exhilarating highs followed by shuddering tumbles
to earth, an arc familiar to anyone who engages in high-risk endeavors. One
week, he'd be driving Tommy Jr. and Adam around in a "really cool" El
Camino, and the next it'd be gone, sold for quick cash to cover expenses. "I
took on too many cases that were impossible to win given the circumstances
of the times," he explained. At one point, Tommy was so discouraged
Rosser grew worried. "He suggested I see a friend, D. C. Campbell Jr. [son
of Dougherty County Sheriff Cull Campbell], a great lawyer doing criminal
defense." Campbell, whose law office was around the corner from the
Malone firm, told Tommy he'd gone through similar losing streaks and the
way to break out of a slump was to keep on swinging. "You don't have
anything to do with the outcome of these cases," Campbell insisted. "All
you can do is your best." Superstitious as any baseball player, Campbell
then reached behind his desk and grabbed a lucky red tie he kept hanging
there. "I, uh, changed my tie and started winning 'em," he confided. "See if
it helps." Tommy was ready to try anything. "I borrowed that tie," he said
in 2016, "and won the next case. Then I started winning cases every now
and then. Mr. Cull's red tie took on real meaning in my life. By the time I
finally gave it back, it had some stains on it."

Pursuing dreams, Tommy was blind to day-to-day reality. His
marriage to Joan Beall was showing signs of distress. Joan had a house to
keep and a rambunctious little boy to raise, and it wouldn't have been easy
for any woman raised in Atlanta to relocate to the very different world of
southwest Georgia. Tommy, immersed in work and surrounded by old
friends and colleagues, was in his natural element. The malaise ran deeper.
Given the tenor of the times, it was not uncommon to turn to alcohol to

mask marital problems. Drinking made Tommy mellow, if anything, more easygoing and gregarious, a fun drunk. "Joan was very insecure," remembered an Albany native who knew the Malones very well. "Once she got going, she'd tear Tommy down rather than build him up. Her insecurity worked against Tommy and what he wanted to accomplish in his own life." Rosser and Toni Malone were old-school in-laws. Joan was bored, they decided, and needed to keep busy. Another baby might be in order. In November 1972, a second son, Rosser Adams (Adam) Malone, was born.

Six months later, Tommy filed for divorce, opening a wound that he and his sons still suffer today. "I never knew what it was like to have mom and dad under the same roof at the same time," remembered Adam, "at bedtime or when I woke up in the morning." Tommy now joined the legions of divorced fathers, seeing his boys on weekends and for a month each summer, doing his best to indulge them in every way possible to make up for his absence. Like his father, Tommy had trouble expressing affection, the hugs and pats on the head little boys crave, but he was a dutiful, if occasionally preoccupied, dad. "My brother and I cherished these times," Adam recalled. "Dad was a giant of a man to a little child. He rode horses and taught us how to ride. He took us to the ocean and the beach and had a beach house and a farm with animals."

True to the pattern, Joan, stuck with the day-to-day duties of raising the boys, the dirty laundry and lunches and arguments, grew bitter and more resentful. "My mother was jealous of the fun we'd have with Dad," Adam said. "We'd be talking about the circus we'd just been to and then get dumped off, all rambunctious, for her to deal with." Joan would later marry a railroad engineer, a Vietnam veteran plagued by the particular demons of that conflict. "If you woke him up while he was sleeping," Adam remembered, "he'd grab you by the throat." Soon, Ken and Joan were having violent altercations, the two boys standing by, terrified and powerless. In his tranquil moments, and there were many, Ken did his best to be a father, playing catch and coaching the boys' Little League teams. Adding to the psychic confusion, Joan constantly demeaned Tommy and insisted that Tommy Jr. and Adam address their stepfather as "Daddy." "My mother would describe this man she said was my father, a man I never saw," Adam recalled. "I couldn't have loved my real dad any more than I did, and this only made me distrust her." After a shaky start, Adam would graduate from college, flourish in law school, become his father's law partner, and be named a "Super Lawyer" himself.

Chapter 20

*"Son, when I need your advice about politics you'll be the
first one to know."*
—Rosser Malone

In 1967, Rosser Malone arrived back in Albany after serving three years as Georgia's Fish and Game Commissioner (today, the Department of Natural Resources, overseen by a board appointed by the governor). His patron, Carl Sanders, was gone; Lester Maddox, he of pickaxe and fish-wrapper fame, was Georgia's new governor. Rosser, 65, was eager to resume his practice. While he was away, things had changed at the firm. The metal logo in the glass case at the foot of the stairway leading up to the law office read "M, D & M." Bob Drake, the associate who'd researched abstracts and titles at the county clerk's office, was now a full partner. He was handling real estate transactions, Rosser's bread and butter. Beyond new paint and carpet, Tommy had expanded the practice on all fronts, a number of them unfamiliar and unsettling to his father. In today's youth-driven culture, Rosser would be labeled a "beached white male," another robust, middle-aged man drifting and struggling to get back into the swim of things. In an odd way, Rosser had fallen victim to his own image-making. The Malones had always lived well—"So well that people in the community thought we had plenty of money," as Tommy recalled. "Nobody felt like Daddy needed the business when he came back."

He did need the work. More importantly, Rosser needed the prestige and power he'd enjoyed as county solicitor, a position he'd held for more than two decades. Instead, he found himself sitting at his desk staring at the new carpet Tommy had installed while contractors and builders who'd come to him for help on construction loans and closings came down the hall, took a right instead of a left, and walked into Bob Drake's office.

"Hey, Rosser," they'd say, passing by.

One day, Tommy, preparing to try a case, approached his father with a copy of the jury list, a public record. As solicitor, Rosser had gained vast experience in striking juries.

"Daddy, I want you to go over the jury list with me."

"All right, Son."

They get to the third name, "Suzy Jones."

"Don't take her."

"All right, Daddy, but why should I not take her?"

"God damn it! Because I said, 'Don't take her!'"

"Daddy, you've done mainly criminal cases and struck more juries than anybody in this county. What I'm trying to learn is why do you let one go and keep another? I'm trying to learn..."

"God damn it, because I said so! That's why!"

"I never again asked him his advice about the law," Tommy said in 2017.

At the time, Tommy watched his father's mood swings with increasing trepidation. Rosser lived and breathed lawyering and politics, the campaigns and coups, intrigues and endless jockeying. In the circumscribed world of southwest Georgia, he was hardly a man to go gently into the dark night of political obscurity. One day he walked into Tommy's office.

"Son, I'm going to run for county commission."

Rosser believed he had an "ace in the hole." He was friends with Jim Gillis, Georgia Department of Transportation commissioner. The Georgia DOT was (and remains) a kind of shadow government within state politics wielding enormous backroom power and influence. "I know Jim on a first-name basis," he told Tommy. "I can do more good for Dougherty County than anybody just in what I can do with the roads if I'm on the commission."

"Great, Daddy!" Tommy enthused. "I'll get my Jaycee friends. I've got this printer who's a client of mine. We'll do posters and..."

"Son, when I need your help with politics you'll be the first one to know."

The years Commissioner Rosser had spent on the grassy banks of north Georgia trout streams had not endowed him with any measure of serenity. "He just shut me up and I stayed out of it," Tommy remembered. "And he didn't ask a single person to vote for him. You see, Daddy was offering to serve." *Noblesse oblige* didn't cut any mustard in South Georgia. As Tommy remembered, a local boy, a high school graduate who happened to be the scion of an Albany moving business family, "beat the hell" out of Rosser Malone.

Like Achilles in his tent, Rosser shut himself in his office and brooded. A day came when Tommy came across his father glumly drumming his fingers on his office window.

"Shut the door, Son."

"What's going on, Daddy?"

"Promise me you won't tell your mother." Here followed a long, pregnant pause.

"Tell her what, Daddy?"

"I've got the cataracts."

"Daddy, cataracts are not so bad. They do lens implants these days and they can take cataracts off."

"Son, you come to a point where you've just outlived your usefulness."

"Cataracts...outlived usefulness...depression," Tommy recalled. "It was really all about losing that race and nobody coming to see him to be their lawyer anymore."

Rosser had the cataracts removed but he declined an intraocular implant. When he got home from the procedure, Tommy noticed his father bumbling around like Mr. Magoo with "Coca-Cola lenses on his glasses." It was time for an intervention. "I was gonna find something to keep him busy," Tommy said. "I'd worked in pretty much all the political campaigns down here because I was active in the Jaycees." So active that during one hard-fought mayoral race, he served as a TV interviewer. Apparently, Tommy did such a puff piece on Motie Wiggins, another of Taxi Smith's law partners, that the other candidate cried foul. "I didn't do it on purpose," Tommy said. "It just came out that way."

When Motie Wiggins won, Tommy showed up to ask a favor. He asked the new mayor to name *him* city attorney. "What I'd planned," Tommy explained, "was not to really be city attorney but to let Daddy sit with us for the meetings and all that. Then I figured I'd ease out and let him take over."

Motie listened to Tommy's proposition. "Get three votes and you're it," he promised.

"Well, I went and got three council votes," Tommy remembered. "It was a tie and Motie voted *against* me."

As fate would have it, a state court judge decided to step down so another opportunity blossomed. Two young lawyers were vying for the position when Rosser jumped into the race. "All of a sudden, Daddy agreed to let me and my mother run his campaign," Tommy recalled. "We taped posters, and I got my Jaycee friends working and carrying my father to churches and union meetings, shaking hands and stuff like that. He beat both of them without a runoff."

Judge Rosser Malone served for the next sixteen years. In 2016, Tommy, now a veteran of innumerable courtroom encounters, reflected on Rosser Malone's career on the bench. "I'd put him at 9 or 10," he said. "He was seldom reversed and had a good, common-sense approach to justice. He was not an intellectual in terms of books and study of the law. In fact, I asked him, 'Are you sure you want to be a judge?' I'd seen all the dusty books in his library and I thought you had to be an intellectual to sit on the bench."

"Son, let me tell you," Rosser allowed. "There'll always be two lawyers arguing a case, one on one side and one on the other. I can read the briefs and listen to the lawyers. I've got a good sense of right and wrong. And anyway, I'll be right 50 percent of the time."

When he was wrong, it could hurt. Tommy's childhood buddy Spencer Lee, at the time an overworked legal services attorney, remembers appearing before Judge Malone. "I had a case where a woman didn't pay her rent," Lee said. "But the reason she didn't pay her rent was because the floors had fallen in in two of her rooms. I went up and argued good law— it's called constructive eviction. Judge Malone didn't know that law but I argued it and showed him the cases. Basically, you don't have to pay rent if a landlord rents you something you can't live in. This place was about half-way destroyed. So we're sitting there and Judge Malone looks up and says, 'Ma'am did you pay the rent?'"

"No, your Honor."

"Well, you're evicted."

"He just couldn't bring himself to understand what Tommy and I were trying to do for people," Lee said. "He'd always land on the side of the landlords. 'You didn't pay your rent, you need to leave.'"

Chapter 21

"Tommy is the better lawyer," he said in 2017. "And he's a
lot more fun than Mel Belli to try a case with.
—Randall Scarlett

Stepping off the plane at San Francisco International Airport, Tommy Malone found himself at the absolute epicenter of the 1960s counterculture—peace, hippies, drugs, psychedelic music, antiwar protests, Haight-Ashbury, concerts at the Fillmore West, love-ins at Golden Gate Park—a five-and-a-half hour journey from Georgia into a different dimension. Grace Slick and Jerry Garcia dressed as a psychedelic Uncle Sam could have floated by and Tommy wouldn't have noticed. He was completely focused on the appointment he'd wangled with Seymour Ellison, a partner in the Belli Law Firm, and hoped to see the great man himself. In his briefcase were the outlines of a lawsuit buttressed by expert opinion and precedent that Malone believed was the key to solving the Bitterman conundrum. This time, he'd fly right over the heads of the cabal of doctors and Albany establishment figures that had thwarted him in the first and second trials. Go after Pharmacia, the drug manufacturer, in federal court with a "breach of warranty of fitness" action. In simple terms, he'd argue the warnings on Azulfidine published in the medical guidance issued by Pharmacia were deficient. "So deficient," Malone said later, "that it permitted all the local doctors to testify that Azulfidine was harmless, when, in fact, it was not." Malone also knew that to gain liftoff speed, he'd need the kind of propellant only a Melvin Belli could provide.

Given the hushed and hallowed ambiance law firms strive to project, arriving at 722-728 Montgomery Street would have been a descent into the maelstrom. A decade earlier, Belli had welded two buildings together—a Turkish bathhouse and an Odd Fellows meeting hall—and decorated the hybrid with inspired madness. Crystal chandeliers hung from the ceiling; red velvet drapes, and religious icons and tribal masks adorned the walls; apothecary jars, hotel keys, restaurant menus, news clippings, awards, and the odd ostrich plume covered every surface. A coat-of-arms bore the legend

"Rex Tortius" (King of Torts), its escutcheon depicting crutches and dollar signs. A Jolly Roger flew and a cannon—barrel poking out a second floor window—roared when Belli won a big case.

There had been many. When Malone arrived *en scene*, Belli's notable clients included Mae West; Errol Flynn; Zsa Zsa Gabor; Lenny Bruce; Ferdinand Demara Jr. (the Great Imposter); Muhammad Ali; Sirhan Sirhan (Robert F. Kennedy's assassin); Jack Ruby, who murdered Lee Harvey Oswald; and a seemingly endless list of victims—and perpetrators—of catastrophe and mayhem. On the civil side, Belli had famously brought physicians and corporate malefactors to task with strings of high-dollar malpractice and negligence awards that exploded like firecrackers across newspaper headlines. "It was a whirlwind," remembered attorney Randy Scarlett, who'd joined Belli as a young law clerk/intake screener in the early 1980s. "We'd literally get eighty phone calls a day, requests for new representation on all different types of cases, all diverse and rapid-fire. There'd be a multimillion-dollar case, and I'd walk into Mel's office and ask, 'Would you like to talk to the client?'"

This was an era, Scarlett said, when a "handful of lawyers across the nation were absolutely revered as rock stars." In this elite group, Mel Belli was king and, oftentimes, knave and joker. He was always in the papers—the *San Francisco Chronicle*, Herb Caen's gossip column—on television, in a documentary film posing with Mick Jagger after the Hells Angels murdered an African American concertgoer at the infamous Altamont concert. His ego and his charm were, even by today's standards of social media-enhanced celebrity, exponential. Belli had gone viral decades before the term existed. He claimed he wore a suit every day because he never knew where he'd wind up at the end of the day. "This was true," Scarlett insisted. "He'd come into the office, a phone call would come in from India, and he'd be on the jet. Next thing you know, he's in Calcutta. It was that type of office, work hard, play hard, and the Playboy Club was just half-a-block away." A flood of supplicants—lawyers and would-be clients—made the pilgrimage to Montgomery Street hoping for an audience with the man. Tour buses filled with out-of-towners eager to catch a glimpse of Belli made regular stops by the green-and-white-striped awning.

There was darker side to Belli fueled by bombast, alcohol, and a personal life that veered precariously to the edge of self-destruction—and then tottered back. Belli hobnobbed with royalty, celebrities—he and Errol Flynn went on riotous binges on two continents—crime figures, preachers and whores, the abject and the saintly, the whole human spectrum. He called his fifth ex-wife Lia Triff, "El Trampo," and accused her having an affair with Archbishop Desmond Tutu. She reportedly threw his dog off the Golden Gate Bridge. "Yet he could be the most gracious guy in the world," Scarlett recalled. "If a lawyer was bringing a case that he wanted Belli to handle, he'd certainly be magnanimous, and not in a bad way. If that person was not the most sophisticated, after he left, Belli might roll his eyes and say, 'Oh my God!' It was business. If you brought a case, Mel was going to be nice even if you were the biggest bore in the world."

Scarlett, who'd go on to try major cases with both Belli and Tommy Malone, paused and then added, "Let me say, Mel could be, and was, absolutely tough on people. If you were in his graces on a particular day, you were on cloud nine. Caesar Belli, Mel's son, is my age. We worked in the office together. For whatever reason, Mel was pretty tough on Caesar. Sometimes I wondered whether he was nice to me just to get under his son's skin. Showering all this affection on me and there's Caesar standing over there?"

***

Into this heady mix, ambled Tommy Malone, 6' 4" and straight off the plane from "Al-baany," Georgia. Tommy had his meeting with gatekeeper Ellison, made his carefully ordered arguments for a third Bitterman case, and passed muster. Now he was ushered in to see Belli. On the surface, two men could not be more different: Belli was pure California, flamboyant, of Swiss ancestry, idiosyncratic as a cheap watch. As a young man, he'd ridden the rails documenting Depression-era America for the WPA. Tommy was red-clay Georgia. At some deeper level, perhaps where striving, pain, and experience coalesce into passion, determination, hunger, and righteous anger, a powerful bond immediately began to form between the two.

"He agreed to take the case," Malone said many years later. "Mel Belli was coming to Albany Georgia." If there's a faint echo of *Macbeth's* premonition "Birnam wood to high Dunsinane hill shall come" in his words, that's how momentous Bitterman was about to become for Tommy Malone and a generation of unknown and unloved medical-malpractice litigators.

The lawsuit against Pharmacia Laboratories, the Swedish manufacturer of Azulfidine (acquired by Upjohn and headquartered in Peapack, New Jersey), was filed in the Middle District of Georgia. US District Judge Wilbur D. Owens Jr. presided. Owens's law clerk, John C. Bell Jr., a newly minted lawyer from Augusta, was part of the entourage that rolled into Albany for Bitterman III. "When the federal court travels," Bell recalled, "it's more than just a judge and a law clerk. If it's a criminal case, you have the US Attorney or an Assistant US Attorney, you have staff people, secretaries and other assistants in the US Attorney's office; probation officers, US Marshals and court-security officers; the judge's secretary, any number of people coming in and staying in the local motels. It's like 'The court's come to town!' Only this time, the main attraction was probably the most well-known, most notorious trial lawyer in the United States, Mel Belli."

In this mix, Tommy Malone was a minor player, a young lawyer who'd tried a few cases in federal court, "none of them particularly memorable," John Bell recalled. And yet the confidence and expansiveness of spirit, the determination to be a man in full that would characterize Malone in his maturity, was on display. "Whenever we'd go to Albany, everybody in the court would get invited to dinner at Tommy Malone's house," Bell said. "It was outside of town and Tommy would have a fish fry or something like that, very informal. Other Albany lawyers, local court personnel would all be there. Malone was probably 30 years old, and there he was entertaining the whole court!"

As expected, Melvin Belli's arrival in South Georgia triggered the kind of uproar Joe Namath got when he showed up in Tuscaloosa, Alabama, after winning the Super Bowl for the New York Jets. However, when testimony got underway, it was the 29-year-old Tommy Malone who'd prepped and studied and thoroughly made a case designed to neutralize the opposition that had stymied him twice before. "I figured we've got a paralyzed local girl," he told Jerry Grillo, a journalist who profiled Malone for the 2010 issue of *Georgia Super Lawyers*. "A world-famous lawyer from San Francisco, the great Melvin Belli coming to Albany, Georgia. A New Jersey drug company—not a local doctor—on the other side. We'd fight the War of Northern Aggression all over again." Beneath the hyperbole was an unassailable fact that the slipperiest and most experienced defense attorneys could not deny or deflect: "Carol Bitterman's injuries resulted from Pharmacia's failure to warn of the dangers," Malone realized, "of giving their drug to a patient who was allergic to sulfa."

Belli watched Malone cross-examine the defense's expert witnesses with the nimbleness of a man picking his way through a minefield. He noted the young lawyer's courtroom style, the eloquence, self-effacing charm, and acuity that drew in and yet challenged jurors. At one point, Tommy underscored a witness's self-damning testimony by literally snapping a pencil; the sound reverberated through the courtroom like a pistol shot. "I wanted the jury to remember that," Tommy recalled in 2017. Tommy was no slouch when it came to alcohol consumption and partying either. A prodigious drinker, Belli certainly appreciated Tommy's eagerness to kick back after a hard day's work.

For Bell, the law clerk, Bitterman III was like having ringside seat at a heavyweight championship fight. He'd done the research and prepared proposed orders for Judge Owens as the trial was getting underway; now, he sat there furiously scribbling notes, absorbing information and courtroom technique like a sponge. "Melvin Belli and Tommy Malone are trying the case," he said in 2017. "It's being defended by excellent lawyers. Both sides have learned experts from afar, medical and pharmaceutical people. Roger Palmer is tall, handsome, and as articulate as he could be, very certain on the stand. The interesting thing was that everybody always talked about the 'flamboyant Melvin Belli' as though he was going to be loud and boisterous. Actually, he behaved more like a college professor. Mel was a big man and wore big glasses. He had the sense of being an instructor more than being bombastic, and a wonderful way of using English to reduce things to simple, understandable bites. I remember one witness, maybe one of the experts, said something using medical terminology, and Belli said, 'Wait, can you put that in terms I can understand?' Of course, Mel knew the terminology, but he got the expert speaking English, *the language of the jury.* I've used that technique many times over the years. In fact, I learned more law clerking than I had in law school."

The plaintiff's case was going so well that six days into the proceedings, Pharmacia's lawyers threw in the towel and moved to settle. Judge Owens shut down the trial. "We got something like $650,000 back when $20,000 was a good verdict," Malone recalled. "That would be about $65 million today. The bottom line is that the defendants were convinced the jury would find against them in an amount greater than we settled for. That's the basis for all monetary settlements: the plaintiffs take less than they may get, defendants pay less than they may be ordered to pay."

With Judge Owens's permission, John Bell, who one day would follow Malone as president of the Belli Society, hurried over to Tommy's office to glean some last nuggets from the great man before he headed back to San Francisco. "I sat next to him on the sofa," Bell recalled. "I said 'How should I be a lawyer? I want to be a successful trial lawyer.' Mel said, 'Just take anything you can get and prepare the hell out of it. And try it.'"

"What do I do next?"

"Take whatever you can and prepare the hell out of it. And try it!"

Bitterman delivered Tommy Malone a measure of respect, but it came with a downside. "The leading plaintiff's attorneys all sucked up to Mel," he said sourly. "And now they knew the way to suck up was to be nice to me. Suddenly, I was invited to speak, become chairman of committees, stuff like that. All these doors opened because of Mel Belli." After Belli left, other doors slammed in Tommy's face. "I heard he'd become *persona non grata* in Albany for doing it," said defense attorney Jack Slover, who was practicing at the time in nearby Camilla. "They'd put out the word that nobody that is, no physicians should treat him or his family. I don't know if this was true, but it was spoken around the courtroom and in lawyer meetings."

Belli and Tommy went on to strike up a lasting and unexpectedly deep friendship. Belli praised Malone as "the best lawyer I have ever been in a courtroom with on either side of a trial." (He also proclaimed televangelist Jim Bakker, convicted of twenty-four counts of fraud and conspiracy, the "finest client" he'd ever had.) Compliments were things Belli dispensed like tissues, but he may have glimpsed a younger, more idealistic version of himself in Tommy Malone. In turn, Tommy came to idolize and emulate the older man, right down to the Western-tailored suits with slash pockets and red linings that Belli sported. Years later, when Ellison noticed Tommy was literally dressing like Belli, he said unkindly, "You can be the best lawyer you can be, but you'll never be Belli."

"I was not around when they did their first case together," said Randy Scarlett, "but whatever happened during that period of time, they hit if off in a way that was really caring for one another and mentoring one another. It was not a threatened relationship. Mel did have a way of using people, but *never* with Tommy. Maybe because Tommy lived all the way across the goddamn country and Mel didn't have to deal with him every day. All I can say is that they had a wonderful relationship. Over the years, they actually missed each other. I don't know whether it was father-son, brother-brother, or what, but it was deep."

Belli and Malone stayed close until Belli's death. In San Francisco, Belli even assigned Malone his own bedroom—ocean view—at the 11,000-square-foot Pacific Heights mansion and entertained the honeymooning Tommy on his yacht in 1987. In 1996, Malone served as a pallbearer at Belli's funeral. (He purchased Mel's Rolls Royce 1983 Corniche convertible, white with red interior, from the estate, and later a new Rolls Silver Seraph of his own. He'd wanted a Rolls much earlier in his career, but Belli shot that notion down. "You can't buy a Rolls Royce and go back to Albany, Georgia!" Malone settled for an English sports car, a Jensen Interceptor, with a Chrysler motor that could be easily serviced at home.) However, he never took Belli's exuberant praise to heart. "I was stupid enough to believe him," Malone often joked.

Randy Scarlett, who'd try cases with both Belli and Malone, saw things differently. "I truly believe that's exactly what Mel thought." Then Scarlett went a big step further. "Tommy is the better lawyer," he said in 2017. "And he's a lot more fun than Mel Belli to try a case with."

Part III

In the Arena

"The credit belongs to the man who is actually in the arena...who does actually strive to do the deeds; who knows great enthusiasms, the great devotions; who spends himself in a worthy cause; who at the best knows...the triumph of high achievement, and who at the worst, if he fails, at least fails while daring greatly."

—Excerpt, Teddy Roosevelt, "The Man in the Arena"

Chapter 22

"I asked Judge Griffin Bell who were the great trial lawyers in Georgia.... The first name on his list was Tommy Malone."
—Mercer University President Bill Underwood

In 2006, William D. (Bill) Underwood arrived in Macon, Georgia, to assume the presidency of Mercer University. At Baylor University in Waco, Texas, his prior posting, Underwood had served as interim president and held the prestigious Leon Jaworski Chair in Practice and Procedure. In Dallas, Underwood had been a trial lawyer whose cases ranged from death-penalty appeals to civil actions in the aftermath of the Branch Davidian catastrophe. Not surprisingly, Underwood wanted a sense of the legal landscape in Georgia. "One of the first people I went to see," he recalled, "was Griffin Bell." At the time, Bell, the US attorney general in the Carter administration, was King & Spalding's former managing partner. "I asked Judge Bell who were the great trial lawyers in Georgia because I wanted to get to know them. The first name on his list was Tommy Malone."

"You may need to go see Tommy," Bell said in his unmistakable rumble. "He's not just a great lawyer, but somebody you need to meet."

Underwood called Malone, who invited him to come by the Ravinia Drive office. "Tommy told me a little bit of his story and how he got to Mercer and that he had a debt to the university he wanted to begin repaying." What followed next was every collegiate fundraiser's fantasy. "Tommy said he wanted to make a million-dollar gift that day." In the years that followed, the two lawyers became colleagues and personal friends. Underwood, who grew up in Oklahoma, discovered more about Tommy's early life and the difficult years he'd had as a trial attorney in his hometown. There is no doubt he became aware of southwest Georgia's terrible civil-rights history and the cases representing African Americans Tommy had argued.

In time, Tommy was named to Mercer's board of trustees and elected chairman of the board in 2015. "He struck me as a guy who cared about important things," Underwood said. "And by how frequently a part of the resolution of his lawsuits was the insistence on changes in practices that would insure that whatever caused the injuries would be adopted so that they were less likely to occur in the future. Tommy cared about things beyond just winning."

As a trustee, Tommy quickly proved he was worth his salt. "We regularly meet with investment advisors who counsel us on our endowment," Underwood said. "So we need trustees who can read through what they're telling us and ask the tough questions that need to be asked. Well, at one meeting, Tommy began very skillfully cross-examining our investment advisors while the rest of the trustees looked on. He quickly cut through all the verbiage to get to the core of the issue. At that moment the rest of the trustees realized how special he was. Sitting to my left while the cross-examination was going on was a very capable trustee, a successful businessman. He turned to me and said, '*Who is that guy?*'"

Ultimately, the question that intrigued Underwood—indeed the core question of this story—is "how this great lawyer who comes to represent important causes, emerges out of this background? What about Tommy Malone led him to be willing to take on the power structure in his community and begin representing people who were injured against prominent doctors and hospitals? It wasn't the money, because there wasn't any money to be made at that time. What led him to do this? There's nothing specific in his background that would cause you to predict that he would become one of the first white lawyers in the Deep South representing his black community members. A kid who grows up in the Jim Crow era in Dougherty County, who goes off to college—not an especially progressive young man—comes back home after he finishes law school and begins representing African Americans against the establishment at a time when it just wasn't done?"

The answers, of course, are as wide and deep and varied as human experience. As far as can be determined, there was no climactic moment, no Saul-on-the-road-to-Damascus conversion in young Thomas Malone's life, though certainly there were signposts. He'd always been a mirror of the world he inhabits, best understood by the reflections he casts on other people's lives. Undoubtedly, the young Malone sensed a "guiding hand" directing him to the good, but there was no teacher or mentor to illumine the path forward, just the gradual accretion of experience, knowledge, insight, and pain on a sensitive soul, kindling a fierce passion and righteous anger. Viewed through this lens, Underwood has come understand Thomas Malone as "a very important figure in the history of this region, and in some respects, the history of the country.

"His is the story of the growth and development of the South."

Chapter 23

"Counselor, do you realize you have 100 years of history to overcome?"
"I'm all right for 10, but I ain't taking no 100."
—Civil rights icon C. B. King to Tommy Malone

With Judge Rosser Malone happily ensconced on the bench, Tommy felt confident enough to open his own practice, one focused strictly on courtroom litigation. He was 30 years old, had a big win under his belt with Bitterman, and no doubt a desire to see how far he could stretch. It may not have been apparent at the time, so immersed was Malone in the hectic day-to-day demands of his practice, but he was breaking new ground, almost single-handedly carving out a niche for medical malpractice and product liability attorneys, very much like the chiropractors had won respectability—and fees—in their pitched battles with the American Medical Association. He needed a roof over his head to hang a shingle, so he and his older brother, Ross, who ran a construction company, set aside their differences and purchased a building on Oglethorpe Boulevard, a modest, mostly completed motel that had gone bust before it ever opened.

The motel truce was temporary. Ross would never get his construction business on track, plagued as he was by money problems, a stagnating economy, and bad decisions. Things between the two would worsen in the decades ahead as Tommy's career streaked across the Georgia heavens and Ross, never the favored son, struggled.

Tommy had a bridge loan in place but needed permanent financing to close the deal on the building. "I applied to one of the life insurance companies my father worked with," he recalled. "They came back and said, 'Tommy it's a 35-room motel and if mom and pop can't make it, we sure can't.' Well, I gave that some serious thought because now I owned a motel with a short-term loan coming due. I had to do something. So I called the same guy and said, 'Listen, I've got this *office* building I want to complete. I'd like to borrow $197,000 dollars,' or whatever it was.

"'I thought you had a motel down there?'

"'No, don't have that anymore. I have an office building.'"

They committed to make the loan, evidence, Malone said in 2017, "of a guiding hand." In any event, things worked out.

***

Now that he had his own firm, Tommy needed work to keep the lights on. Occasionally, he entertained offbeat propositions, the kind of deals familiar to any independent practitioner with an eye on the next mortgage or alimony payment. In the mid-1970s, R. L. Herring, who ran a heavy-equipment business out of Albany, showed up at Tommy's office with an offer that appeared—and proved—too good to be true. In 1977, President Jimmy Carter was embroiled in the highly controversial decision to turn over the Panama Canal, which the United States had built and controlled since 1908, to the government of Panamanian dictator General Omar Torrijos. (Malone's own grandfather had worked on the project.) Meanwhile, the notorious fugitive financier Robert Vesco, accused of embezzling at least $220 million of investors' money, was living in Costa Rica and looking for a way, any way imaginable, including buying an island and setting up his own country, to escape the long arm of the law. As Malone recalled, "Herring said to me, 'Would you be willing for a million dollars to go to Costa Rica, meet with Mr. Vesco, understand his solution to the Panama Canal issue, and then present it to President Carter?'"

"I can't promise you that I can present it to President Carter," Malone replied, "but I can promise that I'll present it to Hamilton Jordan, who is a very close friend of mine."

"I'll get back to you," Herring said.

That was the last Tommy heard from R. L. Herring. However, he was soon visited by federal agents very interested in hearing about the man's peculiar proposition and whether he'd acted on it. Tommy repeated exactly what he'd told Herring.

"Then I was subpoenaed to appear before a federal grand jury in Washington, DC," Malone said. Once again, he described his conversation with Herring. However, the foreman, a hard-charger named Ulmer, came after Malone very aggressively. "What was unusual," Tommy recalled many years later, "was the tone of his voice and his attitude." Tommy, of course, didn't know what was on Ulmer's mind, but he suspects the man felt the prosecutor wasn't going after people aggressively enough.

"Do you expect us to believe that you didn't call Hamilton Jordan and tell him this man had come to you and offered you a million dollars?" the foreman demanded.

"Yes, I expect you to believe it," Tommy answered. "But that's up to ya'll. I'm sworn to tell the truth. I'm a member of the bar. And I am telling the truth."

"Why didn't you call him?"

Now Tommy was in his element, "Well, there are two reasons," he allowed. "One is, he never even showed me any money. Didn't even crack a briefcase open to show me the money. He never got back to me, so I dismissed the proposal as not being realistic. Furthermore, if I had called my friend [Jordan] and told him about it, he might have said, 'I don't care what his plan is, we're *not* going to present it to the President!' Then I could not have accepted the million dollars."

"Well, we learned a lot about lawyer ethics," the foreman shot back. That was the end of it as far as Malone knows. He doesn't think the investigative grand jury ever indicted anyone. For his part, Vesco eventually made his way to Cuba, where he was convicted and imprisoned for conspiracy and drug smuggling. He died in Cuba in 2007.

When Malone arrived back in Georgia, he did field a call from a curious *Atlanta Journal-Constitution* columnist. "Well, Tommy," the man asked after hearing the grand jury story, "if they had given you the million dollars, would you have gone to Costa Rica and met with Vesco and presented the deal to Hamilton Jordan?"

"Let me answer your question this way," Tommy said. "If one of the fallen angels were to approach me and tell me that Lucifer had a plan about how to reenter heaven, and they'd paid me a million dollars to go to hell and meet with the devil to understand this reentry program and present it to St. Peter, I'd be on my way as soon as they gave me the million and worked out the transportation details."

***

In truth, he didn't need such schemes. The Bitterman case had given Malone's reputation a significant boost. As part of his new business outreach, Tommy continued to build bridges to Albany's African American community and attorney C. B. King in particular, once again infuriating James Gray and the white power structure that still clung to the tattered remnants of the past. "It was still not 'proper,' if you will, for a white lawyer in southwest Georgia to be associating, practicing, and handling cases with a black man," remembered Buddy Dallas. "But what the establishment thought didn't matter a lick to Tommy. If he believed in a cause, he was going to be there."

Malone's relationship with King was complicated, representing as much an interaction between two smart, feisty lawyers as an outreach across the racial divide. Despite Judge Malone's objections, Tommy continued to cross Oglethorpe Boulevard to the black side of Albany to huddle with King. "Daddy," Tommy would repeat while Rosser fumed, "I know I disappoint you the way I've been doing things, but I'm just going to have to disappoint you again." Tommy associated King on a number of cases but got not a one in return. The day came when Malone showed up at C. B.'s office and announced, "C. B., you know when I was in high school, if I went out on a first date and I didn't get a kiss that was okay. If I went out on a second date and didn't get a kiss [he didn't say "kiss"], our relationship was in trouble. If I went out on a third date and didn't get a kiss, it was over. Now, I've associated you on two cases, and you haven't associated me on any."

"Counselor," King rumbled, "do you realize you have 100 years of history to overcome?"

"I'm all right for 10," Tommy said, "but I ain't taking no 100."

Grudgingly, King began bringing in Tommy on personal-injury cases. When the victories and settlements began to pile up, the relationship blossomed. "We split up some million-dollar fees over the years," Malone remembered. Many years later, when Tommy was practicing in Atlanta, C. B. suggested his son Chevene King, an attorney, associate Tommy on a very high-profile action involving the negligent death of NFL Rookie of the Year Joe Delaney.

As Tommy remembered it, "Delany died in 1983 during a promotion for the Critter's Creek Water Park in Monroe, Louisiana, his hometown. As a promotion, they were giving away free tickets to the new waterslide at Kentucky Fried Chicken all over town. They had some thousands of people show up, a lot more than they expected. There were busloads of people who came from some of the African American churches.... They [park management] didn't have any real security. Pretty soon, the line was probably 500-people long to get into the waterslide. Nearby was a borrow pit [an area where soil, gravel, or sand has been removed for use at another location] they'd dug out to build the slide. It would fill with water, and they'd installed a pump to pump the water out. It was hot, June or July, and hundreds of people were wading in this 'pond.' Joe Delaney [Kansas City Chiefs' standout running back] and his girlfriend were sitting on the bank. Two 11-year-old boys waded out to where the pump was—there was a drop-off and the water much deeper—and stepped into the hole. They couldn't swim. Joe Delaney rushes in to save them and he drowns too."

Malone paused "It is significant to the story that when he was at Northwestern State University playing football, Delaney got a C in swimming, which probably means he couldn't even dog-paddle. The top athlete in a physical education program doesn't get better than a C, he ain't very good. Knowing he couldn't swim, he still jumped right in to try and save the boys."

The wrongful death/premises negligence lawsuits (*Carolyn Delaney, et al. v. City of Monroe, Louisiana, et al.*) that followed sought a total of $38 million in damages for Delaney's widow, her children, and the mothers of the two boys, Harry Holland Jr. and Lancer Perkins, who'd drowned. Defendants included the City of Monroe, owner of the land rented to the amusement park, Louisiana Amusements of Monroe Inc., Critter's Creek Inc., Gray Communications, Inc., (ironically, James Gray owned the local TV station that broadcast the promotion), and Kentucky Fried Chicken of Monroe. The lawsuit came to a successful verdict in 1987, but what stayed with Tommy Malone many years later was the pure hatred he'd conjured in one of the jurors. "I never will forget *voir dire*-ing the jury and asking the question, 'Are there any of you who have any hesitancy in awarding millions of dollars for the full value of the life of an African American member of our society if you felt the family was entitled to recover?' This white woman looked at me so hard. She was saying, 'You're white and you're asking me a question like that!' She didn't say it, but I can still remember the pure hatred I saw in her face, her scowls and stares." Needless to say, he exercised one of his challenges and excused her.

Justice, however, was blind. "We got a $3 million verdict," Malone recalled.

Chapter 24

"The insurance companies and everybody else realized that I could try a case and damn sure would."
—Tommy Malone, *Phillips v. Meadow Gardens Hospital et al.*

After Bitterman, it wasn't long before Tommy found himself embroiled in another high-profile medical malpractice case, this one against a renowned psychiatrist and, in effect, the quackery and cruelty that masqueraded as "therapy." Word was filtering out of South Georgia that Tommy Malone was a force to be reckoned with—fearless, outspoken, whip-smart, smooth, and seductive as fine whiskey. Well prepared and willing, no *eager,* to represent the little guy against the establishment, the black man crying out for justice in a place where injustice ruled, the mangled millworker, the hapless patient upon whom catastrophe is visited by a physician's negligence...the voiceless, who, lacking opportunity, education, and means, are inevitably denied justice.

Word was out, and not just among the young Turks—the soon-to-be formidable attorneys such as Jim Hiers and Jack Slover paying their dues below the "gnat line"—but also among the major Atlanta law firms, King & Spalding, Kilpatrick & Cody, Troutman Sanders, Alston & Bird; the corporations, hospitals, and health-care systems who demurred at any notion of accountability and hated the glare of bad publicity and certainly any "pipsqueak" lawyer who generated it. More than likely, word was definitely out among the lawyers who represented the St. Paul Companies, the insurers who had issued 90 percent of the medical malpractice polices in Georgia. They undoubtedly found Thomas Malone about as palatable as a dead mouse in a loaf of bread.

***

In 1972, Carolyn Phillips, a housewife in the grip of overwhelming emotional distress, drove herself to Meadow Garden Hospital in Augusta, Georgia, a private psychiatric facility run by Dr. Corbett H. Thigpen and his colleague and mentor, Hervey M. Cleckley, MD. In the 1950s, the two psychiatrists had rocketed to international fame when they published the astounding case history of one of their patients, Chris Sizemore, as *The Three Faces of Eve*. In the eponymous 1957 Hollywood adaptation of their bestselling book, Joanne Woodward won the Best Actress Academy Award for her powerful portrayal of Sizemore, a quiet, unassuming woman suffering from multiple personality disorder (today, Dissociative Identity Disorder). According to documented reports, the pair paid Sizemore $3 for the rights to her story. As the cynics had it, $1 for each personality.

"Carolyn Phillips had two children and a husband, probably a difficult husband," Malone recalled. "She was under a lot of stress and thought she was having a nervous breakdown. She drove herself to Meadow Garden to get help, so obviously she wasn't that bad off. There, they gave her twenty-six shock treatments in six days. Four on the last day, during which she went into a seizure from which she never returned. She lived four or five months before dying." The widower and Carolyn's minor children wanted to bring suit for wrongful death. No doubt because of Thigpen's and Cleckley's notoriety, Melvin Belli was contacted and agreed to take the case. Given his friendship with Tommy and the Georgia locale, Belli associated Malone. As it turned out, Belli was forced to beg off as the trial was about to get underway, leaving Tommy and O. Torbitt (Toby) Ivey Jr., a local attorney known more for death-penalty work than torts, to handle things. (Compounding matters, Malone was in the midst of an IRS audit. "Every day I was in Augusta, there was an IRS agent sitting at my desk," he recalled. "I told my secretary to bring him coffee, donuts, and whatever he wanted.")

In the 1940s and '50s, psychiatrists were rare—Cleckley and Thigpen essentially comprised the entire psychiatry and neurology faculty at the Medical College of Georgia. Meadow Gardens Hospital was their private practice. By modern standards, their protocols were barbarous—lobotomy, coma therapy, electroshock therapy, hydrotherapy (lowering body temperature to between 48 to 70 degrees by the use of ice-packed sheets and tubs), and doses of Thorazine that would reduce patients to a near-vegetative state—and abused. John F. Kennedy's sister, Rosemary, underwent a prefrontal lobotomy in 1941—signed off on by Joe Kennedy himself—that left her in a vegetative state for the rest of her life. According to one published report, Thigpen, an enthusiastic practitioner, claimed he'd performed 200 lobotomies on his patients.

During discovery, Malone realized there was a cost/benefit relationship to administering electric-shock therapy. "The more electric-shock treatments [electroconvulsive therapy, ECT], Corbett and Cleckley gave their patients," he remembered, "the more money they made." Carolyn Phillips endured twenty-six treatments in six days. What Malone didn't fully appreciate—because it was beyond the reach of science or reason—was that the mindset that tainted the Bitterman case was very much alive and well in Augusta. The city was home to the Medical College of Georgia and a number of university and military medical centers and facilities. Hometown juries were going to be packed with health-care workers and retirees likely to look after their own, particularly against out-of-town lawyers and experts challenging the very methods that made Thigpen so widely respected. (Ironically, it turned out that Eve was "cured," (albeit temporarily) because one of her personalities was cognizant enough to resist Thigpen's attempts to subject her to ECT-induced seizures.)

***

Phillips v. Meadow Garden Hospital et al. The defendants were Meadow Garden Hospital owners Thigpen and Cleckley and two pharmaceutical companies. It would prove significant that one of the companies, Eli Lily, was represented by King & Spalding chief litigator Kirk McAlpin. Tommy spent four weeks prepping and assembling his case. At trial, he called one "live" medical expert to the stand, the pharmacologist Dr. Roger Palmer. On the stand, Palmer proved unflappable. "It's my expert opinion based on the facts contained in the record..." He went on from there, buttressing what Malone believed was blatant and obvious medical malpractice. During cross-examination, one of the defense attorneys challenged Palmer.

"Dr. Palmer, you never treated the patient, so everything you're saying is simply your opinion?"

"Yes, but they are opinions to a reasonable degree of medical certainty."

"So, they're just opinions, theories correct?"

Palmer turned to the judge before the defense attorney could cut him off. "Your Honor, may I explain?" (Malone had instructed Palmer to ask that question if the right moment arose, "because almost all judges will let a witness explain.") The judge agreed.

"You can ask me, 'Aren't my opinions just theories?'" Palmer continued. "Yes, they are, but you've got to understand I have two kinds of theories. One is soft theory; the other is hard theory. A soft theory I have is that all the oxygen molecules in this room could suddenly rush to one corner and we'd all suffocate to death. That's a theory and it's possible, but it's a soft theory and I don't believe it's likely. Now a hard theory I have—I can't prove it—is that everybody in this room will die one day. I believe it to be true, but I can't explain to you exactly why everyone will. It's a hard theory. Everything I've testified to you in this courtroom has been hard theory. Nothing has been soft." It was hard to tell what exactly was registering with the jury, a science in itself, where every twitch or yawn or smile can be significant. In any event, the defense kept Roger Palmer on the stand for three days.

The defense was dug in for a long, grinding trial, literally a war of attrition against Malone. "They could have put up all their evidence in a week," Tommy remembered. "Instead, they spent days cross-examining Roger Palmer." Later, he would understand why the proceedings turned into an eight-week marathon. At the time, he was still under the impression—despite all the evidence to the contrary—that a trial was an attempt to arrive at justice.

At one point, an electroconvulsive therapy machine was brought into the courtroom. "At the bottom there were three rheostats like what you might find on a light fixture," Tommy recalled. Cross-examining Dr. Thigpen, he elicited that the renowned expert was unfamiliar with the workings of his own equipment. "They'd hook these leads to the patient's skull then turn these rheostats up until the patient went into a seizure. After they seize for a sufficient period of time, they turn the rheostat down and take the leads off. That's how sophisticated or lacking in sophistication, they were. We were pointing out how silly electroshock therapy was."

He conducted a memorable cross-examination of a defense witness, "an expert from Philadelphia or Pittsburgh," who'd authored a study on hypothermia, essentially freezing a patient out of a psychotic break. "Doctor, I noticed you had ten or twelve people in this study," Malone began. "How many of them did you kill?"

"We didn't *kill* anybody."

"Well, Doctor, I noticed that two people died during the course of your study of hypothermia as a treatment for schizophrenia. You lowered their body temperature down to 70 degrees. Two of them died. (Long pause.) If you didn't kill them, what did they die from?"

"Pneumonia."

"Pneumonia?"

Four jurors burst into laughter, to the point they were elbowing each other in the jury box. Malone let himself relax. "I thought I had at least those four," he recalled.

Both drug companies were voluntarily dismissed early in the proceedings, but not before Kirk McAlpin got a good look at Tommy Malone in action. After seven weeks of testimony, the case went to the jury. After days of deliberation, the foreman sent the judge a note that they were hopelessly deadlocked. "The judge said 'Don't tell me which way you divided, but what is the number of the division?'" Tommy remembered. "It was 10–2. Well, I knew we had those four who'd laughed, so we agreed to be bound by a 'less than unanimous verdict.'" That stipulation in open court was signed by counsel for all parties and approved by the judge.

As it turned out, Malone was wrong. The ten were for the defense. A devastating outcome for Carolyn Phillips's two minor children, driven, in part, by the defense's airing of her husband's unsavory reputation. Somehow, the jury didn't recognize that Carolyn's life had been needlessly and recklessly cut short by the very physicians she'd gone to for help, leaving her minor children to make their way through life without a mother. As in Bitterman, unsettling things soon began to surface. "When the verdict was in and the judge had dismissed the jury," Malone remembered, "a retired nurse who'd sworn she could be fair, came down out of the jury box and hugged Dr. Thigpen in front of everybody." Malone also had an eyewitness report that one of Thigpen's attorneys had been seen visiting the *home* of one of the jurors. "I called the judge," Malone said. "I told him, 'I'm not looking to try this case again. Eight weeks are enough for me, but I feel I've got an obligation to the bar and to you to share this information.'" The judge summoned the defense attorney. The man's explanation was fresh in

Tommy Malone's memory forty years later: "Yes, I was at the juror's home, but that was *after* the verdict, not before. I was personally inviting her to our celebration party."

At that point, Malone stepped away. Co-counsel Toby Ivey pressed ahead with a motion for a retrial, and when that was denied, an appeal that he argued in July 1976. Ivey held that the less-than-unanimous verdict stipulated by all parties was not binding of Phillips's minor children, an argument swatted down by the appellate court.

Like the Bitterman struggle, *Phillips v. Meadow Garden* affected Tommy Malone in unforeseen ways. On the plus side, Kirk McAlpin was so impressed with what he saw in the Augusta courtroom that, a few years later, he was instrumental in Malone being awarded an AV Preeminent rating by Martindale-Hubbell. McAlpin's influence and goodwill would also speed Tommy's admission into the International Academy of Trial Lawyers.

On the other hand, as Joseph Heller put it in *Catch 22*, "Just because you're paranoid doesn't mean they aren't after you." Tommy's growing unease that he'd created some real enemies proved true. The Phillips case cost him a full three months, a quarter of a year's time, and potential revenue off the top of a struggling practice. "St. Paul had almost all the medical insurance in Georgia at the time," he said in 2017. "It later struck me that they *planned* to run me right out of the medical negligence business. At the time, there were only two lawyers in the whole state handling medical malpractice work. Instead, the trial spread my reputation. The insurance companies and everybody else realized that I could try a case and damn sure would."

Chapter 25

"No cocktail party was too trivial, no conference too dull."
—Obituary, Lord Gordon Slynn of Hadley

At an American Bar Association gathering in the late 1970s (the specifics are lost in the mists of time), Kirk McAlpin, the prominent King & Spalding litigator who became a mentor and friend to Tommy Malone in the aftermath of the Meadow Garden trial, was captivated by one of the guest lecturers, a mercurial Englishman named Gordon Slynn. McAlpin, past president of the State Bar of Georgia and a leading contender for the American Bar Association presidency, invited the British barrister with the mop of unruly silver hair to address the Georgia bar's annual meeting in Savannah. Slynn, a man whose dazzling legal acuity was equaled by a love of travel, revelry, and fellowship that could extend to Falstaffian levels, happily accepted. So began an unlikely bond between a blue-blooded Englishman and a feisty band of lawyers, Tommy Malone among them, sprung mostly from the red clay of Georgia,

In the decades ahead, Gordon Slynn, later named Baron Slynn of Hadley (a "Law Lord"), would rise to the highest levels of British jurisprudence, serving, among myriad other titles and positions, as a member of Queen Elizabeth's Privy Council (the highest court of appeal for a number of Commonwealth countries), a Lord of Appeal in Ordinary (equivalent to a justice on the US Supreme Court), and Judge and Advocate General of the European Court of Justice. "A lawyer of uncommon intellectual ability," read one Slynn obituary (*The Telegraph,* April 8, 2009), "Slynn was renowned for his vast reserves of energy and his gregarious, willing nature—no cocktail party was trivial, no conference too dull."

It seems inevitable that Slynn would cross paths with Thomas W. Malone, Esq., also a lawyer who fancied strong drink and roaring good times; they'd become fast friends and undoubtedly "drunk as lords" when the occasion presented itself. At the Savannah bar association meeting, where Malone first met Gordon Slynn, the two shut down the "whiskey bar" at the De Soto Hilton after McAlpin, no lightweight when it came to libations, had staggered off to bed. "It was Slynn and me," Malone recalled many years later, "the last two at the bar. He and I found we had a lot in common, above all, a love of the law. That was the thing we had most in common."

As Humphrey Bogart put it in *Casablanca*, it was "the beginning of a beautiful friendship," one that would last the better part of twenty years. Slynn stayed with Tommy and Debbie when he visited Atlanta, even taking the occasional dip in the Malone hot tub. On one occasion, the two flew to California on Malone's private plane to address a meeting of the International Society of Barristers.

In 1983, Malone, Mel Belli, and a group of Belli Society lawyers rode the train from London to visit Slynn and his wife, Odile, at their estate in Eggington in Befordshire. Slynn, Malone recalled, had a very impressive wine cellar and was "very attached to his dogs." Through Slynn, Malone and John Bell also became good friends with barrister Roderick Noble, a member of the respected firm ("set" in the UK) 39 Essex Chambers, and his wife, Joan. The Nobles entertained Belli Society visitors at their homes in London and in Edinborough. They also made an appearance at one of Tommy's extravagant birthday bashes in Atlanta and visited the Malones in Florida and the Bahamas with their sons, Ian and Jamie.

Gordon Slynn traveled constantly in the course of his professional obligations. (The rumor had it, Slynn would happily show up to lecture anywhere for the price of a first-class plane ticket and expenses.) He developed a real affinity for Georgia and became friends with a gifted fellowship of lawyers and judges—Tommy Malone, Kirk McAlpin, Judge Pope, John Bell, Macon attorney John James (a former president of the Georgia Trial Lawyers Association), Superior Court Judge Tommy Day Wilcox, and the inimitable US District Court Judge Anthony Alaimo among them. In turn, Slynn extended invitations to visit him in London— they happily accepted—and introduced his American colleagues to his fellow peers, arranged for personal tours of the courts' inner sanctum, had them sit in on trials, and hosted grand lunches at the Peers' Dining Room in the House of Lords. Once, he had an assistant escort the group to the royal "Robing Room," where the Queen puts on ceremonial robes and the Imperial Crown in preparation for the State Opening of Parliament.

"Debbie took a seat in the chair," Malone recalled. "To the great chagrin of the lady-in-waiting."

"I'm sorry, no one can sit there but the queen," the woman sputtered.

"I'm already sitting here!" Debbie replied.

The friendship flowed in both directions. When French-born Odile Slynn was injured and hospitalized in a car wreck en route to a party on Georgia's Sea Island, Tommy Malone graciously handled the litigation—a settlement sped by Judge Alaimo—pro bono. In 2001, John James, a Mercer law school graduate, endowed an annual Distinguished Lecture Series at Mercer University. James chose Slynn—who held fifteen honorary doctorates—to handpick an array of international legal scholars and luminaries to present lectures. Tommy particularly recalled the 2005 Lecture, "What Is Islamic Law?" given by Imam Feisal Abdul Rauf of New York. "Slynn would invite people from all over the world to come in and speak at Mercer on matters of worldwide importance in the law," Malone said. "Highbrow talks like that."

"Slynn was an absolutely brilliant guy," remembered John Bell, who helped put together a number of the memorable trips to London, "a gigantic personality who somehow got to know Tommy Malone and this little group of Georgia lawyers."

Chapter 26

*"The thing that really precipitated the move to Atlanta was a
$500,000 verdict in federal district court in Atlanta, a medical
negligence case which was not nearly as strong for damages or
liability as many of the cases I'd lost in South Georgia."*
—Tommy Malone, *Jurysak v. Kennestone*

By 1976, Tommy's law practice was robust enough to allow him to open a
satellite office near Atlanta's Peachtree DeKalb Airport. "I figured I could
fly up there, desk to desk, in about two hours," he said. The expansion
justified bigger, faster transportation, seemingly a theme in Malone's life.
He purchased a twin-engine Beechcraft Baron and later an Aerostar that he
souped-up with dual 350-horsepower engines. Malone Law was also taking
flight, growing to eight lawyers and twelve staffers, with Tommy racing
back and forth between Albany and Atlanta like some kind of airborne
administrator. A day came when he sat down and ran the numbers. "A
lightbulb went off." His net revenue, despite all the business he was
handling, was roughly equal to the two largest fees he'd earned over the last
couple of years—both generated in metropolitan Atlanta.

"The thing that really precipitated the move to Atlanta was a $500,000
verdict in federal district court in Atlanta," he recalled (*Jurysak v. Kennestone
and Dr. Elmer Anthony Mussara II*), "a medical negligence case which was
not nearly as strong for damages or liability as many of the cases I'd *lost* in
South Georgia. It occurred to me that there must be something different
about trying malpractice cases in metropolitan areas than in rural areas: if
you prove to a big-city jury that a doctor is a butcher, they're happy to run
him out of town because they've got many more doctors to take his spot. If
you're in a town of 12,000 people and you prove their *own* doctor is a
butcher, they'd rather have the butcher than nobody. I decided to close my
Albany office. I'd probably been thinking about leaving, but those big verdicts were in metro areas."

Jurysak v. Kennestone grew out of a plastic surgeon's reconstruction of a
painful mastectomy site gone terribly wrong. Kennestone Hospital's lead

defense attorney was Roy Barnes, Democratic state senator, later governor of Georgia. Barnes remembered the case very well. "This was in the late 1970s, early '80s, in federal court," he recalled. "Tommy was the plaintiff's lawyer. Robert [Bob] Tanner represented the surgeon [E. Anthony Mussara, MD]. During the trial, I could see that the doctor's case wasn't going too well, so one morning I came in and moved to another table. The judge [US District Court Judge Robert Hall] came in and said, 'Mr. Barnes, you having a little problem in paradise over there?' I said, 'Well, Judge, I just need a little more room.'" Tommy Malone's courtroom work assured things would continue to go downhill for Dr. Mussara. "In my closing argument," Barnes remembered, "I told the jury, 'I don't know whether Dr. Mussara is negligent or not, but I know this, I don't have a dog in this fight.' It's an old Southern saying. So they let my client out. They hit Dr. Mussara for $500,000 dollars, which was a big verdict forty years ago."

Malone picked up the story. "During the trial, Roy and I developed a friendship even though our interaction was adversarial in nature. We respected each other. When lawyers find themselves friends even though they might be on opposite sides, truth is always the common denominator. You can believe that what they say is the truth."

Over the years, the two became close personal friends. When Barnes quit defense work, he and Tommy collaborated on a number of cases. "It's one of those unique things that used to happen that I don't see as much anymore," Barnes said. "Lawyers on both sides are best friends. That's what happened here." In the summer of 2017, Roy Barnes and his wife, Marie, were among the guests gathered at the Breakers in Palm Beach to celebrate Tommy and Debbie Malone's thirtieth wedding anniversary.

***

Malone's pulling up stakes was complex and deeply felt, not simply a prudent career strategy. Experience taught North Carolina novelist, and observer of all things Southern, Thomas Wolfe that "you can't go home again," a truth that encapsulates the myriad forces swirling within Malone. No one can go home again, not really. Exposure to the larger world transforms, propels, and sometimes repels us from what was familiar and acceptable. Physically, Tommy had never left Albany, but intellectually and emotionally, he'd emerged from the chrysalis that had entangled him in the last vestiges of a dying culture. The Albany establishment would never forgive him for Bitterman or his outreach to C. B. King, Billy and Helen Jennings Black, and others in the African American community, nor for the lawsuit to enjoin the excessive bid for construction of the new governmental center. This anger was real and visceral. As mentioned, after Bitterman, the word was out that no local doctors treat Tommy or his family. This may have been an exaggeration, but the animus behind it was palpable. The unkindest cut came when Tommy felt it necessary to resign as chairman of the Dougherty County Heart Association, a charity to which he'd devoted time, money, and good will.

"None of the doctors would come to our meetings," Malone remembered. "I asked the executive director, where are they?"

"Well, Tommy, they ain't coming back as long as you have anything to do with this organization."

Malone thought this over. "Should I resign?"

"If you care anything about the organization, you will."

"So I quit."

Many years later, Tommy looked back at that moment. "They actually considered me the enemy," he said. "I was not an enemy. I was an advocate for good care...but they also knew if they screwed up, they or their friends would have to face me in court. The Heart Association rebuke was another of those things that made me feel *they* were the small ones. I'm the kind of person who wants everyone to like me, but I also knew that by following my calling, my purpose in life, I was pissing off large segments of society down there. I don't remember being sad about it. I remember feeling sorry for the small-minded folks on the other side of the issue."

Tommy at age 5.

TOMMY – AGE 13
ON TONY

Tommy, age 13, is saddled up on "Tony."

Tommy serving as President of Demosthenian Literary Society,
the University of Georgia.

Tommy interns with Senator Richard B. Russell, 1963.

Tommy graduates from Mercer University School of Law, 1966.

Tommy's great grandfather Reverend John Levi Underwood was Captain Chaplain in the Confederate Army, earned a Master of Arts, and served as Trustee of Mercer University. He also authored *Women of the Confederacy*.

Rosser Adams Malone, Tommy's father (above),
and Petrona "Toni" Underwood Malone, Tommy's mother (below).

Rosser Malone with Governor Carl E. Sanders.

Rosser Malone in typical attire during hunting season.

Tommy's mother, Toni, at a charity ball.

Tommy, Jr. (left), Tommy, and Adam (right)
quail hunting in South Georgia.

Tommy and Adam, law partners.

Photo by Daemon Baizan.

Tommy and Grand Debbie with Adam's children:
Maddie, Rosser, and Emilie.

Tommy, Jr.'s daughter, Kennedy Carter Malone,
with Rosalyn and President Jimmy Carter.

Tommy and Debbie married in Las Vegas on June 27, 1987.

Tommy and Debbie celebrating their 30th wedding anniversary
at The Breakers in Palm Beach, Florida.

Debbie and Tommy at the Shepherd Center Legendary Party.

Christmas Eve Party at the Malone Atlanta home.

Tommy as Santa.

"Santa Tommy" (holding Mollie) and Mrs. Debbie Claus
with Santa and his sleigh.

Long-time pilot Alan Brown (left) with Tommy, and Debbie (holding Mollie) standing next to King Air 350.

Justice, a Striker 70, brought much happiness
to family and friends for more than 25 years.

Tommy and Mollie aboard *Justice*.

Meggie aboard *Justice*.

Tommy and Roger Palmer (left):
medical mentor, big game fishing mentor, and dear friend.

Roger Palmer and Tommy with a blue marlin, 1973.

Fishing club plaque.

Justice docked at Snapper Point, the Abaco Island retreat
where friends and guests made many memories.

(l-r) Jay Cook, Al Corriere, Tommy, and Spencer Lee
after a day fishing out of Snapper Point.

Jody Campbell lands a sailfish out of North Palm Beach.

Herb Phipps, appointed Associate Judge by Rosser Malone,
ultimately became Chief Judge of the Georgia Court of Appeals.

C. B. King, a trail blazing lawyer with whom Tommy served as co-counsel.

Chris and Priscilla Searcy (left) with Debbie and Tommy.

Tommy and Randy Scarlett in Napa Valley.

Randy, Tommy, Debbie, and R2 at home in North Palm Beach.

Lord Slynn visiting Tommy and Debbie in Atlanta (above);
Lord Slynn, DeeDee, and John Bell (below).

Tommy, Tracy Moulton, and Melvin Belli in Early County, Georgia.

Tammy Faye and Jim Baker, Alex Haley, Tommy, Lia and Mel Belli,
Ceasar and Gretchen Belli standing on the dock
next to Mel's boat *The Adequate Award*, 1987.

Tommy, Meri Benoit, Adam, and Tucker Sutton.

Tommy, Buddy and Denise Dallas, and co-counsel Brad Houck
in front of the Washington County Courthouse in Sandersville, Georgia.

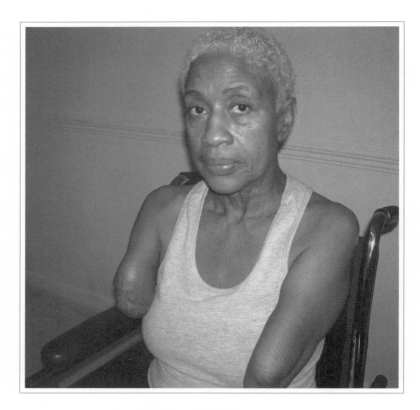

Caroline Palmer.

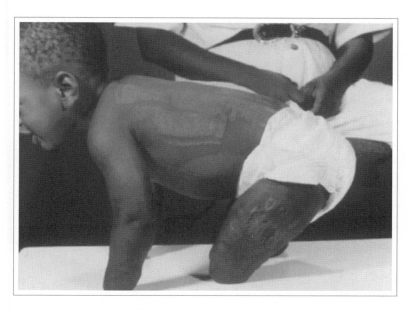

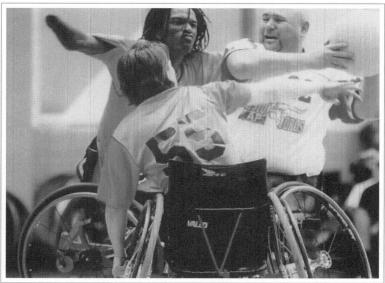

James Adams in 1995 (above); James Adams competing
in basketball during the Special Olympics (below).

Rex and Rhanelda Jones, Tommy, Priscilla Searcy
at Tommy's 70th birthday celebration.

Debbie, President Jimmy Carter, and Tommy
at Mercer University Board of Trustees retreat.

Ray Persons and Tommy co-chair the Just the Beginning
Foundation Atlanta event with President Carter.

Governor and Mrs. Roy E. Barnes, Debbie, and Tommy at Atlanta home.

Senator Max Cleland, Debbie, and Tommy at Atlanta home.

Tommy as Chair of Mercer University Board of Trustees.

Tommy's 75th birthday cake.

President Underwood receiving the Southern Trial Lawyers Association's
"Tommy Malone Great American Eagle Award."

Go Bears!

Part IV

Gone Fishing

Chapter 27

"I found myself back on Bimini Island..."
—Tommy Malone

In these years, another significant movement becomes apparent in Tommy Malone's life. A love of fishing expands from casual pastime to magnificent obsession and near addiction that continues for the rest of his life. In his law practice, Malone would craft innumerable crisp and compelling briefs. His 1999 book, *Voir Dire and Summation: The Law and the Practice*, would become a trial lawyer's bible, but at age 30, he turned his attention to deconstructing *Acanthocybium solandri*, a fish. His meditation "Wahoo Bahamian Style," on the combative and wily blue-and-silver-striped torpedo known to the English-speaking populations of the Caribbean as wahoo, opens with the gravitas one might reserve for a brief presented before the US Supreme Court: *"It was in November in 1972 that I found myself back on Bimini Island..."*

In fact, Tommy was standing, or possibly swaying, on the dock of the Bimini Big Game Club in the Bahamas. The club was Malone's kind of place, a magnet for hard-drinking, nonstop carousing, but also serious sport fishermen and the bikini-clad women who attached to them like pilot fish. He was with his go-to medical expert, drinking buddy, and fellow aficionado Dr. Roger Palmer, whom Tommy had met at that first Belli seminar in Miami and called upon in the Bitterman and Phillips cases. The two had formed a close friendship that would remain raucous and rowdy until Palmer's death in 2007. "We had a lot in common," Malone recalled in 2016. "We loved women, we loved drinking, and we loved fishing." Palmer introduced Tommy, angling since his boyhood for bass, brim, and crappie, to big-game fishing—sailfish, marlin, and swordfish.

When Tommy's mainland buddies began showing up, drawn by the rowdy charms of the Bahamas, they certainly didn't have the patience or time for billfish. "You'd go to a four-and-a-half-day tournament and never hook a billfish," Tommy remembered. "A week of boredom with twenty minutes of uncontrollable enthusiasm when the fish hits. But the fish usually doesn't hit. You'd have forty boats in a tournament and catch maybe five marlin."

On blue-water afternoons, after hours of uneventful trolling, Tommy would be staggered by an explosion of boiling water and the hiss of 80-pound test line sizzling off a Penn International 50. A 'Hoo, vibrant blue band and iridescent flanks glistening, had taken a lure and was racing away at near 60 miles an hour before Malone could react, and when he did, the fish had reversed its trajectory and was speeding back toward him, likely as not to spit the hook back in his face. Aggressive and plentiful, with a mouthful of razor-sharp teeth that turn steel leaders into dental floss, a 40-pound wahoo would give any angler an electrifying battle. Malone was instantly hooked. Angler became acolyte and then evangelical zealot. "When you go wahoo fishing, everybody on the boat gets to catch one, two, three, five," he enthused. "Fish that might weigh 100 pounds, but would be at least 15, 20, or 30."

Like film directors, plaintiff's attorneys can have lots of downtime. The Bahamas became the place where heaven met earth for Tommy Malone, a tranquil haven where he'd escape, unwind, and kick back after a hard-fought trial, take his sons fishing or diving, tinker on a marine diesel engine, or party and entertain friends and girlfriends. The islands became a handy barometer of his career: at first, he and Palmer couldn't pay for the Big Game Club's pricey rooms and stayed half a mile south at Brown's Marina, showing up at the club for fuel and fun. After a while, Tommy could afford to rent the house next door to the Bahamian commissioner, Kirkwood Taylor. Then he moored *Justice* (one of four fishing boats he'd similarly christen) at the club's marina. Fortunes still improving, he stayed *at* the club, moving briskly through the ranks of an indeterminate organization chart until he'd served enough sufficiently raucous tours of duty to be elevated to "Commodore." Of all his honors, Malone's designation as a flag officer is among the most prized. "Commodore means you're the president of people who love to fish," he explained. In years ahead, the Bahamas, particularly Abaco Island, would play an even greater role in Tommy's life.

***

In Atlanta, victories, awards, and notices began to pile up. Lawyers moved in and out of the practice with Tommy. (Over his long career, Malone would have no partners other than his father and Bob Drake in Albany and later, Adam Malone.) He became a man of interest in his profession, as Jack Slover aptly put it, "a guy you'd want to get to know." His personal life was less sanguine. He stayed single seven years after divorcing Joan, then married an attractive divorcee with whom he eventually realized he had little in common. When that union dissolved, Tommy began to reevaluate his flash-frozen adolescent notions of a relationship. Suddenly, he was in his forties, and time might not be on his side. Call it luck, coincidence, or a higher power at work, but the woman with whom he'd happily spend the rest of his life was right there on the horizon.

Chapter 28

"I'm single, are you?"
—Tommy meets Debbie at the Kroger

August 30, 1985. Hurrying home from her executive secretary job at IBM, Debbie Blankinship planned to stop at the local Kroger supermarket, then pack and head down to Panama City, Florida, first thing in the morning. "I was going to buy junk food and lay at the beach with some friends," she recalled. It was Labor Day weekend. On the radio, Huey Lewis and the News' "The Power of Love" was racing up the charts. Hurricane Elena, a Category 3 storm, was brewing in the Gulf of Mexico.

Blankinship was single, attractive, and extremely shy. Disinterested in Atlanta's aggressive singles scene, she was self-sufficient but hopeful of finding someone with whom she could build a committed relationship. Her mom had disapproved of the two serious boyfriends she'd had, one of them her high school sweetheart. Debbie was in her thirties, but there was a schoolgirl's sparkle to her, a mix of innocence, mischief, and wariness that men found intriguing.

On Buford Highway in northeast Atlanta, she pulled into the Kroger parking lot alongside a black Jaguar XJ6 with camel interior, her "most favorite car in the world," and headed inside. Moments later, pushing her buggy up and down the supermarket aisles, tossing in random boxes and bags of snacks, she notices this very tall, silver-haired guy in khaki pants and a baby blue Oxford shirt with rolled up sleeves. He smiles as he passes by. Approaching from opposite directions, their paths cross at the midpoint of the next aisle, the next aisle, and the next.

"We've got to stop meeting like this," the guy says with a grin.

"I don't know," Debbie blurted. "It's kind of fun."

He has tinnitus so he doesn't hear a word she says. He pushes his buggy on by. Then she notices he's behind her in the checkout line, too far back to start a random conversation. As she's leaving, Debbie says:

"Well, did you park next to me also?"

"I don't know but I guess we'll see."

Unconsciously, she's patting her pearl grey business suit, wanting to look her best. Then she's in the parking lot unloading her purchases too late for any further clever repartee. The old shyness, a thing she's struggled with much of her life, is kicking in. "I'm never gonna see him again," she thinks, her life's dating experience flashing by in a frustrating five minutes. She turns and looks back one more time, and there he is, smiling ear to ear.

"Hi, I'm Tommy Malone," he says, shaking her hand.

Startled, she looks up. The guy with the buggy is the guy with the Jag.

"I'm single, are you?" Malone says.

In a very few minutes, Debbie discovers "Tommy" is a trial lawyer, divorced, who operates a firm in the Century Center office complex. He's lives in Variations, a nearby condo, and no, she doesn't want "to come over for a drink." She *is* intrigued, and so is he.

So intrigued and such a good fit, they discover, that Debbie and Tommy (who'd foresworn another marriage) will build a loving, supportive, and complementary relationship. Debbie, strong when Tommy is fragile, disciplined when he's heedless, determined, protective, loving, and selfless, will contribute immeasurably to Malone's success over the next decades. "It's no accident," he said, "how things gravitate." In 2017, in the midst of a devastating health crisis, both insist that a random flirtation in a half-empty supermarket on a long-ago Labor Day weekend was no coincidence, but the work of a guiding hand. "I was put here to help Tommy Malone be the best person he can be," Debbie insisted. "I'm secure with my own self so I don't need to be the star or celebrity." Malone's belief in a force greater than himself infusing his life with meaning and purpose is an article of faith and a comfort. Perhaps it's no coincidence that the arc of his life and career finds an echo in Ecclesiastes 3:1–11: "*To everything there is a season, and a time to every purpose under heaven: A time to be born, and a time to die; a time to plant, and a time to pluck up that which is planted.... A time to weep, and a time to laugh; a time to mourn, and a time to dance.*"

***

All this is in the distant future. First, the dance of possibility and heightened expectation that comes with all new romantic relationships. Debbie did not go to Panama City. Hurricane Elena came and went. Tommy never realized

Debbie was in town, didn't call, and she didn't follow up that first encounter. "A true Southern girl would never call a man," she said many years later. However, she sorely wanted to pursue what seemed an auspicious beginning and undertook some preliminary fact-finding, what today is taken for granted in a Google or Facebook search. That first night, she'd confided in her best friend and then called Sara, her mother. By some extraordinary coincidence, Mrs. Blankinship had also noticed a tall, striking, blue-eyed lawyer on TV that evening. He was being interviewed about some high-profile catastrophic injury case. It was Tommy.

On a Monday night when he does call, Debbie is lounging on the sofa about to call it a night. "By the time I get ready," she thinks, "it will be time for bed!" She tells him—it's not easy—that she has "other plans." Undaunted, he invites her to dinner the following night at McKinnon's, a popular Louisiana-style restaurant in Atlanta's Buckhead district. Afterward, Malone discovers Debbie Blankinship is not a *laissez-les-bon-temps-rouler* kind of girl. They continue dating, but Tommy makes his intentions clear.

"I'm not interested in a serious relationship," he insists.

"Fine."

Sixteen months later, he proposes. Now, Tommy cautions Debbie to expect a "long engagement." Not so long, as it turned out, because for the first time in his life, Tommy Malone is in love, entwined in a mature relationship that also happens to be great fun. The two married on June 27, 1987. By all accounts, the wedding was an affair to remember, and Debbie has committed each shard to memory. Tommy's brother, Ross, was the best man; his niece, Carolyn (Ross's daughter), maid of honor. Sara Blankinship had carried a fan at her wedding, so Debbie and Carolyn carried fans. (Debbie painstakingly decorated each fan with sequins, pearls, and orchids.) Nearly seventy family members, friends, and associates flew to Las Vegas for the ceremony at the Little Church of the West, a rustic, wooden structure among all the glitter. Debbie wore a traditional wedding dress with a cathedral-length train and a tiered veil. Tommy was elegant in tails. After their vows were taken, Judge Rosser Malone handed his son a collapsible top hat and cane. Tommy popped open the hat, twirled the cane, and marched arm in arm down the aisle and outside with Debbie to cheers and flights of white balloons.

A champagne-fountain reception followed at Caesar's Palace, and then a sumptuous dinner at Bacchanalia. Wine flowed from lambskins. "They had Roman Geisha girls dressed like 'I Dream of Jeannie,'" Debbie recalled. "They gave the men sensual massages." Afterward, everybody was bused to a Wayne Newton concert where "Mr. Entertainment" himself sent over a bottle of champagne to the happy couple.

Among the wedding presents was, of all things, the "keys to the city of Albany," delivered by Tommy's cousin Bill Underwood. The honor came courtesy of Albany Mayor Larry Bays who'd won a special election in 1986 after longtime mayor James Gray died suddenly in office. The final irony in the Tommy Malone/James Gray head-butting came later after Gray's widow Cleair—she'd been cut out of her husband's will—turned to Tommy for help in securing a portion of Gray's estate. In effect, Tommy filed a lawsuit, grounded in a case Belli had handled, that leveraged a promise Gray had made to Cleair, and that she'd "relied" upon, into a binding oral contract. The lawsuit was settled, and Tommy walked away with a hefty fee. "James Gray probably rolled over in his grave," Malone said in 2017. "The last thing he would have wanted was me getting some of his money."

Tommy and Debbie spent two weeks honeymooning in Hawaii, then flew to Los Angeles and drove from LA to San Francisco for Mel Belli's eightieth birthday party, which happened to coincide with the American Trial Lawyers Association convention. Among the attendees reported to be at the party were Dianne Feinstein, Jerry Brown, Lana Turner, and a handful of San Francisco Giants' players. Belli invited them to lunch on *Adequate Award*, his yacht. They dined with Jim and Tammy Faye Bakker (Belli's "finest client") and *Roots* author, Alex Haley.

***

Tommy and Debbie's wedding vows ("...for better, for worse, for richer, for poorer, in sickness, and in health...") still resonate thirty years later. "Debbie is my life's partner," Tommy said at their thirtieth wedding anniversary ball. "Life partner" is an image far removed from his youthful notion of a wife as a sexy woman who could play bridge, go to charitable events, keep the house, and raise kids (with a nanny). "I didn't know how very important a life partner can be," Tommy added. "Debbie brought this realization to the center of my being." Their partnership is not so much a division of responsibility—breadwinner vs. homemaker—as a commonality of feelings, interests, and ideas willingly shared with those they love and fiercely defended against interlopers. "Tommy will do anything for anybody," Debbie added. "He needs everyone to love him."

Debbie's in charge of the social calendar, runs the houses, plans the grand parties that regularly attract hundreds of guests, and does everything in her power to foster Malone's well-being, a lifelong voyage that would leave most spouses dizzy, breathless, or exhausted on the shore. "Debbie is my sounding board," Tommy continued. "My first focus group in the cases I fight. She comes to court and doesn't hesitate to tell me when she disagrees with what I'm doing." He paused and added with some irony, "Sometimes, I don't do what she's trying to tell me." This was particularly true when he'd pursue another lifelong passion, Crown Royal on the rocks, particularly true when Roger Palmer was anywhere in proximity. "Debbie cleaned up my act a lot," Tommy allowed. ("She made him rich!" insisted one colleague.) Malone recited his next lines from memory:

"Another wife would say, 'If you take one more drink I'm leaving!'

"And I'd say, 'Bartender, bring me two doubles!'

"Debbie never said, 'Don't you have another drink!' Instead, she'd bring me two ice teas. Controlling me but in a smarter way."

And only up to a point. "A bronco can be broken," insisted one of Tommy's old buddies with a laugh, "but it's still a wild horse." Rodeos and seafaring images still recur in depictions of Malone, who, when all is said and done, is no longer a teen hankering to bust broncos but a 74-year-old grandfather with white hair, stiff gait, and gentle manner. "I've tamed him some," acknowledged Debbie, "but no one can tell Tommy what to do. You just have to be a good influence. Tommy is the ship, and I'm the rudder. He says he needs somebody to keep him off the rocks."

Another resonant image of Tommy and Debbie's relationship comes from Dr. Larry Schlachter, a neurosurgeon and attorney who, with his wife, Teri, are close friends of the Malones. "They've had this Ronald-and-Nancy-Reagan relationship for thirty years," Schlachter said. "Extremely intense and from the heart. Debbie is Tommy's best friend. Tommy is 100 percent in love with Debbie. He may have been a wild man the first part of his life, but I never knew that guy. He's lived the rest of his life on the straight and narrow, a good boy, not just a good boy, a very good boy."

Part V

The Company He Keeps

A man is known by the company he keeps. Over the years, Tommy Malone encountered more than his share of brilliant colleagues who inspired, guided, defended, or tried cases with him. Like stars in a galaxy too numerous to name but dazzling to contemplate—Peter Zack Geer in South Georgia, Mel Belli and Randy Scarlett in San Francisco, Chis Searcy in Florida, Tom Carlock, Judson Graves, Jim Hiers, Jack Slover, Lori Cohen, and now, Adam Malone, whose ability and reputation now rivals his father's—skilled and seasoned veterans with outsized talent and reputations of their own. The stories that follow are, of course, incomplete, shards of long-ago memories of events and interactions recalled by individuals whose careers encompass thousands of cases. Jim Hiers and Jack Slover, for example, met Malone a half century ago when he was a young and troublesome lawyer beginning to make waves in Albany, Georgia. Yet by some strange and wonderful alchemy, the man and the attorney shine brilliantly in all their memories. Taken together, they point the way to Georgia's own guiding star, Tommy Malone.

Chapter 29

"Why did Atticus Finch take on the representations he did?"
—Ray Persons, King & Spalding

W. Ray Persons, senior partner at King & Spalding in Atlanta, first met Tommy Malone in the late 1980s when the two found themselves on opposite sides of a bad-faith insurance case. Malone was associated in the action, brought on board by Wendell Willard (later a Georgia state representative). Tommy invited Persons and a female associate to lunch at the nearby Ravinia Club to see if they could iron out their clients' differences and avoid the time, expense, and uncertainty of a jury trial. Malone had his own table in the dining room. "Tommy was unfailingly polite," Persons recalled. "Not that I expected anything different, but each time she got up to leave the table, he stood. This was very uncommon at the time. I also remember Tommy was not boastful even though he had a gigantic reputation. It proved to be a very, very effective approach because we got the case resolved. Obviously, he was talented and knowledgeable, but what struck me is how gracious he was." Oddly, Persons's colleagues had cautioned him that Tommy Malone was "dangerous."

Grace is a virtue that elevates a man. Toni Malone raised her son to be a gentleman, schooling him in everything from proper comportment to the placement of his dessert fork. And grace in word and deed describes Malone a lifetime later. Toni Malone, a gracious woman, was right when she told Tommy that first impressions are lasting, the imprint that people remember and judge you by. No one knows this better than Ray Persons, a talented attorney in a mostly white law firm who happens to be African American.

Eternal opponents before the bar, Malone and Persons became great friends outside the courtroom. There is something tangible in Malone—call it warmth, openness, and an instinct to treat strangers as friends not yet met—that draws others like a magnet. "As a man, you could not ask for a better friend than Thomas William Malone," Persons said. "Loyal to a fault, generous with his time and resources." A line in *The Canterbury Tales*, "Gladly would he learn and gladly teach," captures this aspect of Tommy's personality. "I've learned a great deal about being a lawyer from Tommy, largely from his example," Persons said. "He meticulously prepares his cases. He's very smart. He's a master at reading and communicating with a jury. He has—and it's hard to describe—such great timing. Tommy appreciates the nonverbal aspect of communication, which is so important. Better than 90 percent of all communication is nonverbal. Tommy gets that. He's very, very effective as an advocate and knows how to reach people's hearts, he really does, and in such a way that they don't feel put upon or that it's an act. He's very authentic and genuine. Wherever you meet Tommy, he's the same person. In the courtroom or outside the courtroom you get the same man."

In the political arena, Malone, a liberal Democrat, and Persons, a "pretty conservative man in a very conservative environment," teamed up to co-chair the reelection efforts of numerous state and local judges over the years. "Tommy would appeal to the plaintiff's bar and I'd appeal to the defense bar, so the judge would enjoy support from both sides of the field."

Operating at extremely high levels of performance in a very conservative environment, Persons inevitably gets the fish-in-a-fishbowl treatment. "Sometimes people will have a relationship," he said, "[while] trying to interrogate you as to what it's like to be black or a woman. This makes people very uncomfortable. I've never perceived myself as Tommy's 'black' friend. It never entered my mind. In none of our dealings have I ever felt that my ethnicity or any other immutable trait made a difference. We never talk in those terms. Ours is a pure, pure friendship that transcends race and all of that."

What makes Tommy Malone tick? That question, as Mercer University President Bill Underwood framed it, is the key to the story. "Why did Atticus Finch take on the representations he did?" Persons said. "The essence of Tommy is crusading for victims. He never stops talking about righting wrongs, making sure people who are injured or oppressed are treated fairly. I don't know anyone as filled with this passion over such a sustained period of time. He's one of these people—it happens to the majority of people who go to law school—who set out as idealists with the aim of righting wrongs. They see the law as an instrument to level the playing field. In the course of time, so many lose that belief, or aspects of that belief, until the whole idea recedes and more practical aspects take hold. Tommy *never* lost his idealism, never allowed setbacks, or ostracism, or any number of things to cause him to waver. He remains undaunted in this pursuit of justice.

"Nobody," Persons continued, "certainly not in the state of Georgia, enjoys the stature he does at the bar. It's no accident that Tommy Malone is the perennial top vote-getter in the peer-reviewed Super Lawyers, year-in and year-out. More than 30,000 lawyers in Georgia and he's always ranked number one."

Chapter 30

"Every time I opposed Tommy or dealt with him, I knew I had to be better prepared, more articulate, a better lawyer and practitioner. He exacts the best from you."
—Jack Slover, facing off against Tommy Malone

In the early 1980s, Jack Slover, a former US Army officer ("Not JAG, an armor unit"), was an overworked young lawyer in Camilla, Georgia, the Mitchell County Seat, thirty miles south of Albany. In those years, South Georgia still possessed its own woeful dynamic. James Gray's toxic racism, the courts' and the bar's shameful treatment of African American attorney C. B. King, the reign of brutal sheriffs like Cull Campbell (Dougherty County) and "Gator" Johnson (Baker County), and Tommy Malone's own baptism by fire in the Bitterman case capture the zeitgeist.

At the time, Slover, an associate with Twitty & Twitty, knew Malone slightly from bar-association meetings and the typical small-town lawyerly interactions. The first of their many courtroom encounters took place in the course of an aggravated assault case that began, predictably enough, in the parking lot of a Tastee Freez. A shouting and shoving match between two young swains over the affections of a local beauty ("doing that good-ol'-boy stuff," remembered Slover) ended in a shooting that, in turn, would trigger a political scandal.

Slover represented the defendant. "We were getting ready for trial," he recalled. "In South Georgia, everybody knows everybody, so when the petit jury is being called, you'd know everybody on the list. Obviously, it's very important that you get the jury list [a public record] in advance of the trial so you can go through it and see who's all right, and who are your friends and enemies. So I went to the county clerk's office and got a copy. As I was walking out of the courthouse, somebody called out to me. It was the young lady's father who was also the Camilla postmaster."

"'Jack, you defending so and so?'

"'Yes, sir.'

"'You gonna be able to defend him?'

"'Gonna try my best.'

"'You know, we think a lot of him. He dates our daughter, but it turns out she'd also been dating the other man. You understand how that goes. It's just a really bad thing with me being the postmaster and all.'

"'Well, we'll see. There was a fight and he did pull a gun.'" Slover went on to explain a bit about his planned defense, but the man had stopped paying attention.

"'What's that in your hand Jack?'

"'It's the jury list...You understand we can't contact the jury, but we can see who's on it and it can help our case.'

"'Can I get a copy?'" the postmaster asked.

"'It's a matter of public record. Here you go.'

"Well, the day before the trial, a Friday," Slover continued, "this lawyer from across the street, a very senior lawyer, comes charging into our office. Mr. Twitty is not in. I'm there by myself. He's waving a paper."

"'I know what you're up to young man!' he shouts.

"'What?'

"'You're committing jury tampering! You're calling jurors...!'

"'The hell you talking about?'

"'The story is all over town. People are being called. I know it was you who went to court and got the jury list!'

"'That's a matter of public record.'

"He kept carrying on. So I immediately went to see the judge and the district attorney and reported what this lawyer was saying. I told the judge I was no party to any such thing. 'I'm just trying to defend my client.' Well, next thing you know, the judge and the DA decide to empanel an investigative grand jury.

"As it turned out," Slover remembered, "the Camilla chief of police, Tom Ed Fussell, was a friend of the defendant's mother. Tom Ed had started calling jury members and making it clear that the defendant was a 'good boy who got into an unfortunate fight.' Stuff like that. Fussell was an officer of the law. He should have known better than to tamper with jurors." Sure enough, an indictment came down against the chief. In turn, Fussell hired this up-and-coming hotshot from Albany named Malone to represent him in the criminal proceedings. Malone was apprised of the rumors concerning the jury list.

"Here I am, a witness for the state, one of the DA's prime witnesses," said Slover. "And Tommy Malone comes to see me! Whether you're involved or not, this kind of encounter is always intimidating. This was the first time Tommy and I ever had an in-depth conversation. In the past, I'd seen him at some function or when I was second chair in a case he was involved in. You learn when you're talking to witnesses who may be potentially hostile to try to befriend them, put them at ease, not make them feel you're attacking them or questioning their veracity. Tommy talked to me about all kinds of things. He was very good, authoritative, but accommodating and gentle in his questioning."

Given the facts—a chief of police facing criminal charges—the case attracted considerable local and state media. "Tommy cross-examined me in what was now a big trial with all the press there," Slover recalled. "I gave a straightforward account of what had happened." Malone was facing an uphill battle, but his great gift, Slover noted, was an uncanny ability to forge a deep connection with the jury, to build a bond of trust as quickly and naturally as if they were twelve folks who had come by his farm for a pleasant Sunday afternoon dinner. "Tommy was very good," Slover recalled. "Fussell wound up with a hung jury. No conviction, though as I remember, he resigned and later left the area."

Was politics a factor in the prosecution? Backroom wheeling and dealing by Tom Ed Fussell's political enemies? "Hard to say," Slover admitted. As a native Atlantan, he was an outsider unable to untangle the myriad forces and intricate layers of intrigue potentially at work. Slover did the best job he could, gained valuable experience, and eventually moved on—like Malone—to Atlanta. "In Mitchell County, there was a saying," he remembered with a laugh. "All you do is pay your bills. Everybody else tends your business for you."

***

In the aftermath of the Fussell case, Malone and Slover forged a friendship that was strong thirty years later, despite numerous hard-fought and occasionally acerbic courtroom encounters. When Slover arrived in Atlanta in 1987, Tommy Malone was already burning up the fast track. Jack Slover became a partner in the formidable defense firm Hall, Booth, Smith &

AND THE LIGHT SHONE THROUGH

Slover, and later, senior partner in Slover, Prieto, Marigliano & Holbert. "Tommy and I litigated a lot of heavy-duty medical malpractice cases," Slover recalled. (They successfully negotiated numerous others outside the courtroom.) "We're talking horrific cases. One of the reasons for Tommy's success is that he never overreaches. He's straight down the middle and never plays games. This isn't a guy out for bucks.

"I watched him grow and saw how famous he was becoming," Slover added. "Not to sound like a bunch of money-grubbers, but all the rest of us lawyers coveted Tommy's success. A lot of people are jealous of what Tommy has accomplished. They deflect their jealousy or try to hide it by showing disdain for him." A current of anti-Malone animosity does run through the Georgia bar, low voltage but detectible. "Oh, Tommy has enemies," King & Spalding's Ray Persons agreed and added, "but you can tell a lot about a man by the enemies he has. These are some of the lawyers who've lost big cases to him. Look at them and look at the outcome of these cases, it'll tell you a whole lot. The rest of it is pure envy. People resent him. Even with all of these resentments, he still ends up at the pinnacle every year."

"Tommy Malone has certainly lived the high lifestyle. Palm Beach...the Bahamas," Jack Slover continued. "But damn it, he's earned it! He did it standing in the door when other lawyers wouldn't dare be there."

Chapter 31

"When a paraplegic is rolled into the courtroom in a wheelchair, 'no
liability' flies right out the window."
—Attorney Jim Hiers

1995. One morning, defense attorney James (Jim) Hiers Jr. was sitting at his desk in his Midtown Atlanta office when his phone rang. Over the course of thirty years, Hiers and his partners (Swift, Currie, McGhee & Hiers) had grown their firm from a handful of lawyers to nearly a hundred. Along the way, they'd built a defense powerhouse focused on malpractice, product liability, insurance claims, medical devices, and other areas of civil defense. "People, doctors, hospitals, companies, manufacturers, any other entity," Hiers said. Experience is no guarantee against surprise. "This call was from an insurance company I'd represented a lot," Hiers remembered. "An excess insurance company, meaning they had the excess coverage other than the basic coverage a liability company would have."

"Did you hear about the *$45 million* verdict last night in Fulton County?" the insurance man asked, a plaintive note edging the outrage in his voice.

"Not yet, but I'm sure I'll find out about it in just a minute."

"We have all the excess coverage," the man said. "$45 *million*! We were assured this was a case with zero liability. The defendant [Kaiser Foundation Health Plan of Georgia] was represented by a very good defense firm. They said they weren't going to lose, and we relied on them. How could they lose? How could they say there was no liability?!"

Hiers, a storyteller with considerable charm and a soothing manner, calmed the distraught insurance man as best he could. After a moment, the man collected himself and muttered sardonically, "You know, we have a belief around here [the case involved multiple amputations] that when a paraplegic is rolled into the courtroom in a wheelchair, 'no liability' flies right out the window."

"Well, I guess that's what happened," Hiers said.

The plaintiff's attorney was Tommy Malone. What's it like to face off against Malone? "It means you're dealing with a fella who prepares his cases thoroughly, is reasonable in the sense of being polite and not so unrealistic, and who'll listen and not play a lot of tricks," Hiers said. "Someone whom people respect, judges in particular." Hiers paused and added, "Finally, it means *I'm going to make a lot of money* because it's going to be a long fight!"

The case (*James Don Adams Jr. and Lamona K. Adams, et al. v. Kaiser Foundation Health Plan of Georgia, Inc.*), was tried in the state court of Fulton County, Georgia, in 1995. The jury award represented compensatory damages for the "unnecessary and preventable quadruple amputation of a 6-month-old child due to medical negligence."

Now, it was Hiers's turn to limit the damage. He picked up the story:

"Well, I started dealing with Tommy trying to resolve it." (During deliberations, Kaiser, represented by Alston & Bird, a powerhouse with more than 800 lawyers nationally and internationally, offered a $750,000 settlement, a sad miscalculation as it turned out. The jury came back with the $45 million verdict.) "Let me tell you, Tommy is really formidable in the courtroom but equally formidable when it comes to trying to settle cases," Hiers continued. "The negotiations to work out this disaster went over several months. Sometimes, I'd have to deal with Tommy when he was in Bimini or on his yacht. He never stopped working on his case while he was down there fishing or whatever. He was always on top of things."

Why negotiate when you've hit a $45 million jackpot? Several reasons, Hiers explained. "*Adams v. Kaiser* was a case of questionable liability in many senses of the word. Resolve this sort of case early and you eliminate the uncertainty of what might happen on appeal and how long it's going to take. This would have likely taken several years to resolve. Settling, you know exactly where you are and can have money flowing to the family to take care of the injured party.

"This brings me to another point," Hiers continued. "Tommy is a great trial lawyer who always tries cases to win, *but not at all costs*. You can try a lawsuit in such a way as to charge through everything, bulldoze through the case in front of the court and the jury. You may get their sympathy and all of that, but you might—and probably have—committed several reversible errors en route to the verdict. So an appeal is filed and the case is sent back. You lose a year or two, or three, and you lose the big verdict. Now you have to go back and try it without the benefit of those errors. It's like a football team that scores a touchdown and has it called back because of a penalty. Tommy is the quarterback who'll run through the line if you leave an opening. He's going to take advantage of it. So you've got to respect him and be prepared. Sometimes, you learn that when you have a worthy adversary, and you don't have a very good defense, the best thing to do is to make a reasonable and realistic settlement."

When the negotiations on *Adams v. Kaiser* were finally done, Hiers and Malone planned a lunch. "I arrived at Tommy's office, which was, of course, fabulous, as was his desk and everything there," he recalled. "We'd gotten it resolved. I can't say for how much, but it was satisfactory to all parties. I will say Tommy isn't dogmatic, but he does *hold tight* pretty well." Here Hiers could not suppress a laugh.

"I know this because over the years, *I made him a lot of money.*"

Chapter 32

"It's like coming up to bat and finding out Sandy Koufax is on the mound."
—Defense Attorney Tom Carlock, facing Tommy Malone

Thomas S. (Tom) Carlock (Carlock, Copeland & Stair) has practiced in the civil arena for more than fifty years. At last count, the Georgia Super Lawyer was lead attorney in 500 jury trials and tried to verdict more than 75 wrongful death and 150 catastrophic injury cases. Tommy Malone considers Tom Carlock among the top three best defense attorneys he's ever faced in a courtroom. And he's faced hundreds. Carlock is also one of the very few defense lawyers to set foot on *Justice*, Tommy's fishing boat berthed on Abaco Island in the Bahamas. "We were always friendly," Carlock insisted. "We showed each other respect, were always truthful with one another, and admired each other's ability in the courtroom."

The defense—Tom Carlock's side—prevails in an overwhelming majority of these proceedings. A study by the US Bureau of Justice Statistics estimated that of more than 1,100 medical malpractice cases tried before juries in the seventy-five largest counties in the United States, plaintiffs won just *27 percent*. If one digs deeper, the research indicates that physicians win 80 to 90 percent of jury trials where there is *weak evidence* of negligence against them and approximately *70 percent* of cases with *no strong evidence* of negligence or non-negligence. More telling for Malone and his clients is the fact that doctors win *50 percent* of cases where there is *strong evidence of negligence against* them. "The attitude of most jurors is to lean in favor of the health-care providers because they know they don't set out to harm anybody," Malone explained. "This is what makes these cases more challenging than a car-wreck case. No one loves an 18-wheeler driver. Most everybody loves their health-care provider, or used to."

To belabor another sports metaphor, Tommy Malone should be getting knocked off the mound every time he appears in front of a jury. But odds and statistics fly out the window when he has the ball. "It's like coming up to bat and finding out Sandy Koufax is on the mound," Carlock insisted. "Sometimes you get a hit, but often you'll strike out."

Why does one man soar far above his peers? Malone's lifelong determination to make a meaningful difference in other people's lives, his idealism and compassion, burn brightly. "Integrity," Carlock said, is another key to Tommy's success. "His word is his absolute bond." In the courtroom, Malone's intuition, a near-preternatural awareness of what is unfolding at any given moment, what moves need to be made to buttress or counter, all unfolding in the hyper-intense and unpredictable atmosphere of a big trial or negotiation. His grace. "We represent people who have real losses and real problems," Carlock continued. "If it goes to jury, we have to turn it all over to twelve people we don't know. You get good rulings and bad rulings. It's not surprising that lawyers are likely to get into a panic. Yet in all matters I've had with Tommy, he's always been gracious. He lets everybody have their say and then steps in and says what he wants to in a very few words. Some people 'shotgun' everything; Tommy knows what's important and what's not. There were times I thought he'd push a point but he didn't. He ended up pushing points that were critical. I'm amazed that he's always right."

And finally, perhaps most importantly, the man who was a lackluster student has become a scholar of the intricate workings of the human heart and the human condition.

No one enjoyed striking out against Koufax. "Success breeds jealousy in some people," Carlock added. "On the defense side, where I usually am, people don't take losses very well." The insinuations and imprecations fly, as do gossip and backbiting: Tommy Malone is "controversial." He's "flamboyant." He "cherry-picks" cases to pad his wallet and winning streak. Tom Carlock is having none of it. "Tommy is controversial because he's so doggone good. More power to him. He wants what's best for his client and he usually gets it. People like me tip our hats to him for being ultra-successful. He's shared his success with a lot of people, a lot of charitable organizations. He does enjoy quite a lifestyle, but he's earned every dime of it through hard work and representing his clients well. God bless someone who earns every dime he makes."

At this point, Carlock signs off. He's got much to attend to in his own practice. At that moment, the image he's been searching for to make his case finally comes to mind.

"Tommy Malone is a giant redwood in a forest of us little people."

Chapter 33

Well, did you ever think that a 52-year-old, single woman being asked to go to a strange hotel room with a man she doesn't know might be a little intimidated and not act as she might in a doctor's office...?
—Tommy Malone cross-exam (Shi v. Coach USA)

Randall (Randy) Scarlett (*Scarlett Law Group*) wanted to try a case with his buddy Tommy Malone. The San Francisco-based attorney had been impressed with the dashing lawyer, whom he met in Mel Belli's office in 1981. At the time, Scarlett was a frazzled law clerk/interviewer for Belli, pulled by the great man like taffy in every direction. A friendship blossomed between Malone and Scarlett that now ran all the way back to when hippies walked the Haight and Jerry Garcia and the Grateful Dead jammed in Golden Gate Park. Like Malone, Scarlett went on to build a successful firm and a national reputation focused on catastrophic personal injury—traumatic brain and spinal cord injury, malpractice, wrongful death, environmental and consumer actions. "We'd looked at different cases together over the years and threatened that we were going to do it," he recalled. "Ultimately, the Shi case occurred and I threw it out to him [*Shi vs. Coach UWA, et al.*]. After we'd pretty much worked the case up, I said, 'Tommy, would you come to San Francisco?' To my surprise, he said yes."

Scarlett and Malone represented Xiu Jin ("Celia") Shi, a woman who'd sustained catastrophic brain trauma and intracranial hemorrhaging after being struck by a Coach USA tour bus in the city's elite Nob Hill neighborhood. Neurosurgeons at San Francisco General Hospital managed to save her life, but Shi was left severely impaired. Liability was contested but *the* key issue in the trial Malone and Scarlett argued in San Francisco Superior Court was whether Ms. Shi would require 24/7 attending home care for the rest of her life.

Scarlett picked up the story:

"The defense had flown up a physiatrist [physical rehab specialist] specializing in conditions affecting the brain, spinal cord, and neurologic impairments. The doctor traveled from San Diego to San Francisco to examine Ms. Shi. In his testimony, he indicated that Shi had certainly sustained a severe brain injury when she was struck by the bus, but had the capability of functioning independently in her daily life without need of a round-the-clock care provider." Then the expert went a step further, into a no-man's-land where Tommy Malone stood waiting. "The physiatrist testified," Scarlett continued, "that he believed Shi was not giving her best effort and that she could do a lot better than she'd displayed. We had not even deposed this guy! Tommy got up and took the witness:

"'Doctor, you told the ladies and gentlemen of the jury that Ms. Shi was not giving her best efforts in your opinion when you examined her?'

"'Yes. That's correct.'

"'Well, Doctor, you didn't have an office from which you worked in San Francisco, did you? In fact, you'd rented a suite in a hotel and your examination of our client took place in that hotel suite, did it not?'

"'Yes, I did.'

"'Well, did you ever think that a 52-year-old, single woman being asked to go to a strange hotel room with a man she doesn't know might be a little intimidated and not act as she might in a doctor's office...?'

"To be honest," Scarlett continued, "I don't remember how the man answered because the jury members were laughing uncomfortably over this whole thing."

"That's all I have," Tommy said and sat down.

"Just that simple logic explained away the whole defense argument," Scarlett remembered. "Tommy Malone just has this innate ability to cut through bullshit and simplify certain of life's presentations in a way that a jury can get. It's really extraordinary. It's a gift." In March 2007, that same jury awarded Ms. Shi $22.8 million for past and future economic and non-economic loss, including pain and suffering, grief, anxiety, and physical impairment. At the time, the Shi verdict was one of the highest nonpunitive verdicts for an individual sustaining traumatic brain injuries in California. "It was our deep friendship that drew Tommy in," Scarlett said. "But boy, he brought a lot to the table. And did I learn a lot."

Scarlett and Malone, avid fishing buddies, family friends, and world travelers, teamed up again in the Drew Bianchi litigation in San Jose, California (*Drew Dakota Bianchi v. Gordon Trucking et al.*). In May 2007, a

Toyota Avalon in which 23-year-old Bianchi, a college student, was a passenger was struck by a Peterbilt flatbed careening out of control after sideswiping an 18-wheeler. The accident occurred midway through Pacheco Pass on California Route 152, a winding, two-lane road notorious—some say haunted—for a long string of fatal traffic accidents.

The evidence indicated the trucks collided at or near the centerline of the road and that neither truck driver had taken evasive action when the monster Peterbilt smashed into the 3,500-pound passenger sedan. Drew Bianchi survived, sustaining brain injuries so severe he'd require a lifetime of 24/7 care. The grueling, hotly contested trial lasted six weeks. The question was—as it always is—what would this cost and who would pay. "At one point, Tommy said, 'Randy, I want you to put on this life-care planner. I want you to go through every single Q-tip and include everything in that life-care plan that Drew is going to need for the rest of his life.'"

"Don't make me do that," Scarlett pleaded. "We'll be here for two days just with the life-care plan. The jury is going to go bat-shit crazy. They get it. They don't need this."

"Randy, you're going to do it and I'll tell you why. When we get to closing arguments, you're going to argue in front of the jury, 'Ladies and gentlemen, you recall how difficult it was to sit through hour after painstaking hour of the life-care planner's testimony? You recall how long it took? Well, ladies and gentleman, you only have to sit through a day and a half of it, but Drew Dakota Bianchi is going to have to live that every day, every second, for the rest of his life.'"

The jury came back with a $49.1 million verdict for Bianchi.

"Tommy's greatest strength," Scarlett continued, "is his ability to absolutely connect with and communicate complex issues to a jury in the simplest, simplest of ways. He makes things understandable. He streamlines a case for purposes of presentation. A lot of lawyers get caught up in the trees. Tommy makes things clear. You are not born with these gifts. You must have in your life a great desire to help other people. Tommy has lived this way, a concept I'm still attempting."

***

Randy Scarlett ends a meditation on his long friendship with Tommy with, appropriately, a fish story. It turns out that Scarlett landed his first blue marlin aboard *Freedom*, Tommy's modified Rivera 30 sport-fisher. Some years later, back in the Bahamas, he was sipping the high-octane rum punch at Nippers, a turquoise and pink bar and grill on Guana Cay, off Abaco Island ("They say you get nipped at Nippers"). Scarlett happened to mention how much he liked that Rivera 30. He picks up the story.

"Without batting an eye, Tommy said, 'You do?'

"'It's a beautiful little boat. I don't have a boat out in San...'

"'Tell you what,' Tommy said. 'I'll get it to Florida. That's an easy trip for me and it'll go in the yard there. Take care of the yard bill and the boat is yours.'"

Scarlett was speechless. "The yard bill was nothing," he recalled. "Tommy was as good as his word. Today, the boat is sitting in San Francisco Bay in Sausalito right now. It's the first boat I ever bought and I refuse to get rid of it." He paused then added, "By the way, that's 'bought' with quotation marks, because Tommy gave it to me."

***

Scarlett's 24-year-old son, Randy Jr., is nicknamed "R2," a contraction born as a way to avoid confusion when father and son were fishing in the Bahamas with Malone. When there was a strike, Tommy or a crew member would shout, "R2, grab that rod! It's long left!" Naturally, Scarlett Sr. became R1, and given the *Star Wars* reference, the nicknames stuck. In high school, R2 expressed an interest in getting into the real estate business. (This is San Francisco.) An uncle was quite successful, but real estate was not his parents' first career choice for him. Randy Jr.'s mother is also an attorney and lawyering is a dynastic profession. One day, the three guys were tooling around San Francisco, when out of the blue, Tommy turned to the young man.

"Randy what are you planning to do with your life?"

"Maybe go into real estate. My unc.."

"Why'd you want to go and do that?"

For the next minutes, R2 sat rapt as Malone launched into a heartfelt discourse on the virtues of the law profession and the men and women who ply it honorably. He argued his case with the sincerity that makes him so successful with juries. "Tommy had such a profound effect on R2," Scarlett said in 2017, "that my son rethought his career options. He's now completed his first year of law school at Boston College School of Law on a merit scholarship."

In moments like these, Scarlett and Malone's intricate past—the Mel Belli experience, the travels and trips and adventures, the courtroom successes—melt away like fog under the Golden Gate Bridge until only their intense human connection remains, a bond that will survive whatever else happens to their mortal beings. "Tommy has impacted my family," Scarlett said, his smooth lawyer's voice beginning to crack with emotion, "in more ways than he may ever appreciate."

Part VI

Giving Back

"Life's most persistent and urgent question is,
'What are you doing for others?"
—Dr. Martin Luther King Jr.

Chapter 34

"We were in Tommy's office and he'd just settled a huge case in Cali-fornia. There were gold balloons all the way across one wall spelling out the amount of the settlement. He was so thrilled and we were thrilled for him. He really has a heart for giving back to the people who've been so grievously injured."
—Alana Shepherd, cofounder, The Shepherd Center

1973. Like millions of newly minted college grads, 22-year-old James Shepherd set out to see the world. His journey would take him to Africa and South America. Some months later, his father, Harold, co-owner of the Atlanta-based Shepherd Construction Co., and mother, Alana, a feisty and forward-looking Midwesterner, found themselves on the receiving end of what they'd remember as the "call from hell." Bodysurfing off Rio di Janeiro, James was slammed by the powerful and unpredictable surf to the ocean floor. He sustained a devastating spinal cord injury that left him paralyzed from the neck down. After six weeks on a ventilator in a Brazilian hospital, James was airlifted home and on to the Craig Hospital, a rehabilitation facility in Englewood, Colorado.

Eventually, James returned to Atlanta only to find no local hospital could handle the intensive long-term rehabilitation he and other spinal cord injury patients required. His parents spearheaded the effort and funding to create such a facility. In 1975, the Shepherd Center opened its doors with six beds. Today, the 152-bed hospital is one of the nation's leading facilities focused on the prevention, treatment, and rehabilitation of individuals—including an increasing number of veterans—with spinal cord, brain, and other catastrophic neuromuscular illnesses. Thousands of patients pass through the nonprofit's doors each year. James, now in his sixties, sits on the Shepherd board. Critical to the center's vital work are charitable contributions that average $12 to $15 million annually.

As might be expected, a number of Shepherd Center inpatients have been involved in catastrophic accidents and life-shattering events where negligence was a factor. Though not treated at Shepherd, Drew Dakota Bianchi is one such individual (see chapter 33), a young man who will require 24/7 care for the rest of his life. As mentioned, Bianchi's lawsuit, successfully argued by Tommy Malone and Randy Scarlett, ended with a jury award of $49.1 million, monies that will assure Bianchi has the care and treatment he needs and deserves.

Understanding the vital importance of building and arguing such cases for victims, the Shepherd Center opens its doors to plaintiff's attorneys. "A lot of our cases are liability actions that can take four, six, even ten years to settle," said Alana Shepherd. "We permit lawyers to record 'A Day in the Life of a Patient' videos to help demonstrate the complexity of the care required. I don't think many other hospitals let TV crews come in and present the evidence they gather in court."

At that point, Shepherd paused, then added, "Yet we've rarely had attorneys give back to the hospital that cares for their patients. I've seen lawyers perform. They get a big liability case and they can't wait to get their half. You'd think a few would feel we've helped their patients have a better quality of life and make some quality of recovery, and want to share a part of these huge settlements, but I can think offhand of maybe one person who's given back."

Tommy Malone.

"Tommy feels people who are horribly injured deserve the right care for the rest of their lives," Shepherd continued. "He feels so deeply about this. I believe this is why he doesn't take that many cases. He takes the ones he believes he's going to win, the obvious cases, but they're very complex and big and the settlements can be huge. Tommy sent a number of his patients directly to us and followed them long after their cases were settled. He also feels he needs to give back to those caring for his patients. So he started giving to Shepherd. He's been amazing in this."

So amazing in both the frequency and magnitude of his gifts that Malone was named a Shepherd "Angel." (Angels are individuals, corporations, or foundations that have been major donors in a given year.) He also involved himself in the center's Vital Injury Prevention Outreach program. "He's been in this arena for many, many years," said Donald Leslie, MD, Shepherd's outgoing medical director. "When I got to know Tommy [the two are personal friends and fishing buddies], I asked him to join our board. I must say there are a number of other attorneys on the board, and one of them specifically said, 'You're going to ask Tommy Malone to be on the board of trustees? He sues doctors!'

"'Well, yes, he does,'" Leslie replied. "'I understand that. Quite successfully in some cases. I understand that too, but I'm going to tell you one thing. He's never sued me and he's a good friend and I'd like to serve with him and have him serve with me.' Guess what? Tommy was elected."

In the fall of 2016, Tommy and Debbie Malone were named honorees at the Shepherd Center's Legendary Party, the hospital's largest fundraising event. Tommy, too ill to attend, insisted the honor be bestowed on another worthy individual. "I've known a lot of litigator types," Leslie continued, "lawyers who are tough as nails. Tommy is tough as nails, but his heart is absolutely in the very best place. He is one generous, very loving man with this incredible zest for life."

Malone stayed three years as a Shepherd Center trustee before leaving to become a trustee and later chairman of the board of directors at Mercer University, his law school alma mater. There, by all accounts, he has been an exceedingly generous and very engaged active board member. Generally speaking, Malone's philanthropy is tied to his reverence for the law. "He's always given money, as much if not more than anybody else in our profession," said Adam Malone. "We support lots of different causes that stand for the preservation of the right to trial by jury. We try to help people get elected who'll stay true to the Bill of Rights and other constitutional principles, particularly where there are politicians running who want to dismantle these rights and principles. These are not charitable contributions. It's putting your money where your mouth is."

Chapter 35

"I'm very careful about the cases I take. When I take a case, the health-care providers, their claims' people, and the insurance companies ought to take a very close look, because I took it, and I'm likely going to win."
—Tommy Malone

It is no surprise that few people other than friends and family had ever heard of Silverlene Kindle and how her life came to intersect with Tommy Malone's. Ms. Kindle was an ordinary person, wife and mother, living an ordinary life in an Atlanta suburb, which in today's world can be an extraordinary definition of happiness. Her story begins, as so many catastrophes do, simply and seemingly without warning, particularly given the standards and practices, guidelines and safeguards we all assume are in place in American hospitals. In 2012, Silverlene's husband, Jeffrey R. Kindle, a retired Army officer, underwent surgery to relieve a herniated disc in his neck (in medical terms, a cervical discectomy and fusion, a relatively commonplace procedure that involves removing a damaged disc to relieve spinal cord or nerve root pressure and alleviate pain, weakness, numbness, and tingling). Something went wrong in the operating theater at Piedmont Fayette Hospital in Fayetteville, Georgia; so wrong that Jeffrey Kindle never recovered, never spent another day in the welcoming arms of his family.

It turned out that recovery-room nurses failed to report his difficulty breathing and swallowing to the residents on duty or the attending physician. They delayed calling CODE when Kindle's difficulties became acute. Evidence would show he'd developed a postoperative hematoma (a mass of clotted blood that compromises one's airways) in his neck that went unnoticed and untreated. Jeffrey Kindle was left in a persistent vegetative state caused by cerebral hypoxia (oxygen starvation) much like Tucker Sutton suffered at birth. He was transferred to an acute-care facility, where he remained until his death.

"Any man's death diminishes me," wrote the seventeenth-century poet John Donne. Jeffrey (Ricky) Kindle, as it turns out, was one of those extraordinary individuals—devoted husband, father, coach, scoutmaster—

whose passing leaves a tear in the fabric of a community that can never be fully repaired. Page after page of Kindle's online obituary is filled with tributes from men and women whose lives he positively affected. Nothing would ever heal the damage wrought by a few careless individuals—health-care professionals, not narcoleptic long-haul truck drivers or drunks careening their vehicles into oncoming traffic—in little more than a few distracted moments.

No earthly thing would ever return Ricky Kindle to his family, but there were legal remedies that could, in the fullness of time, ease the pain of his passing. Much like Lori and Landon Sutton, fate, destiny, the phone book, or a guiding hand led Silverlene Kindle straight to Tommy Malone. Given the horrific facts of the case, his negotiations with Piedmont Fayette-ville Hospital administrators quickly led to a settlement, which, like many of Malone's awards, remains confidential. Tommy was willing to say that his efforts guaranteed Silverlene Kindle will be able to look after her family for "the rest of their lives," the "meaningful difference" that has driven Malone's life and career.

***

"I'm very careful about the cases I take," Malone said in 2017. "When I take a case, the health-care providers, their claims' people, and the insurance companies ought to take a very close look, because I took it, and I'm likely going to win. There might be a verdict much bigger than what they could settle for early on." These words are the closest Tommy Malone ever comes to acknowledging the peerless lawyer he'd become and the vital role the trial lawyer, indeed, all lawyers play, not only in the well-being of his clients, but in civil society itself.

Part VII

Snapper Point

Over the years, Malone's heady introduction to the joys of Bahamian fishing matured into a desire to put down deeper roots, to continue the floating party on a grand scale, and refine his fishing skills and expertise. Inevitably, he departed Bimini for Abaco Island.

Chapter 36

"Bahamian wahoo fishing changed forever."
—Tommy Malone's Revolutionary Expose

In 1998, Tommy Malone cast his gaze 140 miles northeast of Bimini to Great Abaco Island. There, he and Debbie purchased Snapper Point, a 15-acre compound on a pristine peninsula near Marsh Harbour, the island's commercial center. Over the years, Malone's heady introduction to the joys of wahoo fishing matured into a desire to put down deeper roots, continue the floating party on a grand scale, and refine his fishing technique. The two painstakingly renovated and refurbished a property fragrant with hibiscus, bougainvillea, and wildflowers, alive with chittering parrots and peewees, and surrounded on three sides by turquoise waters. Secluded, but just a few minutes' drive from town, Snapper Point encompasses three pale blue-and-white-trimmed villas, thirteen bedrooms, twelve baths, a swimming pool, a six-boat marina, and a protected deep-water anchorage.

Those thirteen bedrooms, pool, and marina are not extravagancies. The Malones are given to extreme acts of generosity, a heartfelt desire to share the blessings in their lives with others, but also, in Tommy's case, an eagerness to be the orchestrator of every party, get-together, outing, trip, or adventure, a trait that runs all the way back to his childhood. He clearly remembers his father, Rosser Malone, a Georgia Bulldog devotee, handing out tickets for the games and putting together Saturday-morning bus junkets to Athens during football season. "Must have rubbed off on me," Malone allowed.

In him, kindness is ingrained, even compulsive, from an outsized tip to a transcendent commitment to those he cares about. When a check arrives, be it in Atlanta, Palm Beach, or at Mae's Oyster Bar in Albany, Malone swoops it up quick as an osprey while eliciting a quick life history of every waiter, bartender, and valet driver he engages. Stories abound of his generosity to struggling clients. Tommy helped the Suttons through a devastating cash crisis one year with an outsized and "anonymous" Christmas gift. It's the same with employees, boat captains, and lawyers going through a bad patch, and, doubtless, never-to-be-revealed random acts of kindness to strangers. "Tommy never expected the kind of success he's had," Debbie Malone explained. "More than most, he needs to give back."

Over the years, the Malones have hosted hundreds of friends, family members, and colleagues at Snapper Point. Spencer Lee and Buddy Dallas, who've known Tommy since their schoolboy days, are still on the VIP list. Randy Scarlett, wife, Mary Anne, and Randy Jr. have had extended vacations in the Bahamas with the Malones. Today, guests arrive via commercial airlines at Marsh Harbour International Airport. In the old days, they flew in by private plane with Tommy in the cockpit. "There was a stretch," he recalled, "where I spent fifty out of fifty-two weekends in Bimini flying myself and my friends." The Southern Trial Lawyers' and the Georgia Trial Lawyers' executive committees have convened at Snapper Point, along with expert witnesses and lawyers associated with many of his cases. In some tellings, Tommy can be generous to a fault.

***

The Breakthrough. In the old days, wahoo championship tournaments on Bimini began like Le Mans starts in grand prix racing. Fishermen would line up in front of the Big Game Club dock and race the instant their start time arrived from channel to fishing grounds. Tommy and the other hopefuls would head out in a long line, fish until they hit 600 feet of depth, and at that point, approximate a right-angle turn, head back in, and repeat the maneuver. The first boat out had a big advantage. "It looked like a circus parade with the leader always being the leader and whatever spot you had in the line, you'd stay in," Malone said. "Everybody fished this way for fifty years."

In the mid-1990s, a small flotilla of Bermuda-based charter fishermen arrived to compete in the Bimini tournaments. To the chagrin of the boys at the Big Game Club, the Bermudians clobbered them. "They out-fished us all, catching twenty fish when all of us locals would catch three or four," Malone recalled. "Worse, we'd become accustomed to three or four." From what Malone could tell, the invaders broke the traditional in-line approach to fishing and scattered like Jesus bugs on a pond. Later winding down at the bar, they were closemouthed about their techniques even after Tommy dispatched Debbie to use her feminine wiles to glean their secrets. "They kept their mode of fishing to themselves," he said darkly. "Nobody knew what they were doing or how. They'd even clean their cockpits before they came in so you couldn't see poles or anything."

Frustrated, Tommy traveled to Bermuda and chartered Allen DeSilva, one of the captains, and Dean Jones, his mate. A legendary figure on his home island, DeSilva still holds the Bermuda record for the largest Atlantic blue marlin ever caught—1,352 pounds. He'd also landed thirty-seven wahoo in one day. As it turned out, there was no secret sauce, just God-is-in-the-details nuance. "DeSilva and Jones taught me everything they were doing," Malone recalled. "I took pictures, made measurements, and stuff like that. There were obvious things: 'He who gets to the wahoo first, catches the most.' They're skittish and will scatter. 'Never get behind another boat.' 'Go in and out between 600 and 200 feet of depth in long S-turns, not right-angle turns.' Instead of covering five miles, this way you cover twenty-five. 'Speed is important.'" (The wahoo is one of the fastest fish in the ocean.) DeSilva countered the fish's velocity by high-speed trolling often approaching 18 knots. He taught Tommy to make his own lures, size 7 hooks embedded in plastic skirts that resembled squid.

The bottom line? It worked. Using DeSilva's technique, Tommy won two wahoo tournaments and, over the years, placed in numerous others. He wrote it all down in "Wahoo Bahamian Style," a "revolutionary expose" published in 1972 in *The Big Game Fishing Journal*. "You know," he said in 2017 with the same joy he derives from winning a big case for a client, "I helped change Bahamian wahoo fishing forever."

Part VIII

Ties That Bind

On occasion, Tommy Malone's busy and complicated life—the struggles of the early years, his meteoric career arc, the successes, personal stumbles and recoveries, peer recognition, paths blazed, the lifestyle and adventures he and Debbie enjoy, the boards and professional associations—recede like the outgoing tide. Another characteristic emerges striking as a granite promontory, the man's fierce loyalty and friendship, gifts once extended, are seemingly boundless. So many examples parade across these pages; friendships binding Tommy to lawyers and judges, clients and colleagues, educators, thinkers, philanthropists, philosophers, fishing buddies, and boyhood friends, lives writ large and small. At a time, when relationships are discarded as casually as last year's shoes, Malone's are enduring. It is no coincidence, for example, that the team at Malone Law—the welcoming faces who greeted Lori and Landon Sutton when they arrived in such desperation—has stayed together for decades. Collectively, paralegals Dee Adams Coleman, Holly Titus, and Denise Asbell have been with Tommy nearly fifty years. Rachel Orlandini, officer administrator and personal assistant, has been with Tommy for eighteen years. Adam Malone has been with his dad for seventeen. Attorney Meri Benoit, the newcomer, for eleven years. "I've stayed because Tommy is an honorable, genuine man, a lost trait in so many people," Orlandini said. "When I met him, I knew it was the only way he knew how to be." Malone's college roommate, Buddy Dallas, takes Malone's friendship a step further: "If Tommy is your friend, he'll be there for you until the bitter end. If there's a cause he embraces, he'll be a warrior for that cause 'till the bitter end."

Chapter 37

"Tommy's got a heart bigger than you can drive a truck through."
—Larry Schlachter MD, JD

In 1998, Larry Schlachter, MD, a frustrated jock still playing baseball in his fifties, was hit in the hand by a100 mph line drive, a career-ending injury for a neurosurgeon. As with anyone whose livelihood is suddenly ripped away, the implications—he had a wife, kids, a big mortgage, partners, a twenty-five-year practice—were devastating. "I was really bummed out," he said. "And it got worse. My self-image shattered along with my hand. I went from chief of neurosurgery to 'No one cares about you.'"

Casting around, Schlachter eventually put the word out that he was available to testify as an expert witness on medical negligence cases. He made no bones about it. "When you become an expert, you do it because you think it's the right thing," he said. "But the underlying reason is to make money. They pay you very well for sticking your neck out."

One day, Dr. Schlachter fielded a call from Malone Law.

"Doctor, would you look at a case for me?" It was Tommy Malone.

The two met for lunch. At first it was awkward—Tommy had sued one of Larry's former partners—but he quickly put the doctor at ease. "I looked at the case," Schlachter remembered. "I supported his argument and felt very comfortable with the issues. I told him I'd be happy to be the expert." The action ended in a settlement.

Schlachter and Malone collaborated on other cases. Gradually, they got to know each other socially, dined at each other's houses. At first it seemed an odd pairing; Schlachter is blue-collar, an up-by-the-bootstraps overachiever—he holds a dental degree, a medical degree, and is a board-certified neurosurgeon—from Brooklyn; Tommy, a notorious slacker in his student days, is the well-mannered son of a South Georgia judge and his patrician wife. Didn't matter. Debbie Malone and Teri Schlachter immediately hit it off—a big selling point with Tommy—and soon the two women were close enough to confide in each other. "Teri decided something needed to be done with me," Schlachter remembered. "Somehow, she was talking with Tommy without me knowing."

The day came when Larry awoke so depressed he couldn't get out of bed.

"I'm whining," he said. "I don't want to do anything."

"Get up! Get dressed," Teri ordered. "We're going to see someone."

She drove her husband to the Ravinia Drive office complex. Minutes later, a bewildered Schlachter was sitting in Adam Malone's office when seemingly out of the blue, Adam announced, "Seems to me you should go to law school."

"What? I'm 52 years old!"

"So you'll get out when you're 55 or 56. You'll be this interesting guy who's got a law degree and neurological training. It's a good thing."

Next thing he knew, Adam was showing Larry his college diploma and the law degree he earned with honors from John Marshall Law School, telling him how he'd worked his butt off as a waiter and a valet attendant along the way.

"Look where I am now." Adam has a number of record jury verdicts, including $24.5 million in a case involving a below-the-knee amputation in Albany, Georgia. He's well regarded in the appellate courts and is recognized annually in *Best Lawyers in America* and as one of the top 100 lawyers in Georgia.

"Get you out of the house," Adam added. "Go at night. Get started. We'll help you any way we can."

Schlachter was sitting there "hemming and hawing," trying to process one of the damnedest proposals he'd ever heard. As if on cue, Tommy strolled into the room.

"We'll all be really happy if you did this."

"*We?*" Schlachter had begun to see Debbie Malone's hand at work.

"It'll be great for everybody, but *best* for you," Tommy added

Schlachter was still spluttering when Tommy looked at his watch and cut him off.

"The dean of the law school is waiting on you right now at John Marshall. I just spoke to him. Go on down there and talk. He'll show you around."

Schlachter picks up the story: "Okay. Teri and I drive down to the law school on Spring Street. Next thing I know, we're sitting there talking to the admissions dean."

"School starts in three weeks," he says. "I've got you signed up for contracts and torts in the evening. So you're all set." He pauses. "Oh, you've got to take the LSAT. It's being given next Saturday..."

"I...I'm not ready!"

"Just show up. Sign your name. Answer as many questions as you can and walk out. You're done. Accepted."

"But I haven't filled out an application?"

"You don't have to. Go buy the books. Pay your tuition. School starts in three weeks."

"You're kidding me, right?"

Schlachter's shock was beginning to meld into interest and the distinct notion—he hadn't felt it for a while—there might be a way out of the mess he'd gotten himself into.

"If you don't like it, you quit," the dean added. The interview was over. The dean was a busy man. "If you like it, you keep going. No problem."

Needless to say, Larry Schlachter, a bright guy, kept going. Technically, he's a triple threat—dentist, medical doctor, and attorney with a healthy law practice. (Actually, he gave up dentistry when he was admitted to medical school.) While Schlachter was at John Marshall, Tommy Malone continued to employ him as an expert witness. And then Tommy went further. "He referred other lawyers to me who needed experts on cases," Larry said. "He put my name out there and it really helped me."

When Larry passed the bar, Tommy arranged for a private swearing-in ceremony with then-Fulton County Judge Gino Brodgon, another of his good friends. "Anything Tommy could do to help, he did," Schlachter remembered. "He put lots of work in front of me when I went out on my own, so I had stuff to do. He'd invite me to different things, to join different organizations, attend meetings with him, and meet people. He promoted me like I was his protégé. And Tommy's range is far and deep."

The salient point is that Malone has extended a hand to any number of Larry Schlachters, men and women, no matter their class or stature, in need or jeopardy. And so it is no surprise that years later, Larry Schlachter, a busy man, drops everything to invite a reporter to lunch and spend many hours talking about all the good that is in Tommy Malone.

"He's got a heart bigger than you can drive a truck through."

Chapter 38

"[It's] something that has endured so many years and marriages and births of children and divorces. We've gone down the road separate and apart, but always together."
—Albert "Buddy" Dallas on his friendship with Tommy Malone

November 21, 2011. At dusk, Buddy Dallas, Tommy's old UGA roommate, was driving home, heading south on GA 171 after a day at his law office. No cell phone or satellite radio to distract him, just the quiet of an early winter's evening in the country with his wife, Denise, awaiting his return. Driving a new Dodge Ram pickup, Dallas was approaching Landrum Road (a red brick church and adjoining cemetery mark the intersection) when a logging truck, massive and imposing as an aircraft carrier, turned right onto 171 straight into his path. Sixty-eight-year-old Dallas swerved left to avoid crashing head on into the Freightliner, but it was already too late. The truck was now blocking both lanes. The pickup rammed into its side and caromed into oblivion.

"I remember thinking," Dallas said in 2017, "God, it all ends here."

It didn't end that Monday night, but it came close. Battered, bleeding profusely, and suffering extensive neurological injuries, Dallas was airlifted fifty miles by medical helicopter to the Georgia Health Sciences Medical Center in Augusta. Surgeons stopped the bleeding and stabilized him, but X-rays and other scans revealed his back was broken in four places, the C-2 and C-3 vertebrae were crushed, and the seventh cranial nerve—controlling facial muscles—damaged. Dallas spent the next five months bedridden. After further months of rehab, the cervical damage proved permanent, a persistent condition called torticollis, in which the head is turned to one side. Torticollis is typically associated with painful muscle spasms.

Dallas v. Bass Logging

Bass Logging, Inc., operators of the truck, immediately blamed the incident on Dallas—he was speeding, on his phone, distracted, etc. However, the evidence indicated the truck driver, Bennie Lee Dixon, had an unobstructed view of Dallas's pickup—headlights piercing the dark—as it approached on a long, arrow-straight section of GA 171. The company's insurers and their attorneys also downplayed Dallas's injuries, suggesting, however subtly, that the subsequent lawsuit he filed was an attempt to cash in.

Fifty years had passed since Dallas, the ambitious and overachieving UGA student-body president from Lincolnton, Georgia, and Tommy Malone, the party boy from Albany, had been roommates at the ATO frat house. Dallas never became governor of Georgia, but he'd built a thriving law practice in Thomson, Georgia, twenty-five miles from where he'd grown up. Tommy and Buddy stayed friends. Malone never stopped crediting Dallas for architecting his academic revival. Indeed, Dallas had encouraged Tommy's better angels, assigning him the secretary's spot in UGA's Pre-Law Club. He'd helped young Malone land a summer position with Georgia Senator Richard Russell.

In turn, Tommy convinced Dallas to apply to Mercer Law School. No slouch when it came to drinking or carousing, Dallas was a fixture at Malone's legendary Atlanta parties. "We've always had this kind of mutual admiration," Dallas said in 2017. "Something that has endured so many years and marriages and births of children and divorces. We've gone down the road separate and apart, but always together."

Like Spencer Lee and Randy Scarlett, Buddy Dallas had crossed a threshold—not easily defined, expandable, but real—from buddy, classmate, colleague, fishing or drinking crony to *friend*. "If Tommy is your friend," Dallas insisted, "he'll be there for you until the bitter end. If there's a cause he embraces, he'll be a warrior for that cause 'till the bitter end." And as Buddy Dallas lay broken and fighting the despair that is the handmaiden of catastrophic injury and illness, it was no surprise that Tommy Malone rallied to him. "This was not a Tommy Malone case," Dallas insisted. "It was not medical malpractice. At the time, I didn't know whether the trucker had a $1,000 worth of insurance or a $100,000 worth, but that was beside the point. Tommy *seized* the opportunity. He told me, 'Buddy, you know I want to handle this for you.' Tommy was going to be there for Denise and me, no matter what. This was his personal commitment. Whether we got paid or not, he'd fight the war for us."

***

Early on, the insurers of the trucking company spurned any attempt at negotiation, refusing, say those familiar with the case, a proposed settlement well below Bass Logging's $2 million in coverage. Malone engaged a former associate, Atlanta attorney S. Bradley Houck, a personal-injury specialist with whom he'd tried many cases in the past. They prepared for trial with the meticulousness that is Malone's trademark.

March 2015. The trial got underway in Sandersville, Georgia (Washington County Superior Court), where Bass Logging is headquartered. Buddy Dallas, now 72, was seeking damages for permanent injuries and the loss of his livelihood—he was forced to scale his practice back dramatically—and his wife, Denise, a probate court judge, sued for loss of consortium. The proceedings ran three days. In simple terms, the defense argued that if Buddy had paid closer attention he could have avoided the crash. Therefore, he was equally responsible, a defense Malone and Houck shredded. "A log truck doesn't stop at a stop sign, pulls in front of you, and they try to blame you?" Malone said with considerable understatement. "That, in itself, is not appealing to citizens sitting on a jury."

Tommy Malone's singular courtroom skill is his ability to appeal to a juror's decency and common sense. No flimflam or fireworks. No talking down, no country or cornpone, just an Everyman sitting around your kitchen table explaining complex chains of events or arcane facts in the simplest way possible. Dallas, for example, testified that he believed the rig was going 20 to 30 mph at the time of the crash and had blown right through the stop sign. The defense jumped on that, insisting the truck could not have made a 90-degree turn at that speed. Malone countered by proving—using the defense's own expert witness—that the driver had not stopped at all. "The expert acknowledged the driver didn't stop, because if he'd stopped and looked to the left," Tommy said, "he would have clearly seen Mr. Dallas coming."

Instead, Malone demonstrated, the driver kept going, his turn so wide "he took over the highway."

During cross-examination, Malone stipulated that the defense's expert witness was a qualified accident reconstructionist, then elicited that the defense didn't allow their own expert to reconstruct the accident. "He hadn't examined the truck," Malone said. "He didn't know whether the lights were on or off. He simply took the driver's word that the lights were on."

Then came the coup de grace: "Do you have a smartphone?" Malone asked the witness.

"I do."

"Well, I asked Siri this question the other day: 'On a dark night, how far would a passenger vehicle's high beams illumine the roadway ahead?'"

"Oh, she probably said a lot of different things."

"No, she said 451 feet." (This was approximately half the distance the defense had argued and undercut their case.)

"I'm probably the first lawyer in the country," Malone said later, "to use Siri as an expert witness."

The jury was swayed by the forthright testimony of Buddy and Denise Dallas. They completely undercut the defense attorneys' intimation that they were trying to cash in on a tragedy. "They underestimated Buddy's popularity, his charm, and how seriously he was injured," Malone said. "And the impact it had on his relationship with his wife." As the jury began their deliberations, it was exceedingly clear how skilled a lawyer Tommy, the lackadaisical, beer-swilling, carefree frat boy, had grown up to be. After a three-day trial, the jury swiftly arrived at a verdict, awarding Albert Dallas what many considered a staggering *$15 million* in compensatory damage and $1,500,000 to Denise Dallas for loss of consortium. The defense appealed, but it was quickly apparent that there were no grounds for a reversal. The case settled.

Summer 2017. Buddy Dallas will never fully recover from the psychological trauma of the crash or his physical injuries. He still suffers from sleeplessness, exhaustion, and pain, but it was no surprise that upon learning that his great friend Tommy Malone was facing a daunting medical crisis of his own, Buddy and Denise Dallas got in their car and drove more than 500 miles south to North Palm Beach to spend time with Tommy.

Chapter 39

"The reason so many people love [Tommy] *is because of his desire and ability to help. He does this in every aspect of his life."*
—Randall H. Scarlett

San Francisco. As mentioned, the bond between Tommy and Randy Scarlett stretches all the way back to their first encounter at the Belli Law firm in in the 1980s. Over dinner one night—it may have been after Belli's 1996 funeral—Scarlett mentioned that he was interested in joining the Association of Trial Lawyers of America's Traumatic Brain Injury Litigation group (today, the American Association for Justice). "Randy, I'm a board member on that litigation group," Malone replied. He thought a moment and added, "If you're willing to work hard, I'll give up my seat so you can have it. You can develop yourself that way, but don't let me down." Scarlett wasn't about to let Tommy, whom he considers a brother, down.

This was typical Tommy Malone. Do whatever you can to help a friend. No questions asked and nothing required in return. For Scarlett, a tremendous opportunity was couched in Tommy's seemingly casual remark. Of course, Tommy knew that. He doesn't miss much. "He gave me his board position, which I took over with the blessing of the rest of the group," Scarlett recalled. "Since that day, I've focused my practice on TBI [traumatic brain injury] and I've gotten a ton of cases. Saying Tommy's friendship has had a remarkable influence on my life is an understatement. His impact is *profound*."

"Tommy, Debbie, Mary Anne, and I traveled the world together," Scarlett continued. They toured Italy in a Mercedes and stayed at the 5-star Hotel Splendido in Portofino on the Ligurian coast. In the United Kingdom, Tommy introduced the Scarletts to his drinking buddy, Gordon Slynn, who arranged for the couples—traveling as part of a Belli Society trip—to lunch at the Peers Dining Room and dinner at the Garrick Club in Covent Garden, a venue exclusive enough to once count Charles Dickens and John Gielgud among its members. What Scarlett remembers long after the fabulous meals and fine wine is his friend's common touch, the grace he'd observed over and over in Tommy. It didn't matter if they were on Abaco Island or the fog-shrouded moors of Scotland. "Everywhere we'd go, Tommy would talk to people and they'd describe a problem in their lives," Scarlett remembered. "It might have absolutely nothing to do with law, but he'd bring that simplicity and logic with the goal of helping folks. The reason so many people love him is because of his desire and ability to help. He does this in every aspect of his life."

Part IX

Organization Man

Chapter 40

"Man, this is useful stuff!"
"I've gotta be a member!"
—Tommy Malone,
Georgia Trial Lawyers Association Seminar

In his very first year of practice, Tommy Malone showed up at a Georgia Trial Lawyers Association seminar. Among the tidbits he gleaned from an accident reconstructionist's presentation was a way to determine potential negligence in rear-end auto collisions by checking the taillight/brake-light filaments for telltale carbon deposits indicating the lights were burning at the moment of impact. The automobile has come a long way with onboard computers constantly recording every imaginable byte of data in real time, but at the time, Malone was more than willing to grab a Phillips screwdriver and pull a taillight lens if it gave him an edge that helped win a case for a client. "Man, this is useful stuff!" he thought. Joining, serving, and leading professional associations would be a theme in Tommy's personal and professional life, a key to his success.

When he got back from Atlanta, Malone called his friend John James, the Macon attorney who was GTLA president at the time. "This organization is made for me!" he gushed. "I've gotta be a member!" Tommy waited for an invitation. And waited some more. At the time, he says, the GTLA was essentially a referral network for big-time Atlanta lawyers and the occasional Savannah plaintiff's attorney. Albany was a legal backwater filled with go-along-to-get-along lawyers. Never shy, Malone kept pestering James. "Still, it was two years before they finally let me in," he recalled.

Fifty years later, Malone has served as president, ranking officer, board member, or honoree in the GTLA and numerous other top-drawer professional organizations—the American Bar Association, National Trial Lawyers Association, International Academy of Trial Lawyers, American Association for Justice (formerly the Association of Trial Lawyers of America), International Society of Barristers, National Association of Trial Lawyers, Southern Trial Lawyers Association among them—but that same rush of excitement, interest, and enthusiasm he felt at his first GTLA seminar is still vibrantly alive.

"There's always learning going on," Malone said in 2017. "I've never left a seminar without learning something I didn't know before. The organizations serve the greater good by educating lawyers, particularly young lawyers, attending the meetings. Hearing people with experience, you gain knowledge that helps you do *your* job better." Often that message is lost in the daily pressures and distractions of the profession, with some lawyers opting to take, for example, their mandatory continuing legal education (CLE) hours online or by listening to an audiotape rather than real-world peer interaction. "I've been with lawyers who took their CLE on the last possible day on a speaker phone in their offices with papers scattered all over the place," said the Augusta lawyer John Bell, who, like Malone, is a committed organization man. "You can bet they've never gotten a case, never learned something unexpected, never met someone in the hallway..."

Tommy Malone has been a fixture at the Georgia Bar, Belli Society, GTLA, STLA, and other seminars for decades, gladly learning, gladly teaching. His success made him a hot commodity, but he kept his eyes on the prize. "When I reached the level of being an invited speaker I was able to give back the important things I'd learned," Malone said, "but I still continued to grow." The greater good is not learning how to become rich, well known, or the greatest marketer. "Our job as trial lawyers is achieving justice for the injured and the survivors of those killed by the careless hands of others."

Professional memberships build friendships and nurture fellowship, often in unexpected locales—Lord Slynn's welcoming Belli Society stalwarts with hospitality and libation-fueled tours of Parliament and the English courts comes to mind. For plaintiffs' lawyers, a slice of the profession besieged by crusading politicians, tort reformers, self-appointed media watchdogs, and the relentless enmity of the corporations, health-care conglomerates, and other mainstream institutions (whose negligence and occasional malfeasance have called the plaintiffs' bar into existence), kindred spirits and experienced mentors play a vitally important role in survival of the species.

Malone has always been an organization man: he joined the Boy Scouts, the ATO fraternity, UGA's Pre-Law Club, the Belli Society, and the International Society of Barristers. Back in his Albany days, he joined the

Jaycees in southwest Georgia and then statewide (a platform from which he once planned to launch a political campaign for state attorney general, flying his own airplane to canvass the state. Mel Belli arrived and forever changed that career arc). He's always been a bomb-thrower willing to take risk and make enemies in pursuit of that elusive greater good. "Throughout his career, Tommy has been involved in things to make the civil-justice system better and fight off those who'd make it worse," insisted John Bell. "Very involved in efforts to protect, preserve, and improve the system because he's passionate about it."

To that end, a much younger Malone engineered a coup against the State Bar of Georgia's General Practice and Trial Section. Today, it doesn't sound earthshaking, but it mattered tremendously to his fellow trial lawyers. In his words, here's how it unfolded: "At that time, the state bar was really controlled by the defense firms and the corporate bar in Atlanta. Every meeting was held in Savannah. My first two or three years in practice, I wanted to go, but my father said he wouldn't allow it."

"Only defense lawyers and chamber of commerce lawyers can afford it," Rosser Malone grumbled. That was that. Actually, Rosser Malone was not far off in his assessment. The bar *was* stacked against plaintiffs' attorneys. He assumed the issue had been laid to rest, but once Tommy got his teeth into something, he'd never let go. "Because I was a trial lawyer, there was a check off," Tommy said. "I could pay 5 or 10 dollars a year in addition to my state bar dues to join these sections. One was the General Practice and Trial Section (GP&T).

"In the late 1970s, after eight or ten years of paying dues, I'd never heard from them. Never any meetings or anything! No minutes of any meetings. I can't say I was surprised, but then I learned they'd *combined* the GP&T programs with the bar's Insurance Section programs. Defense attorneys were giving the presentations! I called the bar headquarters and asked, 'How much money is in the section bank account?' [Funds set aside to pay for seminars, publications, programs, and newsletters, etc.] It was something like $40,000 or $50,000. So, what I did was arrange for a group of trial lawyers to join the General Practice and Trial Section, show up at the mid-year meeting of the bar in Atlanta, and vote me in as chairman."

As it turned out, John Bell was one of the lawyers in town for the meeting. He remembers it well: "I run into Tommy. He's got one or two guys with him. He says 'John come on with us! We're going to take over the General Practice and Trial Section.'

"'Why are we doing that?'

"'They've got $40,000 in their account they haven't spent. Lets' go!'

"We get there and the guy in line to be the next chairman and his buddies are all upset," Bell remembered. "We have enough people by then to outvote them because there were very few people there."

Next thing, Robert "Bobby" Brinson, an attorney from Rome, Georgia, calls Malone and informs him the nominating committee would be happy to name *Tommy* secretary of the section.

"'Bobby, that's not what I came to do.'"

They went round and round, as lawyers are wont to do. "Finally, I told Bobby 'I'm a team player,'" Malone said. "So I'll accept the secretary's position." An agreement was hammered out naming Malone, a plaintiff's attorney, section chairman the following term. (John Bell would win the job two years later.) But Tommy wasn't done.

"When I became secretary, I got a copy of the section's bylaws," he said. "There was supposed to be one board member from each Georgia congressional district, and maybe two at-large members. Guess how many we had? None! They'd never been filled or had been allowed to expire. I kept my mouth shut until I was chairman and then appointed my friends throughout the state to the board. There might have been a bankruptcy judge or a friendly defense lawyer, but primarily these were plaintiff's attorneys. We took the section over."

Why does it matter? Malone and his conspirators immediately hired Bob White, executive secretary of the Georgia Trial Lawyers Association, to be the section's part-time director. GT&P came vibrantly alive, putting on an array of programs and seminars and creating awards and other programs recognizing both plaintiff and defense lawyers, general practitioners, and judges. Over the years, Malone would serve on numerous committees providing input on proposed rule changes and statutes, spearheading efforts to fight bad legislation in the state house, supporting sympathetic candidates—Governor Roy Barnes perhaps the best known—recruiting lobbyists to represent trial lawyers, and writing very large checks. "The trial lawyers now have a voice in the state bar," Malone said. "When I started, we really had nobody speaking for us."

In a perfect world, Tommy Malone, the ultimate organization man, would be welcomed on all sides for his commitment and hard work. For example, Tommy literally revived the Belli Society, which had gone into a long decline at the time of Mel's death. This is not always the case. Over the years, Malone made some enemies with long memories. Before he died, Griffin Bell, former US Attorney General and a former president of the prestigious American College of Trial Lawyers, let it be known that he would like to see Tommy admitted to that organization. The membership is thick with corporate lawyers.

Instead, Tommy Malone was blackballed. "It only takes one," he said, shrugging off the slight. A lesson he learned in too many courtrooms over the years

Part X

Rosser Malone

Chapter 41

"Daddy needed to boss somebody because he'd been the ultimate bosser
when he was judge of the court."
—Tommy Malone

When he turned 86, Rosser Malone once again turned to Tommy for career advice. He'd served sixteen gratifying years as judge of the state court of Dougherty County and twenty-five years prior as that court's solicitor. He still wasn't ready to let go.

"Son, do you think I should offer for reelection?"

"Daddy, I don't know."

Tommy thought a moment, running the possibilities through his head. Among other hurdles, he suspected that Rosser's intellectual capacities were diminishing.

"Okay, Daddy, let me and Bill Underwood [a cousin, not the president of Mercer University] send out a letter with both our signatures to all the members of the bar. We'll ask if they think you're doing a good job and whether you should offer for reelection. If so, 'Please sign the bottom of this letter authorizing us to use your name in our campaign materials and so forth.'"

"Son, that's a great idea, a brilliant idea. Thank you."

"Next thing I know, I get a call from Albany," Tommy said.

"Son, I've paid my qualifying fee. Come on down and run this campaign for me."

"Daddy didn't want to know what all of them thought," Tommy realized. "He ran and he got beat."

The election was a tipping point. Rosser Malone, perhaps the most significant figure in Tommy's life, went into a steep decline. He'd arrived at the stage in life where parent inexorably becomes dependent and childlike, a burden many offspring cannot or will not deal with. Tommy, no matter how complex, frustrating, or, on occasion, uproarious his relationship with his obstinate father could be, was forever the dutiful son. Toni Malone, also in her 80s, struggled to care for her husband. Rosser and Toni were still living essentially independently in the house on Hilltop Drive. Rosser's forced retirement created additional challenges. "Daddy would come home, sit in front of the TV, and watch *Days of Our Lives* and stuff like that," Tommy remembered. "He'd tell my mother, 'Change the channel.'"

"'Rosser, you've got the remote, you change it.'"

"'I can't change it!'"

"Daddy needed to boss somebody," Tommy added, "because he'd been the ultimate bosser when he was judge of the court."

Rosser's decline was physical as well. His knees were so ravaged by arthritis he'd fall down and find himself unable to get up without assistance. Toni, unsteady herself and unable to lift her strapping husband, was forced to call the sheriff's department to send an officer by. A deputy would help Rosser off the floor and into a chair or bed, a courtesy that ended a year or so after Malone lost his judgeship. Toni, a woman of great circumspection, now found herself on the street flagging strangers to come help her pick her husband up.

Rosser grew so debilitated he was eventually moved to a preferred-care home. Not much later, he made one of his signature phone calls to Tommy, announcing he wanted a divorce. "After fifty years of marriage," Tommy said. "At that point, I knew his mind wasn't long for this world." When in town, Tommy would collect his father and drive him home for Sunday dinner with Toni and the family. Sure enough, Rosser now demanded to move back with Toni. To spare his long-suffering mother, Tommy again intervened.

"'Daddy, what do you think about me buying a small house and getting a housekeeper to stay with you all the time?'"

"'Son, I told you I ain't interested in none of that sex stuff!'"

Eventually, Tommy persuaded both his parents to relocate to Wesley Woods, an extended-care facility run by Emory Healthcare in Atlanta. Inevitably, death came calling. Toni Underwood Malone died there on May 30, 2001. She was 91 years old. Judge Malone outlived her, passing away on April 26, 2002. Tommy's older brother, Ross, died of cancer in St. Petersburg, Florida, on April 23, 2003. He'd been best man at Tommy and Debbie's wedding, but things between the two, never affectionate, had deteriorated further. Rosser grew so bitter he forbade Tommy from attending his funeral. "It breaks my heart," Tommy said, "that my brother didn't love me like I loved him."

Part XI

Closing the Circle

Chapter 42

*"Tommy was not stupid. I've met some very stupid attorneys before.
Over the years, I came to realize that if you treat Tommy right, he's
going to treat you right."*
—Laura Deane, director of claims management
Emory Healthcare

March 2013. After being diagnosed with prostate cancer and running the discouraging gauntlet of PSA tests, biopsies, and Gleason scores, Robert Helms dutifully reported to Atlanta's well-regarded Emory University Hospital. There, he would undergo a radical prostatectomy, surgical removal of the metastasizing gland and surrounding tissue, a procedure performed more than 138,000 times each year in US hospitals. According to hospital records, the operation was completely "uneventful." Later, after being transferred to a room in the hospital ward, Helms, a 64-year-old grandfather, told his wife Susan he was having trouble breathing. A day later, when the surgeon arrived to check on him, he advised Helms (saying words to the effect), "You need to start moving around. You should have been up and walking for the last four or five hours."

"I...can't breathe," Helms gasped as Susan attempted to walk him around his room.

The following morning Susan arrived to find Robert, stomach distended and very short of breath. When the urology resident showed up, she noted his discomfort, raised his bed to a sitting position and turned to leave to continue her rounds. According to Susan, she stopped and scolded, "I want you out of the bed and into that chair." Susan again tried to assist the gasping Robert. For whatever reason, no one took Helms's continuing complaints seriously. That afternoon (the second post-operative day), Susan Helms found herself in an unimaginable situation: alone and helpless in a state-of-the art hospital surrounded by doctors, nurses, and medical professionals.

"I'm really, really having trouble breathing," Robert gasped. In medical terms, he'd developed tachypnea, abnormally rapid breathing.

Panicked, Susan rushed into the corridor shouting for assistance. According to one account, the resident told her, "I've got really sick patients to attend to." In the room, Robert Helms had fallen out of his chair and was choking in his own vomit. As his wife watched in horror, Robert arrested. Alarm bells clanged, staff members rushed in, a Code was called. Helms hurried to the ICU. That night he died. An autopsy, requested by the family, revealed he'd developed a post-op ileus, an arrest of intestinal peristalsis—a treatable condition—that can occur after any surgery. In layman's terms, Helms's bowel was obstructed and his distended belly was compressing his lungs. Among the symptoms of ileus are nausea, vomiting, and abdominal discomfort, indicators that didn't register with the resident.

***

"A patient died," recalled Laura Deane, director of claims management for Emory Healthcare in 2016. "At the time, the hospital felt his death was a consequence of the cancer, so I didn't hear anything about it. This was not one of those cases where you knew something had happened and you went and investigated and gathered all the information to share with the family." A former nurse, Deane oversees all medical malpractice litigation for Emory. Her decades of experience in critical care and risk management had convinced her that the best way to handle potential or alleged legal liability issues when they occur is to be open, plainspoken, and forthright with patients and their loved ones.

Susan Helms, who went from hopeful spouse to grieving widow, was so devastated by the loss of her husband she continued to post achingly sad messages on Robert's online obituary months after his death. As often happens, loved ones, once past the initial shock of an unforeseen, life-altering loss, ask a simple question: why? At some point, Helms requested Robert's medical records and began to suspect something had gone terribly wrong that day at Emory, something acute and very different from the cumulative insults of metastatic cancer. Why had Robert arrested in the aftermath of a relatively low-risk surgical procedure? Why had no one at Emory even taken the time to discuss this catastrophic event or series of events with her after his death? She realized the answers to these critical questions were beyond her ability to determine.

It could have been word-of-mouth, a tip from a family lawyer, the annual issue of Georgia *Super Lawyers*, or Malone Law's own website, but Susan Helms came across Tommy Malone, an attorney experienced in handling "wrongful death" and "medical negligence" lawsuits. The two scheduled a preliminary meeting, after which Malone decided he'd heard enough to formally request the hospital's records to examine whether negligence might have been a factor in Robert's death. In simplest terms, did the overworked attending or resident deviate from standard practices and procedures?

At this point, Malone, indeed, any other plaintiff's attorney, would have been on the verge of bringing a medical malpractice action against Emory Healthcare. Given the facts surrounding Robert Helms's last hours, Laura Deane, once apprised, would not have been surprised. "My job *exists* because health-care systems get sued," she said. "Sometimes it's because we've done something wrong. Sometimes it's because people think we have a lot of money. Let me tell you, people are trying to come after Emory about something every day."

As it turned out, Deane and the administrators, insurers, and attorneys who oversee the health-care conglomerate were completely in the dark, a very precarious legal position. "As I said, people die in hospitals all the time. We had *no* idea anything was wrong," insisted Deane. "No red flag for me. Nothing to suggest we needed to worry."

The lawsuit was never filed.

***

At Emory, Malone had forged a deep personal friendship with Laura Deane that ran back more than a decade. Deane was new on the job when Tommy first appeared on the scene putting out feelers on a case, the details of which both have long forgotten. After an incident (or alleged incident) occurs at Emory, Deane's job as director of claims management is to try to read where things are heading and decide whether one of the hospital's defense attorneys should be engaged. Back then, she'd never heard of Malone. "Just another guy showing up," she said. Deane is one of those individuals whose blunt talk conceals a keen intellect and a tender and compassionate heart. When she did ask about Tommy Malone, she got an earful, particularly from the administrators at MagMutual, a hard-nosed, Atlanta-based insurer that provides malpractice coverage to physicians throughout the Southeast. The red flags ranged from "You've got to watch him, he's got the biggest verdicts and he's dangerous" to "He's a pluperfect asshole who won't deal with anybody.... It has to be his way or no way."

In person, Malone seemed the opposite of the bogeyman the defense attorneys described. "He was as nice as he could be," Deane recalled. "Tommy was eloquent. When he did his [discovery] interviews, he made doctors feel comfortable because of the respectful way he treated them. He never talked down, and obviously Tommy was not stupid. I've met some very stupid attorneys before. Over the years, I came to realize that if you treat Tommy right, he's going to treat you right."

***

In the 1990s, the leadership of Emory Healthcare arrived at a momentous decision—adopting a policy of full disclosure in interactions with patients. In Deane's no-nonsense words, "We decided to be transparent. We'd start telling people exactly what happened, why it happened, and what we'd do to try to make it right. In the health-care industry, you didn't really hide these things, but you didn't tell patients all the details of whatever happened because you didn't want them to go out and sue and cost you that money."

Not surprisingly, full disclosure was vehemently opposed by Emory's stable of high-testosterone defense attorneys. "Wait a minute!" they protested, "You used to not tell anybody anything, now you're telling everybody everything?" Nonetheless, it was an approach to patient relations that became the aspirational goal for the health-care industry. "It's a really good thing," Deane insists. "You can tell patients what happened and they'll still maintain trust in your institution and want you to care for them. If you really did them harm, you're gonna make it right. Isn't that the way it should be?"

Deane did not arrive at her job by chance. "Who better," she realized, "to advise Emory on how its full-disclosure policy should work than the number-one malpractice attorney in the state?" Tommy Malone was invited inside the walls. "He was the only choice," added Deane. "And he helped write our policy." Malone was hardly an unknown at the Emory University complex. He was a familiar figure at the law school across Clifton Road, where he and noted defense attorney Lori Cohen would engage in very spirited ethical debates ("I've never understood how you can represent these people!") while teaching point and counterpoint techniques. In essence, Malone advised Emory decision-makers to do the right thing by their patients. "Tell them everything that happened. If a patient or family member wants an attorney, you need to bring one in too." Ironically, when Robert Helms walked into Emory University Hospital a decade later, full disclosure was the system's policy.

***

Malone called Laura Deane inquiring about Helms's death. He didn't file papers or start proceedings. "This is on my radar," he simply told her. "You might want to look at it." That early heads-up, Deane said, was something most plaintiffs' attorney would instinctively avoid. For his part, Tommy's first thought was not "Here comes another high-profile, big-dollar jury verdict." "Most of my clients are looking for acknowledgment of responsibility," he explained. "An apology, if you will." In simple words, justice for the injustice they needlessly suffered. "Monetary compensation," Malone added, "represents a true admission that the doctor or hospital has some responsibility for an outcome. Together, acknowledgement and compensation go a long way to make victims' lives a little better."

"You need to hear Susan Helms's story," he told Deane.

"Well, this doesn't sound good," Deane remembers thinking after getting off the phone. "So we started at square one and investigated." What she discovered was very unsettling, pretty much *the* textbook definition of medical malpractice: "Negligence by a health-care professional or provider in which treatment provided was substandard and caused harm, injury, or death to a patient."

Based on the strength of her relationship with Tommy, Deane decided that the disastrous chain of events that unfolded in the aftermath of Helms's surgery might be turned into a learning experience for Emory Healthcare staff. What follows are direct quotes:

"The physician missed signs that the patient was in distress," Deane said. "She was a resident, not first year, and had some experience. The patient's wife tried to tell her, 'There's something wrong, something wrong...something wrong.' And she just blew off the wife. Everything sort of escalated from there. There were two urology residents and nobody called the attending physician to come over because they didn't think it was anything. The nurses were sort of, 'I think there's something wrong,' but they couldn't get anywhere because the doctors were like, 'Ah, don't worry, it's okay.'"

One of the points Deane underscored: "We tell our people that if the family tells you something is wrong, there's *something wrong*. They know more than anybody. So you need to look further. Prostate cancer is slow-growing. Mr. Helms shouldn't have died so early. We'd missed the signs and he was dead. So we offered to go to mediation."

Here again, Malone's relationship with Deane was a factor. In mediation, Emory avoided the negative publicity a malpractice lawsuit would bring as well as the risks inherent in a jury trial. For his part, Malone believed that no financial award, no transfer of assets from one entity to another, would provide the closure Susan Helms needed. "We all meet in a room with a neutral party [the mediator]," Deane recalled. "Tommy tells her story and we give our side. Typically, at this point, you'd go your separate ways and the mediator tries to come to a happy number. Well, we got to the number. We resolved it, but Tommy kept saying, 'Susan Helms has a story to tell.'"

Deane gathered Emory's clinical risk manager, a small group of Emory physicians, administrators, and one of the hospital's defense attorneys. She invited Susan Helms to address the group. "It was just heartbreaking!" Dean recalled. "She was so powerless. It was just her in a hospital where everybody else *was out for the greater good of Emory* [italics added] and she was trying to get attention for the husband she dearly loved. She gave us some background about her marriage, but it was mostly about how threatened and alone she felt in *our* hospital. It's what we wanted our people at Emory to hear because they never hear that side of the story."

Susan Helms's story was so powerful and provocative Deane asked if she might use it for broader educational purposes. Helms agreed to sit for a video presentation. "The urology chair, the attending, the residents, and the chief quality officer all looked at it," Deane recalled. "Then the dean of students and the dean of the medical school wanted to see it. They invited Susan to participate in the discussions her story generated." The gist of the video—which is still used as a teaching tool more than a decade later—is that "physicians need to put themselves in the patient's and the patient's family's shoes."

This is a precise description of what Tommy Malone, the feared malpractice lawyer, believes he's contributed to the well-being of the health-care profession.

"*Imagine me*," he said in 2017, "being involved in a film used to teach doctors how to pay more attention to their patients?"

Epilogue

"People suffered in silence. Now they have a voice...a voice that was trained by Tommy Malone.... If I had to pick five people in the last fifty years who have changed trial practice in Georgia, Tommy Malone would be right at the top of the list."
—Roy Barnes, trial lawyer and former governor of Georgia

July 2017. It's odd the way things turn out. Tommy Malone set out to be a rodeo rider and wound up a pioneer. This may be the most intriguing irony in a life studded with outsized accomplishments and unexpected achievements. "No one would have ever picked Tommy as the guy most likely to succeed," his college roommate remembered with a laugh. Yet Malone went on to hobnob with governors and English lords, and, of course, the King of Torts. He answered the call, the voice crying out in the desert. Uncertain but determined to press on. Stubborn, willing to bang his head against a wall again and again until the wall collapsed and the light shone through.

He walked away from the society that birthed him, shielded him, and ultimately began to suffocate him. Of course, Tommy did not journey alone. "His mother gave him compassion," Governor Roy Barnes said. "His daddy gave him grit and perseverance." Debbie Malone became anchor and soul mate. The suffering and injustice he saw all around, particularly among the African American community, outraged him. There was something more, a thing that became clearer as his own mortality began to weigh upon him, a guiding hand.

Lawyer extraordinaire, but ordinary man, Tommy Malone did the impossible. He changed things. "He's one of the pioneers," Roy Barnes continued. "He was in rural Georgia representing victims of medical malpractice when nobody else would take their cases, a measure of his strength of character and courage. The skills Tommy portrayed in the practice of law and the new types of methods he used showed us these cases could be won. He has a towering physical presence and a towering personality. If I had to pick five people in the last fifty years who have changed trial practice in Georgia, Tommy Malone would be right at the top of the list."

Mercer University's Bill Underwood sees Malone as nothing less than an avatar whose life and career parallels the rise of the New South itself. The same might be said of Malone's close friend and contemporary Judge Herbert Phipps, who soared above the poverty, segregation, and racism of Jim Crow Georgia to be elected statewide three times and named chief judge of the Georgia Court of Appeals. "Tommy had the skill to represent people who'd been terribly injured against all kinds of foes, no matter how rich, powerful, or influential," Phipps said. "To make them whole again. He used the civil justice system to achieve justice for people whether they were black or white or rich or poor. Early on, he appreciated the value of having jurors who represented a cross-section of the community, the value of black jurors, female jurors, white jurors, rich jurors, poor jurors. Other lawyers had these skills and abilities, but they lacked Tommy Malone's courage. He's special and unique in the legal profession because he has that combination of skill and courage needed to achieve great things, not for himself, but the people he represents."

***

Sometimes Even a Hero Needs a Hero is the name of a little book Lori Sutton put together after Tommy Malone's skills and persistence transformed her life and the lives of her husband and children. (The story depicted in the opening chapters of this book.) Lori's book is illustrated with pictures of Tucker, Landon, and their two other sons now living in a bright, spacious—though modest—house fully equipped to handle Tucker's needs, and a specially equipped van. And a photo of Tommy. *Hero* is dedicated to Malone, "the man who took our world from upside-down to comfortable and hopeful."

In North Palm Beach, the Malones keep the book on the coffee table in the living room of their house "so all who visit can see it and understand." At a moment when tributes are raining on the 74-year-old Malone like Mardi Gras beads—the Southern Trial Lawyers Association hosted their "Salute to Tommy Malone" at Galatoire's in New Orleans in February 2017—Lori Sutton's *Hero* is a treasure, as significant as the honors and acclamations that line his office walls.

A roadmap of a life in the law. And a life well lived.

VITAE of

THOMAS WILLIAM MALONE

PERSONAL

Born November 2, 1942, in Albany, Georgia

Married Debbie Blankinship Malone June 27, 1987

Children: Thomas William Malone Jr.

               Rosser Adams Malone

Interests:

Bimini Big Game Club, *Commodore*

Bahamas Wahoo Championship, *Founder*

Ravinia Club, *Board of Governors*

Shepherd Center, *Board of Trustees*

Mercer University, *Board of Trustees*

Instrument-rated pilot for single-, multi-engine piston and turbo-prop planes, *approximately 4,000 hours flight time*

EDUCATION

Albany, Georgia public school system grades 1 thru 12 with exception of sophomore high school year at Georgia Military College in Milledgeville, Georgia. Merit list at GMC; Junior Varsity football at Albany High; Thespian Club at Albany High.

University of Georgia undergraduate and Law School 1960 through 1963
Alpha Beta Chapter of Alpha Tau Omega Fraternity secretary, Pre-Law Club secretary, X Club, Demosthenian Literary Society president, Gridiron Society.

Passed the Georgia Bar Examination and admitted to Georgia Bar: 1965
Walter F. George School of Law, Mercer University
BACHELOR OF LAWS DEGREE/JURIS DOCTOR DEGREE : **1966**

EXPERIENCE

Tommy Malone has been a trial attorney in courts throughout the state of Georgia for more than fifty years. He is the founder of the Malone Law office, where he practiced law with his son, Adam Malone, in Atlanta. Their practice is devoted to the representation of the catastrophically injured and survivors of those who have died as the result of the negligence of others.

PROFESSIONAL HONORS

Litigation Counsel of America: 2016 Tommy Malone Outstanding Verdict of the Year Award

Georgia Trial Lawyers Association: 2016 Tommy Malone Award for Excellence in Advocacy

Daily Report: 2015 Daily Report Verdicts Hall of Fame Lifetime Achievement Award

Best Lawyers in America
All editions, 1989 to Present

Best Lawyers in America
Cover spotlight, 2009

Knights of the Bar
Lifetime Diplomate, April 1, 2007

Georgia's Super Lawyers
Included as a Georgia Super Lawyer every year since first published in 2004. Cover spotlight: "The New King of Torts," by Jerry Grillo, 2010.

Georgia's Super Lawyers "Highest Rated Lawyer in Georgia"
2009, 2010, 2011, 2012, 2013, 2014, 2015, 2016, and 2017

Georgia's Top 10 Super Lawyers
2007, 2009, 2010, 2011, 2012, 2013, 2014, 2015, 2016, and 2017

Georgia's Top 100 Super Lawyers
Every edition since inception in 2004 to 2017

Compassionate Gladiator Award
Florida Justice Association, 2009

Mel Award
Melvin M. Belli Society, 2009

Tommy Malone Great American Eagle Award
Southern Trial Lawyers Association, February 2007

Pursuit of Justice Award
American Bar Association/Tort Trial and Insurance Practice Section, 2004

Trial Lawyer of the Year
Melvin M. Belli Society, 2001

Top 100 Georgians
GEORGIA TREND MAGAZINE, 1999

Tradition of Excellence Award
State Bar of Georgia, 1999

Warhorse Award
Southern Trial Lawyers Association, February 1996

Trial Lawyer of the Year
American Board of Trial Advocacy, Georgia Chapter, 1995

Most Powerful and Influential Georgians
GEORGIA TREND MAGAZINE, January 1996; January 1998

Small Office Hall of Fame, Initial Inductee
American Trial Lawyers Association Small Office Section, February 1996

"One of the most highly-feared malpractice attorneys of all time."
THE ALBANY JOURNAL (August 26, 2004) 1

"One of the Best Personal Injury and Litigation Lawyers"
ATLANTA MAGAZINE (August 2002)

"A brilliant medical malpractice attorney."
Ron Rosenbaum, *End H.M.O. 'Telephone Triage': Pass the Patients' Rights Bill*, THE NEW YORK OBSERVER (June 25, 2001) 23

"One of the state's top malpractice attorneys."
Carrie Teegardin, *Cody's Story: A medical ordeal, a life upended*, THE ATLANTA JOURNAL-CONSTITUTION (April 29, 1999) A20-A21

PROFESSIONAL MEMBERSHIPS
THE NATIONAL TRIAL LAWYERS: TOP 100 LAWYERS
Executive Committee, 2011; admitted to Hall of Fame 2017

SHEPHERD CENTER FOUNDATION BOARD OF TRUSTEES
Board Member 2011 to 2014
2017 Angels of the Year: Debbie and Tommy Malone

THE CARTER CENTER BOARD OF COUNCILORS
Board Member 2013 to 2017

MERCER UNIVERSITY BOARD OF TRUSTEES
Member 2006 to 2017
Chairman of the Board, 2015 to 2017

AMERICAN BOARD OF PROFESSIONAL LIABILITY ATTORNEYS
President, June 2006 to 2010
Diplomate—Member, Board of Governors
Board examiner, 1992, 1994

BRAIN INJURY ASSOCIATION OF AMERICA: Member

BRAIN INJURY ASSOCIATION OF CALIFORNIA: Member

NATIONAL HEAD INJURY FOUNDATION
Georgia Chapter: Member

INTERNATIONAL SOCIETY OF BARRISTERS
Fellow, elected September 1995

INTERNATIONAL ACADEMY OF TRIAL LAWYERS
Fellow, elected 1982

JAYCEES: President Albany Jaycees, President Southwest Georgia Jaycees, National
Director Georgia Jaycees. First place regional Speak Up competition, second place state Speak Up competition.

LITIGATION COUNSEL OF AMERICA
Member: 2016 Outstanding Verdict Award

AMERICAN ASSOCIATION FOR JUSTICE
Life Member
Presidents Club
Leaders' Forum
Board of Governors, 1980 to 1983
State Committeeman, 1971 to 1975
ATLA Traumatic Brain Injury Litigation Group
ATLA Consumers Coalition
ATLA Birth Trauma Litigation Group
National College of Advocacy, Advocate, 1993

THE ROSCOE POUND-AMERICAN TRIAL LAWYERS FOUNDATION
Lifetime Fellow

AMERICAN JUDICATURE SOCIETY

Member

TRIAL LAWYERS FOR PUBLIC JUSTICE
Sustaining Founder
Board of Directors, 1991 to 1993

AMERICAN BAR ASSOCIATION
Member 1965 to present
Trial Techniques Committee, 1971 to 1972

THE BELLI SOCIETY
Treasurer, 1981 to 1982
Vice President, 1985 to 1986; 1988 to 1991
President, 1991 to 1993

NATIONAL INSTITUTE OF TRIAL ADVOCACY
Faculty 1994

MEMBER STATE BAR OF GEORGIA
Member 1965 to present
General Practice and Trial Section Chairman, 1979 to 1980
Chairman Elect, 1978 to 1979; Secretary 1977 to 1978
Medico-Legal Committee Chairman, 1978 to 1979
Trial Practice General Advisory Committee Chairman, 1979 to 1980
Committee to Reduce Court Costs and Delays
Committee to Preserve Oral Argument and Advocacy
Medico-Legal Conference Committee
No-Fault Automobile Reparations Committee
Standardized Jury Instructions Committee
Supreme Court Special Overview Committee for Mandatory CLE

GEORGIA BAR FOUNDATION, INC.
Fellow

GEORGIA TRIAL LAWYERS ASSOCIATION, INC.
Life Member

President, 1980 to 1981
President Elect, 1979 to 1980
Executive Vice President, 1972 to 1978
Malpractice Committee Chairman, 1975 to 1977; 1984 to 1986

SOUTHERN TRIAL LAWYERS ASSOCIATION
Member
Board of Governors, 1988
Treasurer, 1994
President-Elect, 1996
President, 1997

GEORGIA ASSOCIATION OF CRIMINAL DEFENSE LAWYERS
Charter Member
Vice President, 1974 to 1977

DOUGHERTY CIRCUIT BAR ASSOCIATION
President, 1976 to 1977

ATLANTA LAWYERS CLUB
Member

THE ATLANTA BAR ASSOCIATION
Member

THE GEORGIA LEGAL HISTORY FOUNDATION, INC.
Member

ACADEMIC HONORS
UNIVERSITY OF MIAMI SCHOOL OF MEDICINE, DEPARTMENT OF
PHARMACOLOGY
Adjunct Assistant Professor, 1977 to 1979
Lectured on Medical/Legal Aspects of the Practice of Medicine

WALTER F. GEORGE SCHOOL OF LAW, MERCER UNIVERSITY
Member, Board of Visitors, 1991 to 1994

ALBANY STATE COLLEGE
Friend of the College Award, 1994

SIGNIFICANT VERDICTS

$49,123,375.87 representing compensatory damages to a 23-year-old student who suffered catastrophic traumatic brain injuries as the result of a road wreck involving two commercial truck drivers on a two-lane highway in San Jose, California. The award provided compensation for $35.6 million in economic damages, which included past and future medical expenses and lost wages, as well as $13.5 million for pain and suffering. *Drew Dakota Bianchi v. Gordon Trucking, Inc.*, Samuel Ortega Bimbela and Michael Anthony Demma, C.A.F. 1-08-CV-104548, Superior Court of Santa Clara County, San Jose, California (2009).

$45,000,000.00 representing the parents' claims for medical expenses for their child until age 18 and for loss of services and the minor's claims for future medical expenses, pain and suffering, and lost income. *James Don Adams Jr. and Lamona K. Adams, et al. v. Kaiser Foundation Health Plan of Georgia, Inc.* State Court of Fulton County, C.A.F. 93VS79895 (1995).

$25,000,000.00 representing compensatory damages for a 38-year-old man's claims of medical malpractice against a doctor and two hospitals for injuries suffered as a result of an untimely diagnosis of a stroke plus $1,035,616.50 in prejudgment interest. The verdict included $1,000,000.00 for a loss of consortium claim. *Rex Leroy Jones, et al. v. Robert Glenn Bashuk et al.*, C.A.F. 98VS0137930C Fulton State Court, Atlanta, Georgia (1999).

$22,800,000.00 representing compensatory damages for a severely brain damaged 51-year-old who was struck in the crosswalk by a tour bus making an illegal left turn. *Xiu Jin Shi, individually and by and through her Guardian Ad Litem Rachel Deist, v. Coach USA, Inc., et al.*, Case Number

CGC-05-444417, Superior Court of California, County of San Francisco (2007).

$16,500,000.00 verdict in Washington County, Georgia, against a logging-truck company to compensate a 68-year-old man for injuries he suffered in the collision. $1,500,000 was allocated to his wife's loss of consortium claim. *Albert Dallas and Denise Dallas v. Bass Logging, Inc.*, C.A.F. 12-CV-432, Superior Court of Washington County, Georgia (2015).

$16,500,000.00 representing compensatory damages for minor child who suffered liver failure requiring a liver transplant at age four months caused by a failure of her health-care providers to follow-up on an abdominal cyst detected on ultrasound in utero. *Brooke Yamada, A Minor, by and through her Guardian, Mina Leigh Yamada, and Takahiro Yamada and Mina Leigh Yamada, Individually vs. Northside Hospital, Inc., Northside Pediatrics & Adolescent Medicine, P.C. and Women's Health Associates, P.C.*, State Court of Fulton County, Atlanta, Georgia C.A.F. 2005VS076354G (2006).

$12,000,000.00 representing compensatory damages for a severely brain injured child who suffers from hypoxic ischemic encephalopathy, including cerebral palsy, seizure disorders, and global developmental delays as a result of an untimely cesarean section and mismanagement of labor by a nurse midwife and an obstetrician. *Tate v. Clark-Holder Clinic et al.*, C.A.F. SU01CV2528 Muscogee County Superior Court, Columbus, Georgia (2002).

$7,828,455.30 representing compensatory damages for the wrongful death of 31-year-old mother of two who died from being crushed between two tractor-trailers while performing her duties as a security guard for Kmart Distribution Center in Newnan, Georgia. *Kierra Elaine Garrett and Davante Rashad Purdy by and through their guardian and next friends Betty Garrett and Charles Keith, et al. v. MVT Services, et al.*, C.A.F. 04-SV-381, State Court of Coweta County, Newnan, Georgia (2006).

$6,250,000.00 representing 32-year-old male who suffered loss of 70 percent of his abdominal wall. Physicians performed colostomy stapling digestive tract shut bringing the distal end of the colon to the colostomy bag. After seven days, the colon exploded spilling digestive product resulting in massive infection. Result, he was rendered permanently physically incapacitated. *Krenson Edward Kniphfer and Jennifer Harry Kniphfer v. Memorial Health University Medical Center, Inc., and MPPG, Inc.*, C.A.F. 1010574F State Court of Chatham County (2001).

$6,177,454.00 representing the parents' claims for medical expenses for their child until age 18 and the minor's claims for future medical expenses, pain and suffering, and lost income. *Jennifer and Gerald Garland, et al. v. Phoebe Putney Memorial Hospital, Inc.*, C.A.F. 92-CV-4038 , Dougherty Superior Court, (1993).

$5,537,420.00 representing compensatory damages for a brain-damaged 49-year-old retired US Marine Corps master gunnery sergeant plus $623,000.00 in prejudgment interest, *Baker v. Brown Transport Co., et al.*, Fulton Superior Court, Atlanta, Georgia (1986).

$5,250,000.00 representing compensatory damages for the wrongful death of three children who burned in a propane explosion due to the negligence of an agent for Blossman Gas, Inc., in illegally filling an out-of-date 100-pound propane tank with a defective valve. *Ginger Evans v. Blossman Gas, Inc., Blossman Gas, Inc., of Georgia, and H&H Shoppette, Inc.*, C.A.F. 03-VS-050554 Fulton County State Court, Atlanta, Georgia (2004).

$3,003,000.00 representing a 76-year-old woman's claims of medical malpractice against a thoracic surgeon for injuries she suffered as a result of the surgeon's severing her esophagus during surgery, leaving her struggling to swallow and eat solid foods, and requiring repeated procedures to expand the scar tissue to reopen the esophagus. *Nina K. Spurlock v. James M. Freeman and Cardiovascular Surgery Associates, P.C.*, Dougherty County Superior Court, C.A.F. 97-CV-1083-1 (1998).

$3,000,000.00 wrongful death verdict for NFL Rookie of the Year and two young boys, *Carolyn Delaney, et al. v. City of Monroe, Louisiana, et al.*, State of Louisiana, Parish of Ouachita, Fourth District Court (1987).

$2,250,000.00 wrongful death of a 41-year-old automobile mechanic, father of three, *Davis v. Cooper, et al.*, Fulton Superior Court (1991).

$1,950,000.00 verdict for a 73-year-old lady who suffered paralysis due to a failure to promptly diagnose and treat an epidural hematoma following withdrawal of an epidural catheter. *Roe v. Heidary, et al.*, Chatham Superior Court (1992).

$1,625,000.00 verdict for the wrongful death of 37-year-old single mother of two, plus prejudgment interest of $198,700.84. *Wainwright v. Wendell E. Phillips, M.D.*, Fulton Superior Court (1992).

$1,250,000.00 verdict for the wrongful death of a 60-year-old wife and mother, *Austin v. Kaufman et al.*, Fulton Superior Court (1990).

$1,200,000.00 verdict representing the full value of the life of a 7-year-old child, *Avant, et al. v. Bridges, et al.*, 168 Ga. App. 874 (1984).

$1,015,538.20 verdict representing compensatory damages equaling the full value of the life of 43-year-old male who was killed in a collision with a tractor-trailer carrying a load of logs. *Leslie Phillips, et al. v. Meeks Logging Co., Inc.*, C.A.F. 01-CV-211 Emanuel County Superior Court (2002).

$926,000.00 verdict representing the wife's claims of medical malpractice against a neurosurgeon and hospital for brain injury suffered by her husband as a result of post-operative bleeding in the neck. The verdict was against the defendant hospital only. *Debra Avant v. Fred Achecar, Fred Achecar, M.D., P.C., and Southern Regional Medical Center, Inc.*, Superior Court of Fulton County, E-35510 (1995).

$800,000.00 wrongful death verdict for a 26-year-old husband and father, *Vickie Ray, et al. v. Summerford Truck Line, Inc., et al.*, United States District Court, Middle District of Georgia, Albany-Americus Division (1988).

$700,000.00 verdict for the wrongful death of a 26-year-old man, *Irish et al. v. Lane et al.*, Dougherty Superior Court, Albany, Georgia (1988).

$600,000.00 verdict representing the full value of the life of a four-month-old infant, *Kisner v. Saucier, et al.*, Sumter Superior Court, Americus, Georgia (1987).

$575,000.00 verdict representing compensatory damages for a 28-year-old female whose great left toe was amputated after being run over by a MARTA bus while crossing the street in an Atlanta crosswalk. *Gaffron v. Metropolitan Atlanta Rapid Transit Authority, d/b/a MARTA*, Fulton Superior Court, C.F.A. E-32365, Atlanta, Georgia (1999).

LEGAL PUBLICATIONS
VOIR DIRE AND SUMMATION—THE LAW AND THE PRACTICE, Thomas William Malone, reprinted from a 1999 second edition, The Reprint Company (2006).

TOMMY MALONE ON MEDICAL MALPRACTICE CASE EVALUATION & REVIEW MANUAL—INTAKE TO FILING, PESI Law Publications (2004).

"Structured Settlements," Association of Trial Lawyers of America, TRIAL MAGAZINE, June, 2003.

"Changes in Medical Negligence Cases: An Overview of Handling Medical Negligence Cases for the Past Thirty Years," ATLANTA MEDICINE, JOURNAL OF THE MEDICAL ASSOCIATION OF ATLANTA, March 2002.

"The Law of Managed Care in Georgia," GAZETTE: NALS OF GEORGIA XXVIII/2 (August 1999–January 2000).

VOIR DIRE AND SUMMATION, 2nd edition, The Harrison Company (1999).

"Developing Themes in Cases Involving Managed Care Organizations," PROFESSIONAL NEGLIGENCE LAW REPORTER 13/8 (October 1998).

"Access to Emergency Services Under Managed Care—Tort Aspects," THE GEORGIA HEALTHCARE LAW REPORT, 1/2 (Winter 1997).

"Disasters in Managed Care—A Plaintiffs' Perspective," David L. Leitner, editor, MANAGED CARE LIABILITY, 231 (1996).

"Disasters in Managed Care—Recipe for Liability," THE VERDICT, 21/2 (Summer 1996).

"Managed Health Care: Plaintiffs' Perspective," TORT & INSURANCE LAW JOURNAL, 32/1 (Fall 1996).
"Carriers," GEORGIA JURISPRUDENCE, PERSONAL INJURY AND TORT, Lawyers Cooperative Publishing, 13/30 (1995).

"Medical Malpractice—A Disaster in Managed Care," THE TENNESSEE TRIAL LAWYER, 15/2 (December 1995).

"A Paralyzing Case of Pneumonia," ENDGAME, American Lawyer Media, L.P. (1994).

"Using Safety Regulations in Tractor-Trailer Cases," TRIAL (March 1994). Request for reprint by Great West Casualty Company for educational purposes.

"Voir Dire and Conduct of Judge and Jury," GEORGIA TRIAL LAWYERS ASSOCIATION TRIAL PRACTICE MANUAL, Georgia Trial Lawyers Association, coauthored with Hon. Frank M. Eldridge, May 1993, revised April 1994.

"Voir Dire and Establishing Rapport with the Judge and Jury," TRIAL DIPLOMACY JOURNAL, 15/4 (July/August 1992).

"Suggestions for Summation," SOUTH CAROLINA TRIAL LAWYER BULLETIN (Spring 1990).

"Handling The Plaintiff's Case," MEDICAL MALPRACTICE: HANDLING UROLOGY CASES, Shepard's/McGraw-Hill, 1990.

"Suggestions for Summation," THE VERDICT, 15/1 (June, 1989) Journal of the Georgia Trial Lawyers Association.

"How to Evaluate and Settle Personal Injury Claims in Georgia, Professional Education Systems," 1989.

MAXIMIZING DAMAGES THROUGH VOIR DIRE AND SUMMATION, Thomas Wm. Malone, The Harrison Company (1988).

"Direct Examination of a Neuropsychologist," Personal Injury Review, Part III, PREPARATION FOR SETTLEMENT OR TRIAL: TRIAL PRACTICE AND TECHNIQUES, Matthew Bender Publications, 1987.

"Closing Argument—Case Involving the Wrongful Death of a 7-Year-Old Girl," PERSONAL INJURY DESKBOOK, Matthew Bender Publications (1985).

"Understanding the Medical Malpractice Problem," THE VERDICT, JOURNAL OF THE GEORGIA TRIAL LAWYERS ASSOCIATION, 10/10 (December 1984).

"Summations in Medical Malpractice Cases," Videotape Educational Package, Matthew Bender, 1982.

MEDICAL AND LEGAL PRESENTATIONS
Mr. Malone is a frequent lecturer to medical and legal groups, including the American Association of Medical Assistants, Medical Association of Georgia for Practicing Physicians, Georgia Association of Legal Secretaries, and numerous presentations to lawyer groups on medical malpractice, products liability, and vehicular torts.

"Handling Big Cases Professionally," Institute of Continuing Legal Education, State Bar of Georgia, March 3, 2016.

"Voir Dire and the Selection of a Fair and Impartial Jury," Institute of Continuing Legal Education Webinar Series, February, 9, 2016.

"Golden Age of Torts," Institute of Continuing Legal Education Superstar Personal Injury Lawyers Best Verdicts: 2015, State Bar of Georgia, January, 21, 2016.

"Summations," AAJ Weekend with the Stars, New York, New York, December 12, 2015.

"Handling the Medical Negligence Case," AAJ 25th Annual Conference, Professional Negligence Section, Montreal, Canada, July 14, 2015.

"Remembering Mel," AAJ 25th Annual Conference, Melvin M. Belli Society Seminar, Montreal, Canada, July 10, 2015.

"Voir Dire for the Plaintiff," Institute of Continuing Legal Education 14th Annual General Practice and Trial Institute, St. Simons, Georgia, March 12, 2015.

"Truth through the Story," Southern Trial Lawyers Association 27th Annual Conference, New Orleans, Louisiana, February, 13, 2015.

"Cross-Examination," Mercer University Walter F. George School of Law, Macon, Georgia, February 2015.

"Birth Injury Odyssey: Observations from Both Sides of the V," GTLA Champions Trial Skills, Atlanta, Georgia, April, 24, 2014.

"Qualified Protective Orders: Staying Protected During the Safari," Institute of Continuing Legal Education 13th Annual General Practice and Trial Institute, Pine Mountain, Georgia, March 15, 2014.

"Summation: Motivating the Jury," Mercer University Walter F. George School of Law, Macon, Georgia, 2014.

"Lawyers Can Make a Difference," Mercer University Walter F. George School of Law, Macon, Georgia, November 12, 2013.

"Qualified Protective Orders and Life Expectancy in TBI Cases," 14th Annual Neuroscience of Brain Injury Seminar, Napa, California, November 13, 2013.

"Voir Dire and Qualified Protective Orders," Institute of Continuing Legal Education 24th Annual Urgent Legal Matters Seminar, St. Simons, Georgia, August 30, 2013.

"Lessons Learned from a California Road Wreck, What Works...and What Doesn't," New Jersey Association for Justice Boardwalk Seminar, Atlantic City, New Jersey, April 19, 2013.

"Voir Dire for the Plaintiff," 12th Annual General Practice and Trial Institute, Amelia Island, Florida, March 14, 2013.

"Brain Injuries: Mild, Moderate and Severe," Southern Trial Lawyers Association 25th Annual Conference, New Orleans, Louisiana, February 7, 2013.

"Summation: Motivating the Jury," AAJ Weekend with the Stars, New York, New York, December 8, 2012.

"Strategies for Catastrophic Injury Cases," Institute of Continuing Legal Education 23rd Annual Urgent Legal Matters Seminar, St. Simons, Georgia, August 31, 2012.

"Medical Liability Reform," AAJ 2012 Annual Conference, Chicago, Illinois, July 27, 2012.

"Does Medical Malpractice Improve/Worsen Quality of Care," GTLA 2012 Annual Convention QCOR AHA Quality Conference, Atlanta, Georgia, May 11, 2012.

"New Thoughts on Voir Dire," GTLA 2012 Annual Convention QCOR AHA Quality Conference, Atlanta, Georgia, May 10, 2012.

"Brain Injuries: Mild, Moderate & Severe," 11th Annual Neuroscience of Brain Injury
Seminar, Napa, California, November 6, 2011.

"Voir Dire," Mercer University Walter F. George School of Law, Macon, Georgia, January 25, 2011.

"Voir Dire" Qualified Jurors and the Duty to Provide," Georgia Trial Lawyers Association 2010 Holiday Seminar, Atlanta, Georgia, December 10, 2010.

"Selecting a Jury in a Conservative Venue," Santa Clara County Trial Lawyers Association, San Jose, California, November 8, 2010.

"The Challenges of Two Different TBI Cases," Tennessee Association for Justice TBI Seminar, Nashville, Tennessee, November 4, 2010.

"Q and A: Medical Malpractice Issues," Premier Anesthesia Directors Educational Program, Alpharetta, Georgia, October 22, 2010.

"Voir Dire: Qualified Jurors and the Duty to Provide," Georgia Trial Lawyers Association:

2010 Fall Workshop, Savannah, Georgia, October 1, 2010.

"Making a Difference," Kentucky Justice Association: 2010 Annual Convention, French Lick Springs, Indiana, September 16, 2010.

"Combating Life Expectancy and Other Defenses in Brain Injury Cases," American Association for Justice Professional Negligence Section: 2010 Annual Convention, Vancouver, British Columbia, July 11, 2010.

"Cross-Examination of Defense Experts in a Traumatic Brain Injury Case," American Association for Justice Traumatic Brain Injury Litigation Group: 2010 Annual Convention,
Vancouver, British Columbia, July 11, 2010.

"California Justice—Traumatic Brain Injury," joint presentation with Randall H. Scarlett, Esq., 2010 Belli Society Seminar, Vancouver, British Columbia, July 9, 2010.

"Forty Years of Trying Medical Negligence Cases," American Board of Professional Liability Attorneys: Annual Seminar, Atlanta, Georgia, June 11, 2010.

"Voir Dire: Qualified Jurors and the Duty to Provide," 2010 Georgia Trial Lawyers Annual Convention: Champion Trial Skills, Atlanta, Georgia, April 23, 2010.

"The History of GTLA," 2010 Georgia Trial Lawyers Annual Convention: Champion Trial Skills, Atlanta, Georgia, April 23, 2010.

"Proving and Maximizing Damages through Experts in Personal Injury Cases," 2010 Georgia Trial Lawyers Annual Convention: Champion Trial Skills, Atlanta, Georgia, April 22, 2010.

"Getting a Successful Verdict for your Client: What Works...and What Doesn't," joint presentation with Randall H. Scarlett, Esq., Brain Injury

Litigation Strategies 2010: Mastering the Science and Trial Strategies, Las Vegas, Nevada, April 29, 2010.

"Qualified Jurors and the Duty to Provide—O.C.GA. 15-12-133(b): Obtaining the Statutorily Required Panel of 24 Competent and Impartial Jurors before Requiring the Parties or their Counsel to Strike a Jury," General Practice and Trial Section 9th Annual Seminar, Amelia Island Plantation, Florida, March 12, 2010.

"Changes in Medicine—An Overview of Handling Medical Negligence Cases for the Past Forty Years," Third Annual War Stories in Litigation Speaker's Series, Litigation Committee, Georgia State Bar Young Lawyer's Division, Atlanta, Georgia, February 24, 2010.

"Preparation and Delivery of Opening Statements and Summations in Mild, Moderate, and Severe Traumatic Brain Injury Cases," Florida Justice Association: 2010 Workhorse Seminar, Orlando, Florida, February 19, 2010.

"Making a Difference," Southern Trial Lawyers Association 22nd Annual Conference: In Pursuit of Justice, New Orleans, Louisiana, February 12, 2010.

"Forty Years in the Med Mal Trenches," American Association of Justice Weekend with the Stars: Justice Counts Seminar, New York, New York, December 12, 2009.

"Voir Dire in Tort Cases," Georgia Law of Torts, State Bar of Georgia Headquarters, Atlanta, Georgia, December 3, 2009.

"Trial of the Catastrophic Case: What Works...and What Doesn't," joint presentation with Randall H. Scarlett, Esq., California Brain Injury Association: 10th Annual Neuroscience of Brain Injury: Research Informing Medical Treatment and Legal Practice, Napa, California, November 20, 2009.

"Lessons from Losing," Holy Innocents Episcopal Church, October 25, 2009.

"Strategies for Selecting and Using Your Expert Witnesses," Brain Injury Litigation Strategies 2009: Mastering the Science and Trial Strategies, Las Vegas, Nevada, May 1, 2009.

"An Overview of Handling Medical Negligence Cases for the Past Forty Years," Virginia Trial Lawyers Association 2009 Annual Convention: Pride in the Past, Strength for the Future, Williamsburg, Virginia, March 13, 2009.

"Second Annual Compassionate Gladiator Address," Florida Justice Association 2009 Workhorse Seminar, Orlando, Florida, February 27, 2009.

"Introduction of Traumatic Brain Injury," Southern Trial Lawyers Association 21st Annual Conference, New Orleans, Louisiana, February 19, 2009.

"The Trial, Jury Charges: Torts, Jury Charges: Damages," Magistrate's Court Council Meeting, Smyrna, Georgia, January 15, 2009.
"Handling Brain Injury Cases," STLA 20th Annual Conference: A People's Practice, New Orleans, Louisiana, January 31, 2009.

"Jury Section" What Really Works," Institute of Continuing Legal Education Jury Trial—State Bar of Georgia, Atlanta, Georgia, January 16, 2009.

"The Value of Graphic Demonstrative Evidence in Proving Brain Injury Cases," South Carolina Association for Justice: Auto Torts XXXI Seminar, Atlanta, Georgia, December 5, 2008.

"Closing Arguments," 2008 Institute of Continuing Legal Education Trial Advocacy Seminar, LIVE Georgia Public Broadcasting, Atlanta, Georgia, November 7, 2008.

"The Prosecution of a Negligent Security Action Against Elected Officials," Institute of Continuing Legal Education Premises Liability—State Bar of Georgia, Atlanta, Georgia, October 20, 2008.

"Preparatory Steps for Jury Selection," North Carolina Academy of Trial Lawyers Mountain Magic 2008, Asheville, North Carolina, October 23, 2008.

"Demonstration of an Opening Statement: HMO Case," Atlanta Bar Association: Litigation Section—"Opening Statements: The Punch of Primacy," Atlanta, Georgia, September 19, 2008.

"Bringing It All Together in Summation," ATLA—NJ Boardwalk Seminar, Personal Injury 2008: Tuning In—What Jurors Need to See, Hear & Feel, Atlantic City, New Jersey, May 2, 2008.

"Just Compensation for the Seriously Brain Injured," ATLA—NJ Boardwalk Seminar, Personal Injury 2008: Tuning In—What Jurors Need to See, Hear & Feel, Atlantic City, New Jersey, May 1, 2008.

"Traumatic Brain Injury," Emory University, Dr. Eugene Emory Law Class, Atlanta, Georgia, April 15, 2008.

"Effective Use of Demonstrative Evidence in Brain Injury Litigation," BIAA Brain Injury Litigation Strategies 2008, Las Vegas, Nevada, April 2, 2008.

"Demonstrative Evidence in the Catastrophic Brain Injury Case," Institute of Continuing Legal Education, State Bar of Georgia, Brain Injury Association of Georgia and Shepherd Center, Atlanta, Georgia, March 31, 2008.

"Demonstration of an Opening Statement in an HMO Case," Georgia State University College of Law, February 28, 2008.

"Handling, Litigating, and Trying the Catastrophic Brain Injury Case," FJA 2008 Workhorse Seminar, Orlando, Florida, February 13, 2008.

"Trying Brain Injury Cases," Institute of Continuing Legal Education, General Practice & Trial Section, State Bar of Georgia, Traumatic Brain Injury Seminar, Atlanta, Georgia, May 11, 2007.

"Proof and Argument of Damages for Loss of Enjoyment of Life in Personal Injury Cases and Proof and Argument of Damages in Wrongful Death Cases," PESI 12th Annual The Absolute Litigators Conference, Las Vegas, Nevada, March 25, 2007.

"Proof and Argument of Breach of the Standard of Care in Medical Negligence Cases," PESI 12th Annual The Absolute Litigators Conference, Las Vegas, Nevada, March 24, 2007.

"Examination of Medical Experts" with Dr. Joel Lavine, Southern Trial Lawyers Association (STLA) 2007 Annual Convention, New Orleans, February 15, 2007.

Panel Discussion of Cases proposed by Dr. Larry Schlachter, Cervical Spine Research Society 2006 Annual Meeting & Course, Palm Beach, Florida, November 30, 2006.

"Unique Theories of Premises Liability—A Case Analysis," Institute of Continuing Legal Education Premises Liability, Atlanta, Georgia, October 27, 2006.

"Trial of a Catastrophic Brain Injury Case," California Brain Injury Association, Napa, California, September 2, 2006.

"Timeless Truths in Winning Cases—An Overview of 40 Years of Trial Experience," Tennessee Trial Lawyers Association 2006 Annual Convention, Memphis, Tennessee, June 16, 2006.

"Plaintiff's Perspective—From Screening to Trial," PESI: Perception, Persuasion and Proof Strategies That Have Won Million Dollar Cases Seminar, Dallas, Texas, June 5, 2006.

"Summation in the Case of the Catastrophically Injured," CLE Civil Trial Excellence, Florida Coastal School of Law, Jacksonville, Florida, March 4, 2006.

"Into the Lion's Den—Voir Dire in the Era of Tort Reform, Caps and Cynical Jurors," Southern Trial Lawyers Association (STLA) Annual Convention, New Orleans, Louisiana, February 23, 2007.

Panel Discussion on the Fulton County Courthouse Shooting; Dealing with Client Problems; Carpe Diem—Seize the Day; and Rules, Regulations, Policies, Procedures & Standards, The Academy of Florida Trial Lawyers (AFTL) Workhorse Seminar, Orlando, Florida, February 9, 2006.

"Maximizing the Efficiency and Effectiveness of the Plaintiff's Expert Witness," Association of Trial Lawyers of America Annual Convention, Professional Negligence Group, Toronto, Ontario, Canada, July 26, 2005.

"Common Problems with the Catastrophic Case," Traumatic Brain Injury Litigation Group, Association of Trial Lawyers of America Annual Convention, Toronto, Ontario, Canada, July 24, 2005.

"Drastic Damaging Changes in Georgia Tort Law," Buckhead Rotary Club, Atlanta, Georgia, June 20, 2005.

"Voir Dire in the New Millennium: Where Have All the Jurors Gone," Georgia Trial Lawyers Association (GTLA), Annual Seminar and Convention, Championing Justice in the Age of Tort Reform, Atlanta, Georgia, May 7, 2005.

"Damages: Surmounting Defense Obstacles to Proving Damages," Association of Trial Lawyers of America, 18th Annual Weekend with the Stars, New York, New York, December 11, 2004.

"Voir Dire and Jury Selection," American Bar Association (ABA) Annual Meeting Seminar, Atlanta, Georgia, August 6, 2004.

"Special Settings and Other Civil Case Management Matters in Medical Malpractice," Institute of Continuing Legal Education, State Court Judges Spring Conference, Brasstown Valley, Georgia, May 12, 2004.

"The Adequate Award," Georgia Trial Lawyers Association (GTLA) Annual Seminar and Convention, Atlanta, Georgia, April 23, 2004.

"An Overview of Handling Medical Negligence Cases for the Past Thirty Years," Association of Trial Lawyers of America (ATLA-NJ) Educational Foundation Boardwalk Seminar, Atlantic City, New Jersey, April 22, 2004.

"Changes In Medicine—An Overview of Handling Medical Negligence Cases for the Past Thirty-Five Years," Georgia Trial Lawyers Association (GTLA) Ultimate Medical Malpractice Seminar, Atlanta, Georgia, March 11, 2004.

"Fighting the Conspiracy of Silence, Neurosurgeons Punished for the Truth," Association of Trial Lawyers of America Winter Convention, Medical Negligence Information Exchange Group, Orlando, Florida, February 15, 2004.

"Proof and Argument: Causation and Damages Regarding Mental Pain and Anguish," The Academy of Florida Trial Lawyers Workhorse Seminar, Orlando, Florida, January 29, 2004.

"Maximizing Damages From Voir Dire Through Closing," Institute of Continuing Legal Education Trial Advocacy Seminar, Atlanta, Georgia, December 19, 2003.

"The Basics on Arguing Damages," Georgia Trial Lawyers Association (GTLA) 2003 Annual Holiday Seminar, Atlanta, Georgia, December 12, 2003.

"Summation," Indiana Trial Lawyers Association, Indianapolis, Indiana, November 20, 2003.

"Voir Dire," Palm Beach County Trial Lawyers Association, Orlando, Florida, November 19, 2003.

"Building a Practice" and "Lessons from Losing," Georgia Trial Lawyers Association (GTLA) 2003 Fall Workshop, Pine Mountain, Georgia, October 17, 2003.

"Jury Persuasion—Get Them to Root for You," Georgia Trial Lawyers Association (GTLA), How to Hit a Home Run In Courtroom, Atlanta, Georgia, August 1, 2003.

"Making Your case on Damages: Arguing from Voir Dire to Closing," Association of Trial Lawyers of America Annual Convention, San Francisco, California, July 23, 2003.

"The Dangers of Physician Extenders in Today's Healthcare Environment," Association of Trial Lawyers of America Annual Convention, San Francisco, California, July 22, 2003, Professional Negligence Group.

"Summation," The Academy of Florida Trial Lawyers, St. Petersburg, Florida, June 12, 2003.

"Summation in the Case of the Catastrophically Injured," Institute of Continuing Legal Education, Winning Brain Injury Cases, Atlanta, Georgia, March 28, 2003.

"Cross-Examination of Defense Expert," Southern Trial Lawyers Association (STLA), New Orleans, Louisiana, February 27, 2003.

"Summation in the Case of the Catastrophically Injured Infant," Association of Trial Lawyers of America, Birth Trauma Litigation Group, Atlanta, Georgia, February 21, 2003.

"Wrongful Death," commentator on "Laymen's Lawyer" show, WPBA Channel 30, Atlanta Public Television, January 10, 2003.

"Settlement of Minors' Claims," Probate Court Judges Fall Seminar, Savannah, Georgia, November 13, 2002.

"Common Carriers Law," commentator on "Laymen's Lawyer" show, WPBA Channel 30 Atlanta Public Television, May 17, 2002.

CNN Cable Network, "Talk Back Live," as a panel participant-legal consultant, 2002.

"Litigating Catastrophically Injured Infant Cases: Cross-Examination of the Defense Expert," Association of Trial Lawyers of America Birth Trauma Litigation Group, Atlanta, Georgia, February 22, 2002.

"Working to Get the Best Possible Verdict for Your Client," The Academy of Florida Trial Lawyers 2002 Workhorse Seminar, Tampa, Florida, February 20, 2002.

"Utilizing the Judge and Record to Control and Neutralize Bullish Counsel," Institute of Continuing Legal Education, "Bare Knuckles with the Judges," Atlanta, Georgia, February 14, 2002.

"Swimming with the Sharks" and "Changes in Medicine: An Overview of Handling Medical Negligence Cases for the Past Thirty Years," Georgia Society of Anesthesiologists, Atlanta, Georgia, January 20, 2002.

"Voir Dire and Jury Selection in Light of *Walls v. Kim*," Georgia Law of Torts, Atlanta, Georgia, December 7, 2001.

"Managed Health Care: Profit vs. Patient," Louisiana Trial Lawyers Association (LTLA) Last Chance Seminar, New Orleans, Louisiana, December 6, 2001.

"Summation: How to Argue and Win Damages in the Traumatic Brain Injury Case," The Brain Injury Association of California (BIAC), San Francisco, California, September 29, 2001.

"Summation—Motivating the Jury," Florida Academy of Trial Lawyers (FATL), Orlando, Florida, August 24, 2001.

"Changes in Medicine—An Overview of Handling Medical Negligence Cases for the Past Thirty Years," 2001 Association of Trial Lawyers of America Annual Convention, Montreal, Canada, July 14, 2001.

"Neurologic and Orthopedic Injury Claims: The Untreated Disc Herniation, Epidural Abscess, or Epidural Hematoma," 2001 Association of Trial Lawyers of America Annual Convention, Montreal, Canada, July 16, 2001.

"War Stories with a Point and Evidence Too," Annual Meeting of the State Bar of Georgia, Kiawah Island, South Carolina, June 13–17, 2001.

"Managed Health Care—A Recipe for Tragedy," Delaware Trial Lawyers Association (DTLA), Dewey Beach, Delaware, June 8–9, 2001.

"Direct Examination—Mastering the Overlooked Trial Skill" and "Summation—Closing with Power," CLE Program Ultimate Trial Skills and Strategies, Dallas, Texas, April 20, 2001.

"How to Try a Lawsuit and Win It," The Academy of Florida Trial Lawyers (FATL) 2000 Workhorse Seminar, January 26–28, 2000.

"Tying It All Together to Make Your HMO Case," Association of Trial Lawyers of America Winter Convention, San Juan, Puerto Rico, January, 2000.

Damages, automobile collisions, torts and personal injury training, Magistrate Court Council Meeting, January 13, 2000.

"Effective Use of Voir Dire and Opening Statements in Tort Cases," Georgia Law of Torts, December 10, 1999.

"An Introduction to Truck Underride and Essentials of Motor Carrier Liability," Annual National College of Advocacy (NCA) Seminar, New Orleans, Louisiana, April 29–May 1, 1999.

"Creative and Innovative Strategies and Techniques in Proving and Arguing Damages in Medical Malpractice Cases Where the Plaintiff Is in His or Her 'Golden Years,'" 13th Annual Workhorse Seminar, presented by the Academy of Florida Trial Lawyers, Orlando, Florida, February 3–5, 1999.

"Corporate Dehumanization of Health Care: How Wall Street Affects Coverage and the Quality of Health Care," Association of Trial Lawyers of America Winter Convention, San Antonio, Texas, January 23–27, 1999.

"Taking on the HMOs: Unique Damages Opportunities," Weekend with The Stars, New York, New York, December 11–13, 1998.

"Demonstration of an Opening Statement in an HMO case," Litigating HMO cases, Nashville, Tennessee, September 25, 1998.

"Professional Liability in Managed Care," Pediatric Nursing Conference, Atlanta, Georgia, October 15, 1998.

"Disasters in Managed Care—A Plaintiff's Perspective," American Board of Professional Liability Attorneys, Charleston, South Carolina, October 8–9, 1998.

"Trial Advocacy as a Calling," Georgia Trial Lawyers Association (GTLA) Annual Meeting, Atlanta, Georgia, May 2, 1998.

"Disasters in Managed Care—The Plaintiff's Perspective," American Trial Lawyers Association, Boardwalk Seminar, Atlantic City, New Jersey, April 16, 1998.

"Liability Issues in Managed Care—The Plaintiff's Perspective," American Bar Association, Boston, Massachusetts, March 5–6, 1998.

"Persuading the Jury through Voir Dire and Summation," Florida Trial Lawyers Workhorse Seminar, Orlando, Florida, February 12, 1998.

"Disasters in Managed Care," The American Association of Nurse Attorneys, Annual Meeting and Educational Symposium, Atlanta, Georgia, October 24, 1997.

"Adams v. Kaiser Foundation Health Plan of Georgia," Academy of Trial Lawyers of Allegheny County, Masters of Trial Advocacy Retreat, Nemacolin Woodlands, Farmington, Pennsylvania, September 25–26, 1997.

"Demonstration of a Closing Argument in an HMO Case," American Trial Lawyers Association, Litigating HMO Cases, Atlanta, Georgia, September 20, 1997.

"Proving Liability Issues in Managed Care: The Patient," Institute of Continuing Legal Education in Georgia, Health Law Section Seminar, Atlanta, Georgia, September 12, 1997.

"Preparation for Trial," Institute of Continuing Legal Education in Georgia, Georgia Law of Torts Seminar, Atlanta, Georgia, August 22, 1997.

"Managed Care Disasters—How to Reach the HMO," Institute of Continuing Legal Education in Georgia, Excellence in Advocacy Seminar, Atlanta, Georgia, August 22, 1997.

"Litigating Managed Care Liability Issues," American Bar Association, Annual Meeting, San Francisco, California, August 1, 1997.

"Managed Health Care: Recipe for Tragedy & for Liability," American Trial Lawyers Association, Annual Convention, San Diego, California, July 20, 1997.

"Managed Health Care: Recipe for Tragedy," Georgia Association of Legal Secretaries, Annual Seminar, Macon, Georgia, April 18, 1997.

"Disasters in Managed Care: Recipe for Liability," Georgia Academy of Hospital Attorneys, 1997 Annual Meeting, Atlanta, Georgia, April 17, 1997.

"The Five Most Important Things I've Learned about Being a Trial Lawyer in the Last Five Years," Florida Trial Lawyers Association, Workhorse Convention, Orlando, Florida, February 20, 1997.

"Litigating the Managed Care Case," Georgia Trial Lawyers Association, Health Care Litigation: Secrets to Winning Seminar, Atlanta, Georgia, February 14, 1997.

"Deposing Adverse Economic Witnesses in the Catastrophic Injury Case," American Trial Lawyers Association, Winter Convention, Boca Raton, Florida, January 20, 1997.

"Managed Health Care: A Recipe for Liability," American Society of Medical Association Counsel, Atlanta, Georgia, December 10, 1996.

"First Impressions: Voir Dire and Opening Statements," Institute of Continuing Legal Education in Georgia, Atlanta, Georgia, November 15, 1996.

"Disasters in Managed Care: A Plaintiff's Perspective," 12th Annual Medical Malpractice Institute—Institute of Continuing Legal Education, Sea Island, Georgia, November 14, 1996.

"Managed Health Care: A Recipe for Tragedy," Colorado Trial Lawyers Association Summer Convention, Vail, Colorado, August 15, 1996.

"Using the Computer: Discovery, Depositions & Use at Trial," Small Office Practice, American Trial Lawyers Association, 50th Anniversary Annual Convention, Boston, Massachusetts, July 27–31, 1996.

"Life Care Plans in Brain Injury Cases," Traumatic Brain Injury Litigation Group, American Trial Lawyers Association, 50th Anniversary Annual Convention, Boston, Massachusetts, July 27–31, 1996.

"Disasters in Managed Care—A Plaintiffs' Perspective: Managed Health Care—A Recipe for Tragedy," American Bar Association (ABA), Liability Issues in Managed Care: A Guide for Litigators, Corporate Counsel, and Risk Managers Seminar, May 16–17, 1996.

"The Crisis of Managed Health Care: Unique Damages Opportunities," American Trial Lawyers Association Weekend with the Stars Seminar, New York, New York, December 9, 1995.

"Disasters in Managed Care—A Plaintiff's Perspective," Insurance Law Institute, St. Simons Island, Georgia, September 28, 1995.

"Recognizing the Post-Concussion Syndrome Case: Screening New Clients," Brain Injury Association, Colorado Springs, Colorado, September 29, 1995.

"Plaintiff's Opening Statements in Brain Injury Cases," Traumatic Brain Injury Litigation Group, American Trial Lawyers Association, New York, New York, July 15–19, 1995.

"Affordable High Tech Trials," Small Office Practice, American Trial Lawyers Association, New York, New York, July 15-19, 1995.

"Handling the Motor Carrier Case," Tortmasters Seminar—Academy of Florida Trial Lawyers and Georgia Trial Lawyers Association, Panama City Beach, Florida, May 26–27, 1995.

"The Jury Charge" and "Using Federal Regulations in Truck Cases," Southern Trial Lawyers Association, New Orleans, Louisiana, February 25–26, 1995.

"Common Carrier Liability," Institute of Continuing Legal Education, Common Carrier Seminar, December 9, 1994.

"Common Carrier Liability," South Carolina Trial Lawyers Association, Auto Torts XVII Seminar, December 2–3, 1994.

"Psychology of Persuading the Jury to Action, Final Argument," American Board of Professional Liability Attorneys, Palm Beach, Florida, November 12, 1994.

"High Tech Trials on a Low Budget," Georgia Trial Lawyers Association Fall Workshop, Savannah, Georgia, October 21, 1994.

Truck Wreck Seminars, Georgia Trial Lawyers Association, August 19, 1994, Albany, Georgia; Chairperson, Atlanta, Georgia, August 26, 1994.

"Opening Statements in Cases of Traumatic Brain Injury," Traumatic Brain Injury Litigation Group, Association of Trial Lawyers of America Annual Convention, National College of Advocacy, Chicago, Illinois, July 24, 1994.

"Demonstration of an Opening Statement in a Mild Head Injury Case with Severe Damages," Traumatic Brain Injury Litigation Group, American Trial Lawyers Association Annual Convention, Chicago, Illinois, July 24, 1994.

Closing argument, Masters in Trial Seminar, American Board of Trial Advocates, April 22, 1994.

"Maximizing Damages through Jury Selection," Georgia Trial Lawyers Association, January 7, 1994.

"Small Town Justice," 51st Annual Melvin M. Belli Seminar, Chicago, Illinois, 1994.

"Voir Dire, Demonstrative Evidence, Expert Witnesses and Summation," Gwinnett County Bar Association, December 17, 1993.

"Common Carrier Liability," Institute of Continuing Legal Education, Common Carrier Seminar, December 3, 1993.

"Premises Liability," Association of Trial Lawyers of America, November 12–13, 1993.

"Attorney Conducted Voir Dire Examination," South Carolina Trial Lawyers Association, August 20–22, 1993.

"Conundrums of the 90s: Addressing the Issues Head-On," Association of Trial Lawyers of America, Voir Dire College, June 17–20, 1993.

"Proving Damages in a Medical Malpractice Case," Institute of Continuing Legal Education Proving Damages Seminar, May 7, 1993.

"Cross-Examination of Lay and Expert Witnesses," Institute of Continuing Legal Education, The Civil Jury Trial, April 30, 1993.

"Affordable High Tech Trials," Gwinnett County Bar Association Luncheon, April 16, 1993.

"Preparatory Steps for Jury Selection," Academy of Florida Trial Lawyers, February 4, 1993.

"Successful Lessons from Unsuccessful Trials," Panelist, American Trial Lawyers Association Winter Convention, January 28, 1993.

"Professionalism in Torts Practice," Institute of Continuing Legal Education Georgia Law of Torts Seminar, December 11, 1992.

"Voir Dire and Common Carriers," South Carolina Trial Lawyers Association Auto Torts XV, December 4–5, 1992.

"Common Carrier Liability," Moderator, Institute of Continuing Legal Education Common Carrier Liability Seminar, December 3, 1992.

"Affordable High Tech Trials," Institute of Continuing Legal Education Trial Advocacy Seminar, November 6 and 13, 1992.

"The Birth of a Lawsuit with a View from the Other Side," Medical Center of Central Georgia Risk Management Seminar entitled, "Managing Risks in Obstetrical and Gynecological Care," September 16, 1992.

"Developing a Theme in Jury Selection for the Criminal Defense Attorney to Use in Opening Statements and Closing Arguments," Georgia State Bar Association, Younger Lawyers Section Seminar, May 29, 1992.

"Panel Discussion on State-of-the-Art Techniques in Jury Selection," Southern Trial Lawyers Association Convention, February 20, 1992.

"Trial Preparation: Discovery Interrogatories; Requests for Production of Documents; Requests for Admissions; Depositions; Expert Witness Preparation; Jury Demand; Trial Settings; Note for Trial; Motion Practice; Exhibit Preparation; Trial Notebook; Jury Instructions; Trial Briefs; Subpoenas; Miscellaneous Forms," Law Seminars International, Personal Injury Seminar for Legal Secretaries and Legal Assistants, Atlanta, Georgia, September 14, 1991.

"Opening and Closing for the Plaintiff," Institute of Continuing Legal Education, 2nd Annual Products Liability Seminar, Atlanta, Georgia, September 6, 1991.

"Examining Witnesses with Questions Designed to Persuade," Georgia Trial Lawyers Association, Start to Finish Seminar—Persuasion, Atlanta, Georgia, August 23, 1991.

"Developing the Client as an Active Participant," "Avoiding Pitfalls in Partial Settlements," "Establishing Credibility and Coaching for Clarity of Plaintiff's Experts," "Employing Psychological Principles in Closing Argument and Rebuttal," National College of Advocacy and Hastings College of the Law Series: Master's in Trial Advocacy, San Francisco, August 10–16, 1991.

"Proving and Defending the Drug Liability Case," The American Board of Professional Liability Attorneys Seminar, Advance Theories and Techniques in the Professional Liability and Products Case Seminar, Williamsburg, Virginia, June 21–22, 1991.

"Motor Carrier Liability," Georgia Trial Lawyers Association, Annual Meeting, Atlanta, Georgia April 4–6, 1991.

"Maximizing Damages through Voir Dire in the Premises Liability and Other Cases," Southern Trial Lawyers Association, Mardi Gras Seminar—Advanced Advocacy in Bread and Butter Cases—The ABCs of Journeyman and Journeywoman Litigation, New Orleans, Louisiana, January 31–February 2, 1991.

"Maximizing Damages in Voir Dire," Georgia Trial Lawyers Association, Proof of Liability and Damages Seminar, Atlanta, Georgia, December 7–8, 1990.

"Jury Selection: Developing a Theme during Voir Dire and Carrying it Through to a Successful Closing Argument," Georgia Association of Criminal Defense Lawyers, Start to Finish Seminar, Helen, Georgia, November 2–3, 1990.

"Recovery of Big Damages Outside the Big City," Atlanta Bar Association, Medical Malpractice Seminar—The Prosecution and Defense of Claims for Big Damages in High Stakes Medical Malpractice Cases, Atlanta, Georgia, November 2, 1990.

"Elements of Damage—Putting the Pieces in Place," Georgia Trial Lawyers Association, Start to Finish Seminar, Atlanta, Georgia, August 10–11, 1990.

"Turning Down a Million Dollar Settlement Offer," Southern Trial Lawyers Association, 1st Annual Mardi Gras Meeting, New Orleans, Louisiana, February 5–7, 1988.

"Voir Dire: An Essential to the Achievement of Justice," State Bar of Georgia, General Practice and Trial Section, Tradition of Excellence Seminar, Atlanta, Georgia, November 13–14, 1987.

"Settlement or Trial—Can You Reject the Million Dollar Settlement Offer?" Georgia Trial Lawyers Association Seminar on Negotiations and Settlements, October 16, 1987.

Georgia State University, College of Law, Seminar on Effective Discovery in Georgia, Atlanta, Georgia, May 26, 1987, and October 13, 1987.

"Plaintiff's Attorney Criteria for Pursuit of a Lawsuit," Sisters of Charity Health Care Systems, Inc., Cincinnati, Ohio; Franciscan Healthcare Corporation, Colorado Springs, Colorado, March 26–29, 1987; and St. Petersburg Beach, Florida, May 14–17, 1987.

"Presenting the Full Value of the Life of the Deceased Child," Southeastern Trial Lawyers Association, Auto Torts VI, 1983.

"Proving Damages in Child Death Cases," 37th Annual Belli Seminar, Washington, DC, 1983.

Committee on Individual and Small Firm Practice of the Section of Litigation, Panel Member, American Bar Association, Annual Meeting, 1983.

"Presenting the Deceased Child (Dart Out Case)," Los Angeles Trial Lawyers Association, Masters III Seminar, 1983.

"Handling Medical Negligence Cases in Small Communities," Kentucky Academy of Trial Attorneys, 9th Annual Seminar, 1981.

"Opening Statements in Medical Malpractice Cases," 35th Annual Belli Seminar, San Francisco, California, 1981.

"Discovery and Preparation in Medical Actions," 34th Annual Belli Seminar, Montreal, Canada, 1980.

"The Health Care Crisis: Hospitals, Doctors and Drug Companies," 31st Annual Belli Seminar, 1976.

"Legal Implications in Prescribing Drugs," University of Miami School of Medicine, Department of Pharmacology, 1975.

The Author

Vincent Coppola has written five non-fiction books, *The Sicilian Judge: Anthony Alaimo, American Hero, Uneasy Warriors: The Perilous Journey of the Green Berets, Dragons of God: A Journey Through Far-Right America, Charlie: Just Do Better*, a biography of Aaron's founder Charlie Loudermilk and *The Big Casino: America's Best Cancer Doctors Tell Their Most Personal Stories*. He co-wrote *Grandfathered In* with oncologist Stanley Winokur and *Risk Revolution* with ChoicePoint CEO Derek V. Smith, a road map for risk reduction and prudent policy-making in the Information Age. A former *Newsweek* reporter, Coppola has written feature stories for *Talk, Esquire, Rolling Stone, Men's Journal, Worth,* and *Atlanta* magazines. Coppola's story of his mother's battle against cancer was awarded the William Allen White Gold Medal by the University of Kansas. He is a 1977 honors graduate of the Columbia University Graduate School of Journalism.